ASCENT INTO HELL

Fergus White

ISBN (paperback): 978-1-97342271-6

Cover photograph of the author by Greg Jack.

Photographs by Angel Ezequiel Armesto, Blake Elliott, Greg Jack, Khalid Al Siyabi, Penba, Roger, and the author.

THE CLIMBERS

Ted (Canada): Team leader, Everest summiteer, professional mountain guide

Angel Ezequiel Armesto (Argentina): Team guide, professional mountain guide

Hugo Searle (Wales): Team guide, firefighter in the USA

Mingmar Sherpa Salaka Okhaldhunga 6 Damar (Nepal): 3 Everest summits, professional mountain guide

Ade (UK): Oil exploration

Amit Kotecha (UK): Dentist

Charlene (Scandinavia): Quit banking career to focus on Everest climb

Doug Stuart (USA): Firefighter captain

Greg Jack (USA): Surgeon

Khalid Al Siyabi (Oman): IT expert for education ministry

Linda (Canada): Nursing

Matthew (Australia): IT

Martin McHugh (UK): Construction business

Nurhan (Turkey): Everest summiteer, professional mountaineer, author

Nigel (UK): Businessman

Pete Solie (USA): US Air Force, retired – space and missile operator

Roger (Scotland): Oil industry

TC (Canada): Second attempt at Everest, physical education professor

Yener (Turkey): Professional mountaineer

Fergus White (Ireland): IT consultant for banks

BECAUSE IT'S THERE

APRIL 1

Into the Himalayas

This is a one shot only deal. I stare at the pilot in front of me. If he lands short, he'll hit a cliff that drops six hundred metres into the valley below. If he needs a go-around on this final approach, he'll smack the high terrain at the end of the runway. Through the windscreen I glimpse the short tarmac of the Tenzing-Hillary airport at Lukla. The encircling mountains, thin air, and its four hundred and fifty metre sloping strip have crafted one of the toughest landings in the world. The History Channel classifies it as the most extreme airfield on the planet.

The small plane is not pressurised. Twenty of us fill it. I smell aviation fuel. Flying in at over 3,500 metres, I already feel a little groggy. I trust the pilot is doing better.

I'm thrown forward with the sudden deceleration. Above the propeller noise, the tyres screech on the runway. We're down. We've stopped. I glance around and share a smile with my fellow travellers. I won't admit it to them, but I'm relieved to be out of the sky. At an altitude of 2,800 metres on the edge of the Himalayas, we've thrust deep into the rural heartland of Nepal.

We kicked off at 5am in Kathmandu. Sleep had not come quick last night. It wasn't the hotel; it was me. My mind wouldn't switch off. I knew today wouldn't be just another day. A year ago I set myself a target. This airport is an accumulation of events that finds me eight thousand kilometres from my home in Dublin and within eighty kilometres of my goal. The maths suggests ninety-nine per cent of the voyage is behind me, but not so. Those first several thousand kilometres were the easy ones.

With every metre that we ascend from here, the comforts of Western living will fade into memory. As we climb higher, we'll penetrate a region where no culture has ever survived. We'll enter an inhospitable environment, where only the briefest of visits is possible before escaping. Many who try do not make it that far. Of those who succeed, not all return.

I trained here last year. We attempted to summit the 7,100 metre Mount Pumori, seven kilometres from Everest. The expedition lasted a month. We failed. We reached 6,300 metres, at which point the leader decided the snow conditions were too dangerous. That ruling annoyed some of the mountaineers on the team; they wanted to risk the summit. But the judgement had been made and no doubt for good reasons. The mountain had already thrashed me. I more or less passed out twice on the day we retreated. Three weeks of depleted oxygen, poor food, worse appetite, and blinding headaches had left me but a shell. Grabbing only a few hours of sleep each night, in a subzero tent, had accelerated my body's collapse.

Most of the team on that trip suffered stomach disorders. Stronger men than me exhausted their supplies of anti-nausea tablets early. One climber recounted how he'd swallowed his last remaining pill and then vomited again a minute later. Alone in the dark outside his tent, he rifled through the dust and bile, by the light of a head torch, to find the undigested capsule. At the time it struck me as hard core, but not now. When the going gets rough up here, mountaineers do whatever it takes to survive. Dignity is an early casualty. I've already written mine off; I know what's ahead. I hope I'll act with integrity, but I'm under no illusions. Virtue untested is no virtue at all. This isn't Hollywood, where heroes perform brave acts and bask in a rewarding finale. This is the real deal. When it hits the fan, and it will, I fear I might not acquit myself as a gentleman.

APRIL 1

Trek from Lukla (2,800m) to
Monjo (2,800m)

"Carry your bags?"

"Porting service, porting service!"

Outside the fence of the tiny airport, scores of Sherpas clamour for business. Trekking and climbing pay the wages in this region. These men earn eleven euros a day to lug thirty kilograms of equipment uphill. Judging by their fervour, they know bleaker ways to make ends meet.

We push through; transport of our mountaineering gear and tents, by yak, has been arranged in advance. We'll rejoin our duffle bags at Everest Base Camp, 2,500 metres above this spot. For now, we'll each just carry a backpack with a week's kit.

We'll hike up through valleys for eight days to Base Camp. We're planning a slow ascent with time for acclimatisation. No prizes will be handed out for sprinting. No one brushed aside Hillary's accomplishment to inquire as to how long he took.

"Head into that teahouse," Ted says. "They're expecting us. We'll take thirty minutes."

Ted leads teams up mountains in the Himalayas, Africa, and America for a living. In his mid-forties and about five foot nine inches, a lifetime of outdoor activities presents a trim physique, the envy of many men his age. This wilderness is his office. He'll bump into many old friends these next two months. He led the training climb up Pumori and ended it on making the call to retreat. He broke a rib on that trip; a chunk of falling ice whacked him through his tent as he slept.

From Canada, he's spent decades as a mountain guide, ski instructor, and outdoor medic. He's scrambled in the Himalayas twenty times and climbed on eight Everest expeditions. He reached the summit once and joined the small elite who've stood at 8,848 metres. When tough decisions have to be made over the next two months, it'll be he who does so and there'll be little dissent.

His team of sixteen climbers, plus two guides, pass flasks of tea across tables. Another six mingle with us and will do so for the next ten days. They aim to summit a mountain called Island Peak. It soars up to 6,100 metres; although, only the last few hundred require crampons. If four of the group clamber to the top, we'll count that as a success. Such is the hardship of performing day to day functions above 5,000 metres that at least one of them may not even get to step on snow.

To complement our numbers, six trekkers will hike up the valleys alongside us. They hope to see Everest and experience a night at Base Camp.

Noise builds in the hostel as the mugs of tea disappear and final adjustments are made to backpacks and boots. Most of us only knew one or two of the others before we met up in Kathmandu two days ago.

"Ok guys, ten minutes and we'll push off," Ted says.

A few Canadians chat at the table in the corner, either trekkers, or climbers aiming for the summit of Island Peak. I've picked up the names of most of the team who are trying for Everest but cannot remember the others. Hopefully I'll get up to speed as we progress higher through the valley. I feel a bit of an ass talking to someone when I've forgotten their name, particularly when they've already told me three times.

"Hey Fergus, a last mug of tea?" a voice beside me asks.

"Thanks." I glance to my right. "Thanks, Nurhan." Somehow I remember his name.

If his accomplishments were shared out among us, we'd be the most experienced squad in the region. He'd summited five frozen 7,000 metre peaks in Russia by the time he was twenty-six. A year later, he hauled himself up Everest and became the first Turk to do so. He was the youngest person in the world to climb the Seven Summits. The pinnacle of the technical and dangerous K2 has had his company. Now, fifteen years after scaling Everest, he's returned to repeat the feat. Only this time he'll climb the hard way: without oxygen tanks.

Nurhan and I are worlds apart, well almost. On arriving in Kathmandu he sported a dark scraggy beard and wild hair. Yesterday he transformed that into a clean, cool goatee and crew cut. He now looks every bit the hard-edged adventurer. I too flash a tight haircut. Our physical builds are the exact same: five foot nine inches and trim. If that's what a world class climber looks like, then I may be more suited to this challenge than I'd given myself credit for. At least I have the hairstyle.

I zip up my black fleece top and recognise that there's no turning back now. Back at home, Dad had spoken little of the climb. He assured me that his prayers would keep me safe. I hope so, but my two duffle bags crammed with mountaineering gear should limit my reliance on luck. I know he thinks I'm crazy to set off on this venture, as my friends back in Dublin also do. But while I reckon my buddies get a kick out of the boldness of the attempt, these two months will only deliver dread to Dad. Our family has no history of climbing; I've even less.

Several years ago I'd read a newspaper article on Everest. It had suggested that climbing it was within the grasp of anyone in good health. Prior to that, in my late teens and early twenties, I'd raced bicycles. I was still putting in over a hundred kilometres a week, although nothing competitive. I pushed the story to the back of my mind and went to work in the office the following morning.

Four years ago, I'd got a burning desire to complete a marathon. I don't know where the idea came from. Others had done it; so, why not me? The furthest I'd ever run at that stage was about ten kilometres, to keep fit. I printed off an eight-month training schedule from the internet, bought a pair of runners, and hit the road. Some training buddies joined me, but life commitments and injuries pulled them off the programme. Later that year, I fell over the Dublin finish line in under three and a half hours. Exhausted, I'd felt I could expect no more from myself physically.

But every few months, an action, a comment, a magazine column would ring that bell within me once again. I couldn't ignore the audaciousness, the nerve, the cheek of pitting myself against something that is so far beyond my reach. I don't know what the purpose of life is; although, I know how it ends. For now, I've something I wish to achieve before that denouement.

Thirteen months ago I'd begun to scour the internet for instruction. Two months later, I'd made email contact with Ted's operation on the far side of the world. Uphill solo hikes with a weighted backpack then filled my evenings and weekends. Not being married or having to support a family left me with no excuses to miss training. The timetable ignored bad weather. I wasn't even certain it was possible for a novice to achieve what I was attempting within a year. I pored over equipment lists and evaluated and purchased kit. Working abroad, on computer projects, had allowed me hide my lunacy from those at home. The opportunity to abandon the plan had remained a possibility. But the night before flying to Pumori for the training climb, my buddies in the pub had posed the obvious question: since Pumori is one of the more difficult peaks on the planet, then what exactly was I training for?

I look around the room in which I now find myself. Ambition drives us forward, takes us to unexpected places, faraway lands. The acceptance of trying and failing defines those who follow a dream. But trying and quitting, I've never been good at that.

"It looks like we're off." Nurhan rises to his feet.

I nod back to him. Now for something that'll be a feature of the next fortnight: comparing my health against how I felt at the same altitude six months ago. Last time, a headache crept in after three days ascending. Within five I knew I'd altitude sickness. A week in and it took all my energies to just stand up straight and perform basic functions. I plan to go much slower on this occasion and hopefully delay the start of trouble. If I can postpone its onset and intensity, that'll give me a shot at reaching the upper camps.

I feel perfect. The crisp morning air has invigorated me. As we ascend to Base Camp, I know my brain will fog over. A dull throbbing sensation will develop that might become a more persistent, intense pain. For the next eight days, we'll retrace the route to Pumori. Just before Base Camp on April 8th, we'll turn off that trail and into new territory for me. If I amble today, then, with a bit of luck, I'll have a sharp, clear head tonight. After that, I'll take it one slow day at a time.

Through the window of the teahouse, the sun is rising into a blue spring sky peppered with light clouds. We'll hike about fifteen kilometres to the tiny village of Monjo on an undulating track. Despite the ups and downs, our altitude tonight will be same as here, at 2,800 metres. But given that we flew in from Kathmandu at 1,000 metres above sea level just an hour ago, this evening will see us a lot closer to 8,848 metres than when we woke up.

I place down my mug of tea and take in the room. Dire memories of this hostel flood back to me. Six months ago we'd hiked off the mountain after the Pumori expedition. Flushed with oxygen and returning appetites as we'd descended, we'd bounded along and ate and drank our fill. But a few kilometres short of the airport here, food poisoning had walloped me. Over and over my stomach had ejected whatever it could find inside me. Very few spend time in this valley and remain healthy.

As the sun had dipped below the hills, I'd no choice but to continue; there was nowhere short of Lukla to sleep. I'd stumbled for three hours, dehydrated, in a near daze. My climbing buddy had held me upright under the weight of my backpack, so I didn't collapse into a pool of my own vomit. The night had drawn around us and the track had emptied. Sometimes I only staggered a few paces before stopping. Eventually, to make any progress, my mate had to carry my pack.

I had slumped onto a bed above this teahouse, while the lads on the team disrobed me. They fed me antibiotics and anti-nausea tablets. I threw up again. Lucky enough, we'd been well stocked and were saved a fishing trip. They nursed me more pills and waited twenty minutes till I'd digested them. Only then did they head to the pub. I'd be fortunate to have those guys on this climb. I must avoid illness on this trip, or my preparations and training will have been in vain.

Thirty of us lift our packs onto our backs and file out of the teahouse. Half a dozen of the others have personal Sherpas, which swell our numbers further. These men will act as individual assistants. They'll carry some of the mountaineer's load. Down here it grants little advantage; a few extra kilos in a backpack won't tire the legs. But up high where the air is thin, the gradient steep, and each step gruelling, every gram will punish. The personal Sherpas should accompany their climbers all the way to the summit. I'll attempt the challenge without a Sherpa as far as Camp 4. On the last day, one of them will assist me with the weight of oxygen tanks.

One of the Sherpas approaches me.

"Hello Fergus, remember me?" He stretches out his hand.

"Ang Nama, of course. How've you been?"

"Very good. Good to see you again. What's new?"

He's much older than the climbing Sherpas, probably well into his forties. He'll bring up the rear on the trek to Base Camp. I've never seen him other than cheery. His smooth face contrasts to the weather beaten visages of many of the locals. Leaving the airport of Lukla behind and to the sound of eighty or so boots meeting hard clay, we chat about our upcoming adventure.

On our right, the green valley wall stretches upwards. To our left, the foliage slopes down to a river. The floor extends for a few hundred metres, and on the far side lies farmland. As we move in deeper, the farms give way to forest. Trekkers, porters, and yaks crowd the trail. Everyone carries something, but the heaviest and bulkiest loads burden the porters. Everything for the villages above must be lugged up, as this trail is the only route in or out. Food, beverages, building supplies, plumbing equipment, detergent, crockery, life's necessities; a yak or a back provides the transport. Some of the loads blow my mind, but regardless, there's a fellow who'll haul it for a price.

After nearly three hours trekking, we pull into a teahouse at a small village for lunch. We take on powdered soup to start and rice with some flavouring for the main. Not appetising, but I eat as much as I can. I must lose as little weight as possible over the next two months. Altitude devastates appetite. In the 1960 Himalayan scientific expedition, most people working at 5,700 metres shed about two kilos a week. Last time I entered this valley, I weighed seventy kilos. I exited a month later at sixty-one. On this undertaking I'll push myself for twice as long. With the exception of rest days, I expect to burn up four to six thousand calories per day. I sense weight loss in my future, lots of it.

Back on the trail we hike past single storey stone homes from a bygone era. A woman has come alongside me.

"Hi Charlene, I hear you're racing to the top," I say.

"Well, not quite racing, but yeah, kind of. I hope to be the first woman from my country to summit."

Up to now we've exchanged little more than pleasantries. Short, shockingly blonde hair complements her red close fitting top, adorned with sponsors' names.

"How long have you been planning this?" I ask.

"I quit my job a year ago, in banking. So pretty much full time since then."

"You'll go back to the job afterwards?"

"I don't think it's there. There's a lot of media coverage back home on this: TV, newspapers, you know. If I make it, I'll guide trekking groups full time afterwards. I'm supposed to write a book about this too. And make some speeches."

"You've started the book?"

"Not yet."

"God, you're going to be busy. Has anyone tried it before?"

"You mean another woman from home?" she asks.

"Yeah."

"They've tried, but none succeeded." She steps around an oncoming mule. "But this year, someone else is also trying."

"What? There're two of you trying to be first? Where is she?"

"Somewhere on this trail I guess. We're both aiming for the same weather window in May."

"Do you need me to break her legs?"

"Not yet."

The trail drops down and crosses the river. Then it sucks us further into the Himalayas. The steeper sections resemble a rocky staircase. Perhaps a motocross rider could penetrate here but nothing else of the motorised variety.

I've been trekking alongside a teammate named Greg for a few minutes. The same height as me, he's also in his late thirties. The short uphill sections don't trouble him. He looks more muscular than me. That difference will show once we get up high.

"How'd you end up here anyway?" I ask.

"It was almost by accident. I've been climbing for years, but I didn't think I was in the Everest category. I'm a doctor and –"

"A doctor? What kind?"

"Surgeon, urology. But anyway, I wanted to get a taste of Everest and work as a Base Camp doctor for two months. I was looking at various team websites. I realised I was as qualified as the rest to climb this. They'll take anyone."

"Tell me about it; how'd you think I got here?" I jump over a puddle. "You've been in the Himalayas before?"

"Nope, I grew up in east coast USA. A few years back I moved to Australia."

"Australia? I thought the States was the place to be a doctor, ridiculous salaries and all that."

"You're right. The salary's a fraction of home. But you can't beat the lifestyle. I don't see myself going back anytime soon."

We chat about our college days, our differing lives, and what the next two months might have in store for us. His repartee will shorten the nights in a mess tent. I hope this guy makes it to the top.

"Listen up, guys. For the next week we'll sleep in hostels," Ted calls out. "It's two to a room. We'll get to Monjo in an hour and a half; so, pair up now or I'll do it for you."

It feels like the month before Prom night. Sharing is more than just crashing out for a few hours every night. Heaps of equipment crammed in a tight space, tired legs and sore heads play their part. One might be having a bad day. Roommates usually end up trekking beside each other. I reckon this Greg bloke will be a fine lad to share with, but I'm not sure of the protocol. He's hiking behind me somewhere. I can't just ignore those around me and shout back to him. A minute passes.

"Hey Fergus, are you up for sharing a room?" Greg arrives at my shoulder.

"Is this an indecent proposal?"

"Whatever you want it to be."

"Sounds great. Good man, thanks for that."

Lumbering, laden yaks announce their presence via heavy Alpine cowbells hanging from their collars. Locals peer at us as we walk past their doors.

We close in on Monjo late afternoon. We leave a trail of tiny farming villages behind us. In places, we hiked through forests where dense foliage blocked out the sun. At other times, the trail was hemmed in on both sides by metre high stone walls. Beyond each lay a small tilled plot, a basic two roomed home, and an outhouse.

I've drifted off the back of the group on a climb up rocky steps. I think Monjo is just a few metres around the next bend, but I've no intention of getting out of breath. The less I stress my body over the next week, the more strength it'll have to acclimatise.

"Ok there, Fergus?" a voice asks.

"Grand, Hugo, thanks. I'm going to take it real slow this week."

"Good plan, you've got the right idea," he says.

He's one of two guides on the team. From Wales, he now lives in the USA as a firefighter. I don't know much about him. A few years older than me, he's well-built and looks powerful. Since his youth, he's enjoyed a passion for climbing. He's mountaineered on several expeditions. He's scrambled in this region before and tried to summit Everest once, from the north side, but didn't make it. This too will be a first for him.

We reach the village while there's still some warmth in the sun. A few houses along both sides of the trail for a hundred metres form the guts of the settlement.

12

We locate our hostel on the left of the track. Just behind it, the river flows fast and white down the valley. On the far side of the water, the green banks rise into the sky.

Upstairs I find Greg who's already settled into a room with two beds. I pull a few items out of my pack and head downstairs. The rest of the group is sitting on benches in the main room. All the hostels employ a similar format: a score of bedrooms, a kitchen, and a large room for eating, socialising, playing cards and team planning. The bathroom facilities are usually Spartan: a shared hole in the ground, or if we're lucky, a porcelain throne. Tonight, our luck is in. Dinner normally runs from 6pm to 8pm. Trekkers and climbers retire well before 10pm; the hostels get cold, and only a few dim solar powered bulbs provide the lighting. The climbing Sherpas and porters hang out in the kitchen. Once the main room has emptied, that makes space for them to sleep on the cushion covered benches under blankets. It seems a little racist, kind of a two-tiered structure, but that's how it appears to go up here.

I wash down as many potatoes and vegetables as I can with tea and a bottle of Coke. Noisy conversations, as people get to know each other, fill the air. After this morning's early start, a gain of 1,800 metres in altitude from Kathmandu, and a day's trekking, our numbers soon shrink. Within an hour of eating, Greg and I also call it a night.

"How's the head?" I ask.

"No problems. And you?"

"Perfect."

Regardless, I swallow a Brufen tablet. In day to day life I refrain from pills, maybe a little Aspirin when struck with a bad cold. But up here the rule book gets thrown out. We'll push our bodies to the limit of their endurance day after day. It's too late taking action once they've broken. The last time in this valley, I woke up with headaches above 4,500 metres every morning. No one understands why this happens. Suspicion falls on a lack of oxygen as the respiration rate slows down while sleeping. Whatever the cause, I can recall the pain, and it lasted most of the day. I must postpone those debilitating problems for as long as possible. I plan to take a Brufen every morning and evening. Coupled with a slow ascent, the pills should resolve any glitches and keep my blood thin and flowing while I sleep.

Lying in the dark at 2,800 metres, I contemplate that day one of sixty has furnished success. I've arrived in the mountains a few kilograms heavier than last time. I feel strong. The bed feels warm. Crucially, I've not picked up any illness. As I drift to sleep, I'm reminded that health in this valley is not something that can be taken for granted. Judging by the sounds coming from the toilet next door, some poor soul will suffer a long night. If it's a member of the squad, our team size could be down tomorrow.

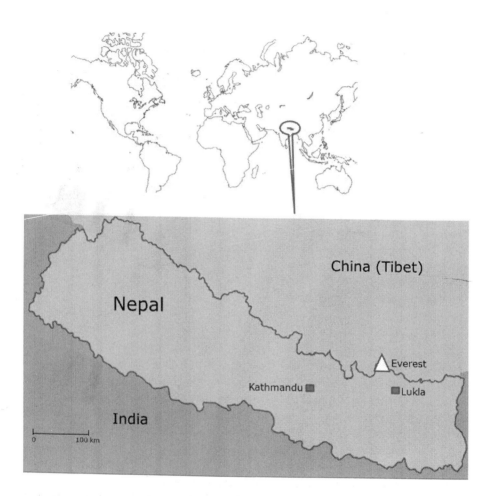

Everest's Location

APRIL 2

Trek from Monjo (2,800m) to
Namche (3,400m)

"God, that was some night." Greg sits up on his bed.

"What happened?"

"The toilet's just on the other side of this wall. My head was up against it. It must be made of paper."

"It woke you?" I ask.

"Woke me? I hardly got a wink. There must have been fifty trips in there, puking and diarrhoea."

"Come on, fifty?"

"I'm telling you, man, it was non-stop. I started to recognise some of the styles."

"Dude, spare me. I've not eaten yet. I hope it was none of our guys."

We head downstairs for a breakfast of toast and cereal at 8am. Within the hour, we carry our backpacks out onto the patio. I'm sitting around a table, chatting with a few of the team, still struggling to remember who everyone is. Everybody looks healthy on this cool morning.

"It must have been another group that got hit," Greg says.

"There were only a few other trekkers here," I say. "Somebody somewhere has been very sick."

All present, we set out. The route flashes back to me from six months ago. It'll undulate to start and then drop down a hundred metres to the river. We'll walk along the bank four or five kilometres. Then we'll cross the river and ascend six hundred metres through a forest to Namche. That incline will chasten us, with no let-up in the gradient. But we're facing a short day and should have it finished by lunch.

I know I must arrive relaxed and place my body under as little strain as possible. Last time I'd rocketed up the hill. I'd been trying to prove my mettle and left our group behind. I recall checking my watch altimeter as I'd gained a hundred metres in altitude every ten minutes. Panting and dripping sweat, I'd climbed from the river to Namche in an hour. I can't remember when the headaches had crept in, but it wasn't too far after that town. That had hampered my body's ability to acclimatise and to consume enough food each day to perform.

The real, challenging stuff won't hit us for many days, but at close to 3,000 metres with a modest backpack, Greg strides over the uneven terrain. Trekking alongside him, it's as if we'd been travelling companions for years.

"I'll take it real slow when we hit the hill," I say. "A snail's pace."

"That's fine by me. I don't want to get out of breath either. We're only starting to acclimatise."

"From what I've read, I think going fast is the main cause of headaches. They killed me last time."

"Speed is a problem," Greg says, "but there's more. As we go up, our bodies will change to send more oxygen around. The changes will start straight away and go on for a few weeks. We'll breathe quicker; it'll make up for the low oxygen in the blood."

"That's what I figured," I say.

"But as well as getting more oxygen into the lungs, it also causes more carbon dioxide to be lost." He steps onto a rope bridge. "The lost CO_2 turns the body alkaline. Some say that's the real cause of altitude sickness."

"It sounds like you've been reading the Lancet. I thought the problem was just a simple lack of oxygen? You're saying that too little CO_2 is the problem? So how on earth do we solve that?"

"You pee."

"Pee? You're joking."

Greg explains that to remain healthy, the body must somehow regain its balance. To achieve this, the kidneys excrete bicarbonate, an alkaline, into the urine. This transformation should occur within a day or two of our increased breathing.

"So I just pee away my headaches?" I ask.

"Exactly, but that's only possible if you're hydrated. We've got to take on about four litres of liquid every day."

"I never read anything like that." I jump over a rock. "So racing and sweating like a dog is just stupid?"

"Now you've got it. We need to be drinking or peeing, never rushing. And a clear stream too."

"Well, you're the bladder doctor."

"If you say so. The more you sweat, the less you pee. The alkaline stays in your system, and your body becomes unbalanced. Altitude sickness kicks in. The next thing you know, you can't hold down food."

"Game over?"

"That's right."

"I'll go even slower than planned. I'll bring up the rear every day to Base Camp, starting now."

"I'll be beside you," Greg says.

We walk through a small village of stone houses. Brightly coloured trekkers sport cleverly designed backpacks and the most modern hiking boots. Porters, wearing tattered, dull clothes, lug massive loads in shoddy footwear or just flip flops. Children, half dressed in rags, stare up at us as we go by. There's no local obesity here.

A few hundred metres ahead, a metal-cable rope bridge stretches far above the river. Colourful prayer flags hang from it. We aim for it. On top of the hill on the other side, six hundred metres higher and hidden beyond the forest, lies Namche. Straining my eyes, I spy the brown track as it winds up through the dense, green foliage. Perhaps a kilometre away and several hundred metres above, we see the dots of trekkers hiking up.

The team gathers, and we snap a few group photos with the bridge behind us. Sitting beside Greg on the banks of the river, I munch a Snickers bar to keep up energy and take a few sips of water.

Bridge across the Gorge
Mules, mountaineers, trekkers, and porters cross the river. A steep pull up to Namche rises to the left of the photo.

"I'm going to stop for ten minutes after every hundred metres we gain," I say.

"I think that's a bit over the top," Greg says.

"I don't care. There'll be no oxygen debt or sweating on this one."

"Ok, count me in."

Backpacks on and break over, the team climbs up the rocky steps towards the bridge.

Greg and I stop halfway across the bridge. A huge drop looms under its hundred metre width. The centre bulges down as we gaze along the valley. The summit of Everest can be sighted from the trail somewhere between here and Namche. When I was last here on an overcast day, there was no chance of a viewing. But under today's blue sky, I hope I won't pass by the observation point.

Now it's time for some serious acclimatisation.

We toil up the steep, dusty, brown trail through the forest. Our pace drops. Breathing under control, talking fades. I'm keeping an eye on my wrist altimeter, counting down a hundred metres.

We sit down in a shaded spot for our first ten minute break. Observers might be puzzled that two would–be Everest climbers have stopped to recover on a slope such as this. Trekkers, mountaineers, porters, and beasts of burden pass us. We watch the world go by and discuss our up-coming challenge. Greg sounds prepared for what's ahead. He knows how gruelling it'll be, and how success and failure are equal possibilities. He'll be a fine man to have on the team. I don't think I could have asked for a better person to be paired with.

"And that's ten minutes. Let's get back to it." I push myself up to my feet.

Gravity forces down on our bodies and backpacks, but the pace does not raise our breathing. We earn another hundred metres and find a grassy bank to sit on.

"Last time I came up here so fast, I never noticed that view down the valley," I say. "What a dick I was."

"How on earth did you miss that?"

"Head down, powering up like a fool." I sip water from my camelbak. "There'll be a lot of new stuff to see over the next few weeks."

"Yeah, here's how I see the next two months," Greg says. "From here to Base Camp is preseason, as they say in football. We've got to keep on track, stay with the program, and stay healthy. Nothing taken for granted. A poor performance and we're off the team."

"Right."

"Then we've got to get from Base Camp to Camp 3, acclimatise, and drop back down again. That'll be the season proper. It'll take us to about seven thousand metres. The thin air will kill us."

"Thanks for reminding me."

"Presuming we make it back down to Base Camp in one piece, we'll qualify for the playoffs: the climb back up to Camp 3." Greg tightens his backpack. "That'll give us a crack at the title, the finals. We'll need the game of our lives. But unlike football, it won't be over if we win. We've still got to get back off the mountain. And we'll have little in the tank."

Greg has laid out some season in front of us. If bookies were taking bets on who'll reach the top, I'm not sure what odds they'd give on these two lads sitting at the side of the trail. Eighty thousand trekkers a year hike in the Himalayas, to catch a glimpse of Everest and perhaps touch Base Camp. By contrast, about three hundred climbers a year try to summit Everest from this southern side. Most are seasoned veterans. Only half succeed. Of those on their way up this month, three or four will not return. If this was a sporting event, I reckon I could back myself at ten to one. The chances of Greg and I both reaching the peak? Probably fifty to one.

"Two hundred metres down, four hundred to go."

I've adjusted to our slow rhythm; my breathing doesn't suggest we're ascending.

"This is almost easy."

"Don't get cocky," Greg says.

Up higher, this mountain will inflict a terrible toll on our bodies. In 2004, three climbers succumbed to exhaustion near the summit and never made it down. I think Greg's three words may become our motto.

We're leaning back against a tree on our third break, three hundred metres above the river. Our guide, Hugo, and Nadia, a Canadian who's aiming to summit Island Peak, join us from behind.

"Hey Hugo, I thought we were the last group," I say.

"Well, you are now."

We explain our plan for climbing this hill and our rest strategy.

"It's a bit leisurely, gents," Hugo says, "but we'll join up."

Once the watch indicates ten minutes has passed, we hoist ourselves back up.

We press upwards, now above the 3,000 metre mark. Several trekkers bust themselves as they pass us. But today, the incline tortures the porters. Eight cases of Everest beer load down one man. At twenty-four cans per tray, nearly two hundred cans sit on his back. Another porter shoulders several twenty kilogram bags of rice. The next local is lugging half a dozen sheets of plywood that are used as room partitions. Who cares about the weight, if the wind gusts, he'll take off.

Nadia ascends alongside me. We pull into a shaded site for our fourth stop. We halt at the edge of the hill we've been climbing. For the first time, we glimpse what lies beyond this knoll. A gap in the trees has drawn the attention of a dozen trekkers. They hold cameras close to their faces. Green valleys and snowy peaks stretch away from us. At the end stands a brick wall of mountain, the Lhotse ridge. What lies beyond it attracts the focus.

I see the reason why those beside me clutch their cameras. Only the brown upper peak of the pyramid is visible. It looks smaller than the nearer mountains. But its near lack of snow indicates it's steep and subject to fierce high altitude winds. There she stands in all her glory. Everest.

For most people standing here, this is their first taste. The camera shutters click away, recording and savouring the moment for their owners. And beyond Everest, hidden from view, sits Tibet.

"I forgot we'd see Everest today," I say.

"Me too." Nadia peers up the valley. "Where is it? Which mountain is it?"

I suspect several of our team passed this point, not realising what was on offer. Everest waits a good thirty kilometres from where we've halted. Nadia lines her eye behind my outstretched arm.

"Ok, follow left from the leaves that are just in front of us," I say.

I draw my arm to the left and talk her through the white peaks that are some fifteen kilometres away. My arm rises up and down, as my outstretched finger draws an invisible line linking us to the Himalayan summits beyond. I trace out the tall white crest of Lhotse and the Nuptse ridge some thirty kilometres away. And just behind, peeps up the brown lump that is Everest. Little snow clings to its sheer side. Against a panorama of white mountains, its brown facade stands aloof.

This is the mountain we've all heard of since we were children. It's a mythical place of adventure and misadventure. Only a few years ago, it had never occurred to me that I'd see it. And now in this forest, through a gap in the branches on a sunny day, Everest menaces ahead of us. And whatever about viewing it, I never thought in my wildest dreams that I'd be setting out to climb it. Sitting under the trees, enjoying a snack, chatting to a young Canadian with the world's highest in the background; it's not a bad acclimatisation day.

My watch nudges us to our feet, and the small window onto Everest disappears behind us. We must gain another two hundred metres before Namche. Greg and Hugo are ascending alongside us. We slip into our unlaboured rhythm. After fifteen minutes we clear the top of the forest and progress under sunshine. I'm tempted to continue into the village but determine to stick to the conservative plan Greg and I devised.

"You've got to be kidding me," Hugo says. "I could hit it with a stone from here."

"Be my guest." I slip off my pack.

As far as I'm concerned it's only 1pm, and we've five hours of daylight to complete the last thirty minutes of our hike. The four of us sit on a wall outside a small, brown single story house. It looks like it was built in the times of Genghis Khan. Perhaps it was, but for the family inside, this two room dwelling is home.

"Why are you guys so afraid?" Nadia places her water bottle on the wall. "This is still low. Aren't you heading for Everest?"

A trickle of porters and trekkers pass by on their way to Namche and beyond. I recount my tales of fearsome headaches and the challenge of taking on food, from when I'd been up higher six months ago.

"But we're still low," she says.

This is where trouble starts, Greg reminds her. It can only be managed by ascending slow, staying out of oxygen debt, and keeping hydrated. In addition, unusual foods, poor hygiene in the valley, and suspect water will all combine to attack any chinks in our bodies' armour.

"And he's a doctor," I say.

"So you're saying our team will get sick soon?" she asks.

"Above Namche, above three thousand four hundred metres, I think so," I say.

She looks at Hugo. He insists we're too cautious, and the debate continues. I'm glad to have the conversation. In a week's time, Nadia will go her separate way, but Hugo and I will climb in the same team for the next two months. A mistake by one, most likely me, could affect both. At some stage I'll need his assistance, in a situation far less pleasant than where we find ourselves today. Back in 1974, six men were swept away in an instant. Five mountaineers fell off Everest to their death in 1984. Five years later, hundreds of tons of snow buried and killed five Polish climbers up higher. We'll ascend into harm's way, but I'm confident Hugo is one of the right men to lead us there.

"Ok, that's the last break. Namche it is."

We trek on, and Namche Bazaar comes into view. Some two thousand people reside here, in five hundred households. To our immediate west, a mountain rises to nearly 6,200 metres. On our eastern flank, another soars to over 6,600 metres. The settlement sits on a crescent shaped mountain slope and presents a stunning vista. It's as if we're staring at stepped paddy fields on the side of a hill, except instead of a sea of rice, we see a barrage of houses and coloured roofs.

In times gone by, locals bartered yak cheese and butter for agricultural goods that were grown further down the valley. But now, serving the needs of climbers and trekkers provides the vitality. The bustling town bursts with Sherpa life. Shops selling climbing and trekking gear press against the narrow lanes.

"Are these the real brands?" Greg thumbs a North Face top.

"I don't think so, but I heard a lot of the kit comes in from China. They come from the same factories that make the real thing."

"This one is about twenty-five dollars."

"It'd be about a hundred and fifty euros back in Dublin. Maybe it's fake, or maybe Dublin's a rip off."

"Watch it, Nadia, step in!" Hugo says.
She squeezes against a wall as two yaks lurch by.

Traders from all around trek here to sell their wares at the weekly market. Tibetan merchants arrive via high Himalayan passes. We'd gone for a look last time on the Pumori trip, presuming we'd be pestered on all sides by vendors shoving their wares in our faces. We may as well have been invisible. As we'd walked past their rows of goods, set out on plastic sheets on the ground, the dealers had cast little more than a glance at us. In all my travels, it was the first time I'd seen such disinterest in a western wallet. It had been relaxing, but I wasn't sure whether to feel relieved, or in an odd way, a touch insulted.

Most travellers spend two nights in Namche to acclimatise, which is what we plan to do. Consequently, it has boomed in the last three decades. It's the only place between Lukla airport and the summit that exhibits any sort of a town feel. We pass several hostels and well-stocked stores. A few bakeries double as internet cafés, making it one of the few spots in the region where trekkers can access the web. Due to the tourist trade, Namche has become the wealthiest district in Nepal. People from all over the world cram the dining room of each hostel, exchanging their stories. For the next two days, we'll be a part of that tale.

The four of us wind through tight spaces up towards our lodgings. A final flight of steps delivers us to the entrance at 3,400 metres. Mingmar, Charlene's personal Sherpa, meets us in the shade at the door. He looks untroubled by this morning's hike.

"Hi guys. How is everyone?" he asks. "They've started lunch inside."
We chat, and Greg mentions that we'll stroll down to the bakeries in the afternoon to fill up on calories.
"No, no." Mingmar points to his stomach and shakes his head. "Do not do that. Very risky."
I'm amazed, given how much the bakeries of Namche feature in any trekking story. But we don't have to be warned twice. There'll be no food stops down in the village.

We relax in the afternoon. The well-furnished dining room downstairs contains a treasure of old climbing and Sherpa memorabilia. Everything we need is provided: good food, laundry, showers, and a deck of cards. Greg and I settle into a bright room with two comfortable single beds. This'll be our home while we acclimatise. The living standards will decline once we ascend out of Namche.

View down to Namche from our Lodgings

In the bedroom next to us, we hear the two Canadians, Des and Blake. Good friends in their mid-twenties, they plan to summit Island Peak alongside Nadia. They seem like nice lads. Streams of laughter penetrate the thin wall.

"It sounds like we got the Chuckle Brothers next door," I say.

They hear me, and it sets off another torrent of titters.

Day two and we've ascended six hundred metres closer to the summit of Everest. Wherever the eventual point of breakdown will be, it will not be today. But the law of averages dictates that at least half of us will break down somewhere along the way.

APRIL 3

Acclimatisation Hike in Namche

(3,400m)

"Climb high, sleep low today, lads?" Roger pulls up a chair at the breakfast table.

From Scotland, I'm just getting to know him.

"Yeah, it should be straight forward," I say. "I think we'll go up about four hundred metres. Then back to the same beds tonight."

"Easy." A grin spreads across his face. "I'll be all set at nine and back before you know it."

We're planning several of these climb high-sleep low days before our summit bid. This mountaineer's tactic will stress our bodies to create more of the red blood cells that are needed to provide oxygen to muscles. But by sleeping back down here, we'll not be pushed beyond our limits and can recover. We must manage getting our bodies ready for the stress of high altitude, without destroying them in the process.

We'll have to tease this delicate balancing game. Go too fast; altitude sickness will result. Not aggressive enough; we'll expose our bodies to the slow, crippling effects of thin air for more days than are necessary. At this altitude, a cautious approach will not be a problem. But next month, we'll live at a height where our bodies are dying, even when acclimatised.

"Heat won't be a problem today." I peer out the window into a cool looking, overcast morning.

"Shame, it'll kill the views," Greg says.

Breakfast goes down well for me. 3,400 metres is not the top of the world, but it tests appetite nonetheless. I swallow a multivitamin and iron tablet with the meal. I won't receive the full range of vitamins with the food available up here; so, I must take this pill to give my body a chance to repair. Iron enables the blood to hold more oxygen. Given what's ahead of me, I ignore the one-a-day warning on the container. I'll pop one every morning and evening for the next two months.

We're ascending a zigzag trail that climbs out the back of Namche. Conversations dry up as breathing rates rise. I cut my pace by half. A near hour of ascent asks questions of me. The slope then eases, and we walk through fields of short, scrubby grass, interspersed with large rocky outcrops. Somehow a few of us at the rear have gotten separated from the team. We can no longer see the rest of the group.

"Some climbers we are," a deep English accent says.

I look around and see Ade, many inches taller than me and sporting a huge set of shoulders.

"I thought you were supposed to be the outdoor expert," I say. "What was all that talk about the jungle last night?"

"I must have lost my touch. Old age might be setting in." He emits a deep chuckle.

"Oh yeah, early forties, I forgot."

But I'm certain this ex-paratrooper from the British army has lost none of his edge. He saw active service in several locations and did a spell in Northern Ireland. As he moved through the ranks, he trained UK soldiers in jungle warfare and outdoor survival in the depths of Belize.

"A bit cooler here than what you're used to?" I ask.

"Yeah, it's a long way from oil drilling in Africa. But it's certainly not my first time getting lost. It won't be the last time either." Ade chuckles again and sets me off.

Beside him walks his English friend, Martin. He's about forty, the same height as me, and just a touch heavier. We've not spoken much. He trained on Pumori with Ade and Ted eighteen months ago. In his youth, he served in the Royal Marines with the British Navy. He didn't make a career of it. Nowadays he runs a construction and scaffolding company in the UK. He looks fit and has as good a chance of success as the rest of us.

"What do you reckon, Ade, which way?" I ask.

"Lost on a grassy slope, Everest mountaineers indeed." He pauses. "It has to be this way." He points to the right. "It's the only route up."

We restart, and I find myself walking alongside Doug. He's a year older than me. A firefighter from southern California, he's climbed before but nothing in the category of Everest. He provided great entertainment at the dinner table last night. He now amuses us with a few of the better tales from his job. His medical, rescue, and rope skills will come in useful over the next two months.

In an attempt to get back on track, one of the lads ahead climbs over a loose stone wall.

"Watch it!" Martin says.

A large rock tumbles down and bounces towards a trekker. She's standing near me, seconds from a broken leg. I'm not able to move. I can't make any intelligible noise to warn her. Doug picks her clean up in both arms. He twirls her around, runs a few metres to safety, and plonks her down again. I guess that's the difference between a firefighter and someone who sits in front of a computer screen all day.

After crossing a few fields, we spot the rest of the group and rejoin them at an old grass airstrip. A ramshackle garden shed has the word "Airport" painted on it. I'm sure the guys who work at Heathrow would have something to say about that. We cut across the runway and follow a track for an hour to the small village of Kunde, at 3,800 metres.

Walled-in fields of sparse looking grass surround stone buildings. Tilling has taken place, but I'd say any crops grown here require sweat. Yak dung in pizza-sized shapes dry out on every available rock. These will be used as fuel. A scree covered slope stretches for hundreds of metres above the back of the village. Tumbling rock avalanches have destroyed the higher pastures.

We aim for the small clinic at the top of the settlement, our highest altitude for the day. Several trekking groups mill around it. Short tours of the facility can be arranged, but we don't wish to over-burden the staff. It was built with the help of Edmund Hillary. He remained close to the locals, after being the first person to reach the summit of Everest in 1953. Our team pales in size to that expedition. That one totalled over four hundred people, with more than three hundred and fifty porters and some twenty climbing Sherpas.

The early morning chill gives way to a weak sun. We kick back as the thinner air, four hundred metres above Namche, nudges our bodies to squeeze out a few more red blood cells.

"Ok, lunchtime," Ted says. "It's just down the trail, that house on the left. It's Ang Nama's place. His wife will fix up a meal for us."

I presume Ang Nama must run a lodging house, as we file into a large room that accommodates the thirty or so of us.

I don't have the appetite I'd expect after a morning's walk in the hills. But I eat as much rice, coloured with chopped up vegetables, as I can. For an hour I recharge my mug with lemon tea. The banter flows in the room. Ade and I exchange memories of our differing jobs in Africa: him in the bush recently, me in a Cape Town bank a decade ago.

"Do we need more tea?" Ted asks.

"Ted, yeah, I could do with some more."

Ang Nama's wife carries in another heavy flask and places it on one of the crammed tables. Last time I was here I wasn't ill. But I feel sharper now: more energetic, a keener sense of what's going on around me. The plan to go slow and flood myself with liquid may be working.

"Has anyone got Aspirin?" one of the trekkers asks.

The hidden enemy stalks us.

"I think I do." I root out a small medical kit from my backpack. "Yeah, here we go. Headache?"

"Yeah."

"That should do the job." I pass over two tablets.

Ang Nama's wife walks back into the room carrying a jug.

"Hey, hey, here's trouble," Ted says. "That looks like Chang to me."

He's offered the local hooch first. I think it's fermented from rice but looks thicker and cloudier than Japanese sake. I've not had a drink for a month, and I don't intend to start now. I'll down my next tipple as I descend the valley, either in celebration or drowning my sorrows. Macho culture suggests we should knock back the beverage. Most of the team swallows a small cup. Ang Nama's wife accepts my polite refusal at face value and passes on. But in what appears to be a well-practiced ritual, she challenges Ted's repeated rejections. She does not respect his manhood until he downs three cups.

After lunch, Ang Nama gives us a quick tour of the house. The large kitchen sits above the stable, where yaks sleep during the cold nights. Over generations in this harsh environment, the Sherpas have determined how best to conserve energy: the heat of the animals drifts upwards and heats the room above. I think the family sleeps in the kitchen; although, Ang Nama might now enjoy a more modern bedroom and the assistance of a hot water bottle.

We say our goodbyes and leave Kunde. We'll descend to Namche by a different route. We amble along, our bodies busy coping in the thinning air near 4,000 metres. We stroll for less than an hour, along a flat track, to a village where Edmund Hillary helped build a school. I loiter at the rear of the gang, enjoying the repartee with the lads around me. An al fresco group pee behind a bush breaks down barriers further in this new team. My mind is on the job that I'm here to do, and I delight in registering a clear stream. The body is hydrated, and my kidneys expel more evil alkaline.

At the village I pick up a bottle of Coke. The liquid and sugar will trump my earlier mass hydration. Everything I do this week is to get me fat and healthy to Base Camp.

"An Irishman who turns down alcohol but then has a coke," Roger says. "They'll take away your passport."

"What can I say, no excuse."

We hike through a small forest. On its far side we stumble upon a building. The large construction looks more recent than the Sherpa homes. It has the air of a castle and a spooky Norman Bates feel. Steps lead up to a mystery door that hasn't been opened in some time.

"What on earth is this?" Doug asks.

"It was a hotel for rich tourists," Ted says. "They could view Everest from here."

Through the clouds, there's no hint the peak can be seen.

"They'd arrive by helicopter and land just over there." Ted points. "Having not acclimatised at all, a donkey and oxygen tank were available, if needed, to get them to the door."

On this grey afternoon, it seems the most bizarre location on the planet to raise a structure this size. Scant grass and green bushes are all that surround it. What insanity led someone to build this here? But the surrounding wall wasn't built in vain. I jump over it for my fourth pee since lunch. Drinking and peeing as much as possible was the strategy, but I must have a word with Dr Greg later about the volumes.

We ramble on and cross the far end of the grassy airstrip we saw this morning. This takes us to a ridge, below which lies Namche. We should make it back to the lodge within the hour.

We follow rocky steps down a steep section, most of the way to the village. Today has taken little out of me. At the edge of town Greg elbows me.

"The woman talking to Charlene."

"Yeah, what about her?"

"That's her."

"That's who?"

"That's the other woman, you dummy. That's the one Charlene's racing against."

"I got you. Are they friends?"

"You tell me," Greg says.

I observe them from a few metres. It's all a bit too polite, a little cold.

"There's no love lost there. I think the race is on. She's in good shape too."

"Yeah, she runs ultra-marathons, and I heard she's got a lot more experience than Charlene. Let's see what happens up high."

"We'll see. By the way," I leave the ladies behind us, "I'm peeing like a race horse, I mean, like non-stop. Is this normal?"

"That's the plan," he says. "Your body has figured out what it needs to do. Just keep drinking."

Metres

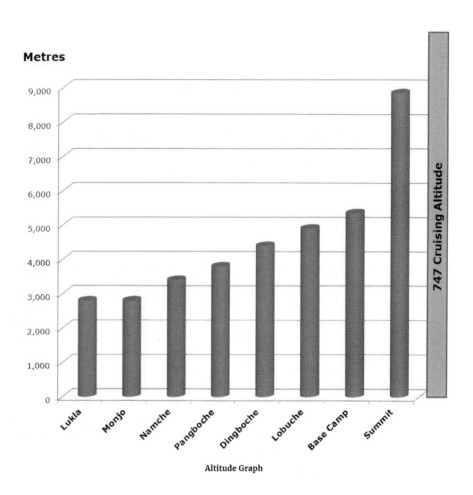

Altitude Graph

APRIL 4

Trek from Namche (3,400m) to

Pangboche (3,800m)

We'll hit the trail again today. We'll push out of Namche and trek up the valley into the wilderness.

I enjoy breakfast with the team and drink as much as I can take on board. Word reaches us that Roger has suffered a bad night. I look around the table but can't see him. He's been vomiting since midnight and might not be out of the woods yet.

"Will he rest here and recover?" I ask.

"No," Ted says. "He'll travel with us."

Roger faces a brutal day. I hope his body is up to it.

The gradient out of Namche with a loaded pack asks more of me than I'd expected. Greg and I toil near the rear. My raised breathing reminds me of the altitude. But my discomfort pales in comparison to the man beside me.

"I heard you'd a bad one, Roger. Take it easy today," I say.

"Bad? Worse than that."

"Has it passed?"

"I got locked in the room while you guys had breakfast. I had to throw up in a plastic bag."

"God, that's some start to the day."

This man should be in bed. I can't understand why he hasn't been left here today to recover. Ang Nama or his personal Sherpa could have kept an eye on him. Greg and I give what reassuring words we can. We remind him that we're not up against the clock today. At times, on the steeper sections, he comes to a virtual standstill.

We drift ahead of Roger. The brown, dusty trail twists along the left edge of the valley, with scrubby vegetation at its edges. Far below us, the white water river snakes through trees, bringing glacial melt to those lower down in the plains. Snowy peaks reach up above 6,000 metres on the right side of the valley. Trekkers fill the route on this cool, bright morning.

We notice the team has stopped at a religious shrine a hundred metres ahead. The sunrays are bouncing off the brilliant white surface of the ten metre high stupa. Colourful prayer flags flutter all around it.

We round a spur and climb up a few steps to join the team. The full valley unfolds in front of us. Spectacular mountain scenery stretches for at least thirty kilometres up the gorge.

The 6,800 metre white flat top of Ama Dablam stands just up ahead on the right. At about 6,200 metres, on its steep side, a hanging glacier sticks out of it. It's hard to grasp how this glacier, weighing thousands of tons, can jut out the side of the face. Expeditions often aim for the summit. Climbers pitch three camps during an ascent, with Camp 3 just below and to the right of the hanging glacier. Ice that calves off it tends to plunge left. On a November night in 2006, a large section collapsed right. It swept away several tents and killed six mountaineers.

"Is that where we're going today?" Greg points to a green knoll a few kilometres along the valley.

"Yeah, we've got to climb up over that. See the building at the top, the colours?"

"Yeah."

"That's Tengboche monastery. That's where we'll be this afternoon."

"It's about the same height as here, isn't it?"

"Yeah, but don't get your hopes up. The trail drops down to the river. We'll cross it and then climb up six hundred metres to the monastery. A killer."

Beyond the forest covered hill, the colours become less verdant. Green makes way for brown as the air gets thin and the cold temperatures support little if any plant life. Further away, as the valley reaches towards the sky, brown gives way to white snow. At its end rears the white ridges of Nuptse and Lhotse. The white yields to brown again, as the slope becomes too steep even for snow to lodge. The pinnacle of the Lhotse ridge, the fourth tallest mountain in the world, clocks in at just over 8,500 metres. A Swiss team first climbed it in 1956. In addition to the main peak, Lhotse Middle soars up over 8,400 metres. For a long time it remained the highest unclimbed named point on earth. Eventually in 2001, a Russian crew sat atop it.

And behind the ridge, Everest stands proud. Cameras catch the moment. For many, this is the first time they'll have seen her.

Viewing Everest from a Stupa
Snow blows off the summit of Everest (left peak). The Nuptse Ridge runs in front of it. Lhotse stands to the right. The summit is about thirty kilometres from this point and more than five kilometres above.

"That's some wind now." Greg shoves his hands into his pockets. "What are we doing sitting down?"

My mind comes back into focus. I've seen all this before, and this year I aim to climb that beast on the horizon. Back in Kathmandu I'd packed my camera into a duffel bag and sent it on to Base Camp, to reduce the weight I'll carry. This week is preseason. I'm here to acclimatise, stay healthy, and remain strong en route to Base Camp. I slide to the sheltered side of the stupa and wait for the last few to arrive. Behind us, Roger drags himself around an outcrop.

Back on the trail and moving, the slope on our left protects us from the wind. Greg and I make steady progress. We push up one of the short, stiff uphill sections.

"Just the nose, just breathe through the nose," Greg says. "If you have to breathe through your mouth, you're going too fast."

On the Trail out of Namche.
From left to right: Me, Greg, Martin, Ade.
The summit of Everest is above my head, while Lhotse is above Greg. The Nuptse and Lhotse Ridges stand in front of those peaks. Ama Dablam is above Ade.

We fire off a quick pee with pride and trek on. As we round a bend, we spy the team up ahead relaxing on a teahouse patio.

"Lunch? Already?" Greg asks.

"Just elevens," I say. "It's time to knock back the tea again."

"Super. That's some view isn't it?"

"It's incredible. This is like a ski holiday, cold air, but you'd be burnt to a crisp in the sun."

The lemon tea flows in the late morning suntrap. With the exception of Roger, smiling faces surround the tables. After a few minutes relaxing back in a chair, I forget we're in thin air.

The Route Ahead

1: We'll trek down through this forest in the next hour.

2: Lunch will be here on the banks of the river.

3: Mid-afternoon should bring us to Tengboche Monastery on the top of this knoll.

4: Over the next few days we'll trek up these valleys and route left around the Nuptse Ridge.

5: In about six weeks' time we hope to stand here, the summit of Everest.

"Ok, let's get moving," Ted says. "We'll have lunch down at the river. See everyone there."

The views change as we move into a forest, and the route winds its way down the incline.

"It's good to have those branches overhead. That was getting hot," Greg says.

"I'm pretty certain we won't have that problem in a few weeks."

We pass through tiny villages en route to lunch. Small clay houses line the trail. Children in threadbare clothes play in the dust. We see no electricity supply cables overhead. I doubt there's much in the line of plumbing underneath either.

A check on my watch altimeter as we stop for lunch puts us at 3,250 metres. Despite the stiff uphill sections this morning, we're a hundred and fifty metres lower than today's starting point. One step forward, two steps back I guess.

Our team crowds around a long table on the patio. Most have been here for some time already. I squeeze into a gap at the end and take on the simple fare. Potatoes form the base carbohydrate. My mouth doesn't want to know about the food. Is the cooking plainer or is it just the altitude?

We haul our packs onto our shoulders and push out. After crossing a metal-cable rope bridge over the Dudh Kosi River, the incline bites. We face a six hundred metre pull up to the monastery at Tengboche. On a dusty trail through a sparse forest, the sun will find us for much of the ascent. The last time I was here, I'd blasted up the hill in under an hour, ahead of the group. Then I'd sat and waited at the top for sixty minutes as the sweat turned cold on my back.

"There'll be no ego today, Greg," I say. "I'll take pride in how long I can stretch out this climb."

"Just sit in behind me then."

Most of the others pull away from us.

We hike past a small military billet just to our right in the forest. A few soldiers with rifles from the World War II era man the sentry posts. I've no idea what they're protecting, maybe positioned in case the Maoist insurgents we've heard about try to shake us down.

With measured discipline, Greg and I continue our climb. Ascending trekkers toil past us. A constant flow of Sherpas with enormous cargos labour up. By contrast we have it easy; although, it doesn't feel it. We never breathe through our mouths. The simple gauge stops us going too fast. Any suggestion of breathlessness or oxygen debt must be avoided. We're already locked in a battle to generate an ever increasing number of red blood cells in this thinning air.

Halfway up the hill, we sit down on the edge of the trail for our third stop.

"I feel fine," I say. "This pace isn't killing me."

"Nor me. Just keep it steady"

He's right. I must remember those words. They must be my mantra, today and every day on this mountain.

As I stop for another timed break, Greg eases on ahead. I recognise the three who close in on me from behind.

"Hey Fergus. It's good to see you. How's it going?" Angel arrives with Roger and Ang Nama. "It's hot man. Whoa. Look at this place."

He's the other guide along with Hugo. He looks like a nutcase with a Ming the Merciless beard that trails ten centimetres beneath his chin. In his late thirties, this Argentinian is of fit build and a little taller than me. He's led some sixty expeditions to the top of Aconcagua, the tallest mountain in South America. Always full of energy, I struggle to keep pace with his bustling conversation on the steep uphill sections. He thrives at this altitude. I don't know anyone who can talk this much while exercising. I'm not sure if I should be glad to have such an able escort on the team or worried there's such a difference between his level of fitness and mine.

"Hi Angel. Hi guys. I'm doing ok. Just seeing how slow I can go. Ok Roger?"

"I'll get there." Roger leans against the ditch.

"I don't know where you're pulling this from, Roger. You've got some balls. I'd have been flattened if it were me."

"Little choice."

"Just keep it handy. No rush."

Angel Relaxes by the Edge of the Trail

We reel in the final quarter. My altimeter is my companion, indicating steady progress. I've slipped ahead of the three. Angel and Ang Nama tweak their pace to ensure Roger's not alone.

I take what will be my last mini-break of the ascent under the shade of a few trees. I turn around to wait for the others. Through the leaves and branches, I stare back down the valley we've travelled this morning. The foliage frames Ama Dablam. It would make an incredible photo. But I've seen this trail before and already have a few photos of it. In one sense, I'm here to enjoy myself, have an adventure, and build memories. But reaching the summit is the aim. If saving a smidgen of energy improves my chances of standing on the peak, by even the tiniest fraction, then that's what I must do. The camera is not being transported in my pack. In my mind I take a good snap of the view. The three rejoin me.

"Hi guys, almost there now," I say. "By my reckoning, it's just fifty metres higher."

I'm well within myself, having accomplished the climb at such a relaxed pace. I'm proud to reach the top in the closing group, taking a full two hours.

"Is this it?" Roger asks.

"Well done," Angel says, "you've made it."

We pass under a colourful stone archway and into the Tengboche monastery grounds at 3,860 metres.

Reds, whites, and yellows abound on the monastery's stone exterior. Prayer flags flutter in the wind, their colours symbolising the five Buddhist elements: earth, wind, fire, water, and consciousness. This is the largest monastery in the valley. Out front lies a camping area and a few lodges.

Several monks potter around on the steps, I'm told about sixty live here, but fewer and fewer boys now join, preferring to work in mountaineering or trekking-related activities. Tenzing Norgay, who summited Everest with Hillary, had been sent here to study as a monk. But the allure of climbing big mountains, particularly a peak that had never been scaled, had been a call he couldn't resist.

Contemplating what lies ahead, I take in the panoramic views of the elevations in every direction, including the spectacles of Ama Dablam, Nuptse, Lhotse, and Everest.

Tengboche Monastery

The sun disappears behind clouds, and the chill wind steals our body heat. The rest of our team is sitting on the grass in front of the monastery. We join them, and I munch on a bar of chocolate. I've just enough time to finish my snack before Ted gives the word that it's time to move on.

"The trekkers will stay here for the night," he says. "The climbers will go on to Pangboche."

He wants the latter group to receive a traditional local blessing tomorrow morning in Pangboche. Then we'll rejoin the trekkers at lunch time.

We saunter down the far side of the hill. I trek alongside Greg towards the rear, our now unofficial position. We drop down a hundred and fifty metres and pass a small nunnery in the middle of nowhere. It's hard not to wonder if there may have been some unscheduled trips over the years from the monks in Tengboche to this convent.

Protected from the wind again, the temperature suits hiking. The trail becomes a slight uphill. We ease off the pace.

"Tough, isn't it?"

"Yeah, it's thinner here." Greg says.

"Anything steeper than flat, it feels like someone's sitting on my shoulders."

An hour passes. We walk across another bridge. Below us, white water thunders through a narrow, rocky channel. Greg and I take a minute to gaze at it from the crossing and enjoy the untamed sights and sounds of nature. The route has become quiet; many groups trek no further than the monastery.

We move on and ascend a rocky section on the other side of the river. We keep the pace even and watch our breathing as we progress up. To our surprise, we reel in Ade, Martin, and Doug. They're sucking in big mouthfuls of air. Could it be that our plan is starting to pay dividends?

"Keep it easy, lads," Greg says.

With controlled movement, Greg and I step up past them.

Demanding section behind us, we get back into a rhythm as the sun loses its heat.

"Preseason's going to plan." Greg takes a swig from his bottle.

"That wasn't too bad today. I thought the pull up to the monastery would be worse. I feel ok. And you?"

"Not too shabby. That's four days trekking in the bag now," Greg says.

"Yeah. And close to four thousand metres. Pity about Roger. Will he recover?"

"He's a gritty Scot. He's got time to come around."

At about 5pm we reach the village, a series of one and two story stone structures along the side of the trail. We find our lodgings, which I recognise from my previous visit, and settle into a small room in an annex. After unpacking and a quick rest, we step back out for the short walk to the main building, where the team has gathered.

"Damn, it's freezing. Where did that come from?" I fold my hands under my arms. "It must be close to zero. We didn't climb that high today, did we?"

"Keep going, keep going, let's get out of this," Greg says.

Above this altitude, frostbite threatens. When that happens, capillaries becomes so cold, the blood crystallises into ice. It afflicts more than a dozen climbers a year on Everest. Fingers and toes get hit hardest, often ending in amputation. Sir Ranulph Fiennes, the English explorer, suffered it on the fingertips of his left hand during a solo shot at the North Pole. On returning home, his doctor had instructed a wait of almost half a year before going into surgery, to allow the surrounding area recover. After an impatient and painful four months, and exasperated by the sight of blackened, shrivelled tips, Fiennes strode down to the garden shed with a saw. He spent two hours performing the unthinkable on his little finger. Over the following four days, he severed off the tip of each digit in turn. I now find myself trying to emulate this man; he too has stood on top of Everest, successful on the third attempt.

A stove burns in the middle of the dining room. Doug and I are sitting beside each other at the table. The two of us laugh our way through dinner. The slices of pizza get inside me, but I have to force them.

We strike up a conversation with a man and women in their twenties. They look like models from the cover of an outdoor magazine. They reveal that they're on some sort of world tour, having set out from the USA.

"So what are you doing here?" Doug asks.

"Ama Dablam, we'll climb it this week," the woman says.

"Serious? Ama Dablam? You're kidding?"

"No, we're all set."

They look too pretty, at least compared to our grubby bunch, for such hardship. Good luck to them. Forget the advertised views from the monastery today; she's the best sight I've seen all week.

APRIL 5

Trek from Pangboche (3,800m) to

Dingboche (4,400m)

After breakfast and a mug of coffee, we stroll to a small monastery for a blessing. It seems a bit late to bank on words in a foreign language to protect us. If there's any karma on the mountain, it'll be based on a life well lived or otherwise. I'm aware that I'm trying to steal a deathbed conversion: to place my faith and hope in the well-meaning consecrations of a stranger, only days before we pitch ourselves at Everest proper. But I'll keep my thoughts to myself and show reverence for the tradition.

"It's the building over there," I say, pointing for Greg, "the one with the red and yellow roof."

"You were here before?"

"Yeah, same deal as last time."

We drop our backpacks outside, file in, and take a seat. Lama Geshi shuffles into the room. His face is an artist's dream, etched by decades of history. The personal Sherpas stoop in his presence. He rattles off prayer after prayer at an unstoppable pace. Handfuls of rice are thrust into the air as the aromas of incense and smouldering juniper envelop us.

In between prayers he giggles, similar to his boss, the Dalai Lama. I'd listened to a lecture by the Dalai Lama in Cape Town a decade ago. I'd been struck by how happy he seemed and his constant schoolboy-like chuckling. The Buddhist monk in front of us struggles to contain another dose of laughs. Perhaps it's a part of their training, or maybe they just study The Beano for seven years.

He bestows an individual blessing on everyone and ties a piece of coloured string around their neck. To complete the formality, he taps his forehead against the recipient's. My eye catches Ade's, and I fight to keep a straight face. I step forward to receive my virtual Kevlar jacket. I must show dignity to the office, if not to this cheery and delightful old man. I imagine he'd be a great gent to share a few drinks with, if there was a translator to hand. What stories he must possess. I presume he's studied in Tibet, perhaps met the Dalai Lama, whom I've heard is just a notch or two above him in the Buddhist pecking order.

Six months ago, I'd sat in this exact seat. At 3,800 metres I'd battled to follow the proceedings. It's the first memory I have of feeling wasted. This morning, I can appreciate what's happening around me.

"That should do us no harm." Ade slips his shades on as we step back outside.

"Yeah, just the small matter of climbing the mountain left. How're you doing today?"

"Top notch. Another beautiful day."

Green ferns brush against our legs as we cut back to the trail proper. Chatter emanates from the group. Charlene and I are chatting about our training, our first chat in a few days. I'm struck that most of us do not know each other, and yet in a week's time, we'll attack Everest as a team. I think the two of us will get on well together over the next two months.

"I've not felt great since yesterday," she says. "I shouldn't feel so bad this low down."

"Oh it's normal-"

"But this low? My stomach has turned against me. I don't feel fit at all."

"You should have seen the state of me here last time. This place thrashes everyone. Look at Roger." I step over a rock. "Most of us will get sick. I'm just trying to put it off as long as possible. Half of us either threw up or had worse problems last time."

"Really?" she asks.

"Yeah, the life expectancy in this valley isn't great. In any case, we're not that low. We'll be over four thousand metres soon."

"So it's not just me?"

"Far from it."

44

Trailside Views

We trek for two hours beneath mountain peaks, before reaching the village where we'll stop for lunch. I remember the high stone walls that enclose this narrow path. The teahouse where we'll eat is still a distance away at the top of the settlement.

I turn a corner and, to my surprise, come upon the place where we'll dine. I remember trudging up past buildings for ages last time.

The midday sun chases us off the patio to a lunch inside. We squeeze in around a few small tables.

"How on earth can you eat seconds, Greg?" I push the rice and small pieces of vegetables around my plate. "It'll be all I can do to clear this."

"Man up, dude."

The meal quality deteriorates the further up the valley we climb, but I force myself to finish what's in front of me. Hydration, though, hands me an easy victory. I down several mugs of lemon tea and sip on a bottle of Coke. I'll de-alkaline my body en route over the next two hours.

"How about you, Roger?" I ask. "You look better. I see your appetite has returned."

"Can't keep me down."

Between bites, he entertains us in his strong Scottish accent. His recovery astounds me. I thought the trek yesterday on a sick and empty body would finish him. He'll strengthen our team.

Lunch finished, we rejoin the trail with the trekkers. Greg and I hike at a restrained pace near the rear of a spread out group.

"What are we at?" Greg asks.

I glance at my watch.

"We've just gone over four thousand one hundred."

"Steady as she goes."

An hour after lunch finds us walking along the banks of a small river. The thinning air, however, has stolen the energy with which I'd enjoy the sight of this Himalayan stream cutting through the landscape. The vegetation becomes sparser. Green yields to stone on the edge of the trail. The team is ascending out of the lowlands.

We reach a split in the river, where the trail diverges at a wooden bridge. Everest lies somewhere to our left, but we persist on straight ahead. Behind the next spur lies Dingboche, where we'll spend two days acclimatising. After our sojourn there, we'll trek parallel to the valley we've just ignored and then merge with that route to the top of the world.

At the far side of the bridge, a steep gradient over dusty rocks faces us.

"I see there's no stopping the Chuckle Brothers."

"Where are they?" Greg asks.

"They've already blasted over those rocks and are around the back."

"The joy of youth."

Each step up bites my thigh muscles. We adopt a drawn-out pace. We place one boot forward, let it rest flat on the ground, and then lift the trailing boot through. We've no momentum. If someone was to glance at us, they'd presume we're standing still. I learnt this technique towards the end of our training climb. We're never compelled to breathe through our mouths. Conversation dries up. My eyes point down. Every few seconds, I force a knee straight.

Half an hour of ascent pushes us higher.

"Ok?"

"Yeah."

"Speed?'

"Fine."

We've each noticed sometimes a tiny, almost imperceptible numbness in the back of our heads, just above the neck. It would be easy to ignore or not even recognise. It signals an approaching headache. If either of us feels this sensation, we ease off the pace still further. The other waits.

Up over 4,300 metres, and we've put the arduous work behind us.

"That's Dingboche ahead there," I say. "We just follow the trail through the grass."

"Cool, same height as us, more or less."

"Yeah, won't be too long now."

Two huge stupas stand above a village of some twenty homesteads. The brilliant white coating and colourful upper sections of the monuments glisten in the sun. A maze of small fields surrounds the buildings. From this distance, the soil doesn't appear too fertile. I can't imagine many crops thrive on it.

The oppressive heat of the midday sun has eased into a fine afternoon. Conversation resumes, and Greg and I return to our normal trekking pace.

"The team is all over the place today," I say. "Most are probably close to the lodge. I think a lot of the trekkers are behind somewhere."

"Suits me, we'll get there when we get there," Greg says.

"It's a pity there're no rocks around here. I've got to go again," I say.

The pee stops are now worn like a badge of honour.

"It's just grass." I look around.

"There's no one ahead or behind," Greg says.

"Right so, I'll try to spell my name in the grass."

Greg and I reach the edge of the village. We pass the imposing stupa and progress to the lodge at 4,400 metres.

"Wow, I never thought I'd feel so good at this height." I drop my pack.

"Yeah, that was a good one," Greg says. "Three more days and we've passed preseason."

"Let's just keep it cool and do nothing stupid."

Most of the lads have already arrived at the hostel. I recollect that the rooms here were comfortable. They even offered an en suite, an en suite hole in the ground that is. Unfortunately the nice ones in the upper section are occupied; the price we pay for our leisurely pace. We stroll down to the lower annex and walk till we find a vacant room, the last one by the toilet. A plain one with two single beds offers us what we need.

"We passed eight doors in the corridor," Greg says.

"So?"

"That's sixteen other people who'll use the toilet. It might be another noisy night."

"I hope not."

He pops into the toilet. He shakes his head on returning.

"Time well spent is not time to be spent in there."

I stride in undeterred, delighted that my kidneys are doing such a fine job. My audible yelp of shock elicits a burst of laughter from Greg next door. I'm standing in a dark room just over a metre square. A hole in the ground looms below. A large barrel of water rests beside it. The aromas of springtime meadows do not float here. Eighteen people, foreign foods, the effects of altitude, a hole in the floor, and no hand basin threaten carnage.

The Chuckle Brothers, Des and Blake from Canada, land in our room. The mountains can't hold these men down.

"We're going exploring in the village. We'll pick up some water. Do you guys want in on the action?"

"Absolutely." I pass them cash. "As much as you can carry."

Greg and I settle in for a mid-afternoon rest on our beds, with our heads raised. The raised head is supposed to lessen headaches at altitude; although, we're unsure of the medical reasoning behind it. The stresses of the day ease out of our legs. When not hiking, we should be hydrating, eating or resting. Better still, we should perform all three at the same time.

"What are we looking at in this place?" Greg asks.

"We've got two days at this lodge. Tomorrow is a climb high-sleep low day. We'll climb up the hill that's just behind here. It goes to five thousand metres. Then return here for the night."

"Sounds good. Now back for a snooze."

The Chuckle Brothers burst in the door.

"Success, we cleared out the shop." Des throws a few bottles at the end of the beds.

"Great stuff, lads, thanks."

I open a bottle, grab a Snickers bar, and lie back on the bed. Water, food, and rest, it's just what the doctor ordered.

Evening time find us all up in the main room. Our group of about thirty swells the population of the lodge. Outside, the temperature drops close to zero. A large furnace in the middle of the dim room keeps the Himalayan night at bay. I'm huddled at a small table with the Chuckle Brothers, Nadia, and her two Canadian trekking friends. I couldn't ask for better company to end the day. The Brothers produce a deck of cards and start to deal. We chat about their five lives in Canada, the rain in Ireland, and everything in between.

Unknown faces surround us at other tables. This hostel is jammed. That toilet will be the end of someone's adventure. I hope it doesn't end mine.

APRIL 6

Acclimatisation Hike in Dingboche
(4,400m)

"It looks like a bright one out there, Greg." I pull back the thin curtains. "How'd you sleep?"

"Pretty good. And yourself?"

"Grand. But there was a lot of action in the corridor last night. They were queuing up to make bits of the toilet."

Just outside, Nangkar Tsrang soars up to 5,010 metres. We'll climb to its peak, some six hundred metres above us, stay an hour for lunch and then descend. That should push the red blood cells in our bodies but not over-stress our systems.

After a breakfast of toast and eggs, we step out onto the patio for what should be a short day. Nadia's already chatting to Hugo outside on this cool, dry morning.

"Set to go?" I tighten my pack. The absence of my bulky sleeping bag, spare clothes, toiletries, and various odds and ends will free me up for today's challenge.

"Nadia will stay here; she's not feeling great," Hugo says.

"I might try to gain a hundred metres later this morning, if I feel better," she says.

This has sprung out of nowhere.

"How're you this morning, Fergus?" Hugo asks.

"Great. And yourself?"

"Never better. Let's get to it."

I hope she'll pull through, but once illness attacks, it tends to persist. I'm not certain she'll get back on track quick enough to attempt Island Peak. Their schedule doesn't allow for rest days, with the exception perhaps of today.

Greg and I bring up the tail of the group. At the top of this hill six months ago, I'd sat at the summit disinterested and groggy. A numbing headache had spoiled the day. I feel none of those symptoms this morning. But this afternoon will provide the best opportunity so far to evaluate the difference in my condition between this time and last. I've been as careful as I can. Slow and steady has been the mantra, Brufen morning and evening, and buckets of liquid. In a few hours I'll know if I've a chance of reaching Base Camp in good health.

Blake starts to race away from Greg and me.

"He's at it again." I look up to Blake. "Hey buddy, take its easy. You'll blow a gasket when we get higher."

"Screw you, old guys."

More for entertainment, rather than thinking it will slow him down, I tell him an old tale I'd once heard.

"A bull and his young son are grazing in a field. In the pasture above, a wagon arrives. It delivers a truckload of young cows and then leaves. Excited, the young bull pounds the ground underneath him and says

"Dad, let's charge up there and have sex with one of those new cows."

"No, son," the old bull replies, "we're going to stride up there and screw them all.""

Blake brushes aside the moral of the story and continues to put space between us.

Up and up we push along the steep clay trail. Each step asks something of me. The altimeter puts us at 4,700 metres, halfway to the top. Dozens of trekkers fill the route, either on an acclimatisation hike or to witness the views from above. Even from this height, as I turn around to take it in, the vista strikes me. Below, the village basks in the late morning glow. Yesterday's valley meanders away into the distance. On all sides, snowy peaks reach to the heavens. I think the snow line begins about the 6,000 metre mark. Today will drag us up to 5,000 metres. Within an hour we'll be higher than Mont Blanc, the highest point in Europe. I turn back, breathe deep, and slog on.

"Relentless, eh Greg?"

"One step at a time," he says.

We gain another hundred metres of altitude. Chit-chat has reduced to the bare minimum. The team is strung out ahead and behind. Nature humbles us near 5,000 metres.

We labour on. It's just after noon. If I gasp, I slow my pace. The thin air slaps me with every step.

"Only the rocks to go now." Greg selects a foot placement among the boulders.

"Another fifty metres." I pull in air.

If this were Europe, we'd be suspended from a sky hook.

"Well done, guys," Ted says as we reach the top. "Watch your feet up here. There's some space over there."

Exhausted, but pleased, we join the climbers who've already succeeded. The mountain continues to bruise the trekkers further below us.

I settle into a little cove out of the light wind. As I busy myself consuming a sandwich, fruit, and water, I take in the panorama. I've seen it before, but that doesn't make it any less special. We can see for kilometres down the valley. Knolls, which had blocked our views before, now paint the lower landscape. Hill after hill, peak after snow-covered peak, it continues to the horizon.

One by one, the rest of the team reaches the finish. Ted congratulates each as they arrive. With some food inside me, I clamber around to take in the spectacle from different angles. I've to remind myself there's a fatal drop off two sides of this apex. Once I've satisfied the tourist within me, I scuttle back to my small sanctuary and settle in, protected from the breeze. The thin air will force the next step in our quest for the summit of Everest.

Greg Takes in the View from the Top

Laying on my back, a tiny pillow of sand comforts my head. The sun finds me and warms my face. I hear camera shutters catching memories. I can now make the first accurate measurement of my expedition progress. Six months ago, this had been the earliest place I felt dreadful. I was weak. I didn't want to move. Right now I don't wish to move either, but only because I'm so relaxed. I'm delighted. I doze off, gaining maximum benefit from this new altitude.

"Ok, team, let's head down," Ted says.

Groups of twos and threes rise to their feet. Greg nudges me.

"Hold on, Greg, ten more minutes, this sun is beautiful."

"Let's go," he says.

"It'll do us good. A little extra acclimatisation, come on."

"OK, ten minutes." He leans his head back against the rock beside me.

The voices of the team fade away below us.

Ten minutes later Greg and I depart. We negotiate the rocks and find the clay track. My speed at times gets the better of me. I keep forgetting to go slow. I don't want to undo our cautious progress, or worse still, twist an ankle. But as the extra oxygen fills me on the descent, it's hard to contain my enthusiasm. My legs and knees are like elastic as I bound down rocky steps.

"This has been our best day so far," Greg says.

"Wow, close to five thousand metres and smiling, I didn't think it was possible. Base Camp is only three hundred and fifty metres higher."

The hike up hurt us, but my appetite was strong at the top. Now on the way down, my legs have found a gear I never knew I had. As we stride off the steeper section, leaving the lunch spot some four hundred metres above us, I can classify the day as a success.

"I feel like I'm at sea level." I skip over a hollow.

"I'm pretty good too, but remember: don't get cocky."

They're wise words, but on this bright afternoon with under an hour to the hostel, I allow myself a moment of cockiness. I feel great. I'm full of energy. If I can make it to Base Camp healthy, then dare I dream how much further, how much higher I might push my luck?

Mid-afternoon finds us resting in the hostel, thrilled with our day's exertion.

"I'm going to pop to the shop. The Chuckle Brothers gave me directions." I sit up on my bed. "A little chocolate and maybe some Fanta, keep the calories going in. Can I get you something?"

"I'm good, thanks," Greg says.

The village resembles the last few we've walked through. Small stone houses comprise the accommodation. More modern two story buildings offer lodgings for trekkers. Wobbly walls a metre high surround fields of poor soil. A dusty track two metres wide provides the main street. Yak dung clings to everything. I can't imagine a lot happens when the sun goes down, not that much seems to occur when the sun is up either.

I'm standing in a small room at the front of a house. It's perhaps two metres deep and four metres wide, with a counter in the middle. Products of all descriptions envelop a brown faced woman behind the desk. I recognise many of the brand names. I'd say some have been here a while. She doesn't speak English, and I've no Nepalese, but with a little pointing and holding up fingers, to indicate quantities, a trade is performed. It feels unexpectedly nice to be separated from the regime of the group and to perform an independent act, even one as mundane as this simple transaction. I saunter back to the hostel, content in my own company.

Back in our room, Greg is resting on his bed.

"Head up to the others about five?" he asks.

"Sounds good, an hour and a half rest will be perfect."

I prop up some blankets and a pillow on my bed to make sure my head is raised. I pull my sleeping bag over me and snuggle in. I'll munch on a bar of chocolate in thirty minutes.

It's 4pm and snack time. The thin air will thump my appetite above here, and I know I'll struggle to swallow proper meals. I'll be beaten when faced with a plate of unappetising rice, but simple snacks and chocolate always appeal to me.

I don't feel like a nibble now though. Regardless, I must consume something. At the very least I need to chomp two bars of chocolate each day, in addition to the set-down meals. I choose a Twix and take a bite. My mouth just doesn't want to know about it. This is a big change from earlier. I'll find it hard to eat what's served at Base Camp in the weeks ahead, and I've placed a lot of reliance on eating two a day. I hope my body hasn't decided it doesn't like cocoa products. Without the fat and sugars that the hundred confectionary bars in my duffle bag contain, I'll have no chance of summiting. Difficult or not, I have to eat this Twix bar, and so I do.

Greg ties up his boots and gets ready for dinner.

"I don't feel good. Not at all," I say.

"Serious? What's up?"

"No idea."

"Dinner?"

"Head up without me."

"God, that doesn't sound good."

"I know."

"Do you think you got something?"

"I hope not."

Yak dung covers the trail. The toilet facilities are grim. There's no hand basin, and a constant stream of trekkers and locals wade through this environment. It only takes one chink in the armour to get whacked. Greg's earlier warning not to get cocky now rings in my ears.

The light fades and turns to darkness. I lie in bed. I grapple with the covers. I don't want to move. My breathing labours, my muscles hurt, and my stomach tightens. This is a rotten end to a wonderful day. Two or three ghastly hours pass. Greg eases into the room.

"How're we doing?"

"Not good." I breathe out.

"Anything I can do?"

"Pray for a quick death."

"Ok, give me a shout if you need anything during the night."

"Will do, night."

I know where this is going. If I stay dead still, I'll continue to feel terrible. If I move, I'll throw up. And of course I'll still feel dreadful. Either way I'm going to be sick. I'll gain nothing by waiting till the last second and vomiting all over my sleeping bag and gear. I stagger to the toilet. My legs wobble. I'm nauseous. I'm doubled over like an old man. I'm back in this dim latrine. There's that hole in the floor. My eyes are squeezed shut to block the pain. Now they're open, now closed again. Perspiration drips off my brow. Damn this valley and the diseases that fester in its every corner. What am I doing here? Why do I push myself to do these stupid things? This is vile.

Hell breaks loose from all angles as my body presses the eject button.

Time passes. About the only thing I didn't do was bleed out my ears. I tidy myself as best as possible using the large barrel of water. To be kind to everyone else, and with the few shreds of dignity I still possess, I clean down the area as best I can. Even in a spotless western toilet, those advertisements on TV remind us that germs can lurk in hidden corners. They'll not be lurking here. The microbes are sitting out sunning themselves, meeting new partners, and bathing in the squalor. Passing within a metre of this toilet could now knock ten years off a man's life.

"Well, that went about as badly as could be expected." I re-enter the bedroom.

Greg chuckles.

"I wasn't sure you'd re-appear. They were some sounds. How're you doing now?"

"It'll be a long night."

He reaches into his medical kit and hands me a tablet.

"Take this. It's Cipro, an antibiotic. It should kill everything."

"God, I wish it would kill me."

I hope this Cipro thing is strong. Anti-acids won't be much use against the might of Nepalese bacteria.

I get back into bed. I feel a little better but know this night is far from over.

As I rest on my back, so glad to be off my feet, I recognise that my stomach and bowels will have to regain my trust from scratch. Farting has now been moved into the high risk category. At the first hint of danger, I'll dash for the exit.

Last night, Greg and I deduced that getting the room next to the toilet was a bad idea. Constant and often unpleasant visitations flourished. Now its proximity gives me reassurance. I've positioned my boots where my feet will hit the floor. All gear and equipment between the bed and the door has been shoved aside. I reckon I can make it from bed to toilet in ten seconds. Soon enough, I receive an opportunity to test my legs. Then back to recover.

I'm wiped-out. How will I walk tomorrow? This will take a lot out of me, perhaps too much. When illness last struck me in this valley, it took a full month to clear. If I've been hit with something similar, my climb is over.

APRIL 7

Trek from Dingboche (4,400m) to

Lobuche (4,900m)

About 4am I paid my last visit to the latrine. Eating nothing since lunchtime yesterday, and then expelling whatever food and water was in my system, has left me feeble.

"How're you now?" Greg pulls back his covers.

"Thrashed, but the last few hours have been better."

"Will you manage breakfast?"

"Better to skip it. Anything could happen."

"Here." Greg hands me a pill. "Take another Cipro. We might nip this thing in the bud."

The sun shines down on the patio, but I'm in no mood to absorb the beauty that surrounds me. A few of the team inquire as to my health. By way of response, I can only shake my head and indicate that the night was far from appealing.

"I'm a little off myself," Hugo says, "and Nadia hasn't improved."

"Man, we're falling like flies."

I've flunked the main objective of preseason. I hope that the improvement I'm feeling this morning is the start of a full and quick recovery.

We set off up the steep eighty metre hill that rises at the rear of the hostel. I complete the tail with Ade and Blake, and set as slow a pace as is possible, without actually stopping. Ang Nama treks a few steps below us. I carry a bottle of Fanta in my hand. I hope that if I can take a sip every ten minutes and hold it down, then I might make it to the lunch target. Blake pulls away from us. I call up to him, reminding him again of the tale about the cattle. He responds that by the time the old bulls plod to the upper field, he'll have had his wicked way and we're welcome to what remains. Ade smiles to me and shakes his head.

"I can feel this," he says. "Even slow is too fast."

Shattered
After a long night, I leave Dingboche below me. Ade accompanies me. Ang Nama, as ever, brings up the rear.

We reach the top and pause for a short break. I lean against a stupa to catch my breath. Blake has waited and takes a photo of us. The Himalayas have thrown forth a photographer's paradise on this bright morning, with the glistening Imja River snaking through the valley. Most of the team has pushed a few hundred metres ahead on the brown trail that cuts through a sparse, green covering.

"What's up ahead?" Blake asks.

"We've got a few kilometres along the trail, where the team is. It's almost flat, just a little against us. That'll take us to lunch."

"You'll make it?"

"I feel better than I expected. Let's see."

I'm hiking alongside Greg, Angel, Ade, and Martin. A stream of Sherpas and heavily laden yaks pass us, also ascending to Base Camp. The bells around the animals' necks, ringing with every pace, give the atmosphere a Swiss Alpine feel. All the time I'm noting that the sugary sips of Fanta I've taken have so far stayed down. Is it possible that the illness has released me so quickly?

We catch up with the rest of the team, who've taken a break outside an abandoned stone hut. They're sheltering on its leeward side. While it's not cold walking, it wouldn't take long once stopped for the light breeze to penetrate a layer of clothing and chill a layer of sweat.

"I'll keep going," I say.

They'll pass me quick enough once their break is over.

Pumori
Pumori is the leftmost peak. It's about two and a half kilometres above me.

Another hour and a half of trekking takes us across a narrow, fast flowing river to the two building settlement of Thukla. Here at 4,600 metres, I spot most of the team sitting outside a teahouse for lunch. I ease into a chair near the end of the table.

"Hi guys. I see you started without me."

"We gave up on you a long time ago," Doug says.

Ade chuckles.

"I'm just glad to make it."

The Fanta now gone, I sip on lemon tea.

"It feels good to sit down." I lean back in the chair.

"Lunch?" Khalid asks.

Prior to arriving in Kathmandu, he was the only climber I knew on the team apart from Ted. We were together on the training climb six months ago. He's a little older than my thirty-seven years. Another newcomer to the mountains, he began preparing at the start of last year. He's carrying a few more kilograms around the waist than me. That'll be a bonus; the demands that lie ahead will burn them up in no time. He's aspiring to be the first Omani to summit Mount Everest. Like me on Pumori, he was also spent by the time we turned back.

"No, I'll skip lunch. It's too risky. I'll grab a bar of chocolate."

I dig a Bounty bar out of my pack. After twenty-four hours without food, it tastes so good. With the weight off my legs and my pack on the ground, I begin to feel human.

One of the trekkers dashes from the table and hurls up her lunch. I'd seen worse at a lower height during our training climb. That time there'd been no warning. One of the team vomited on the table. That expedition had prepared climbers for what happens at altitude; although, I've learnt as much as I need to know about illness in this valley by now.

"Here come Nadia and Hugo," Khalid says.

I lift up my head and stare down the trail. I don't recognise the familiar pair.

"Where are they?"

"Just there, down on the trail." He points.

I recognise Nadia, trudging up towards us, less than seventy metres away.

"I see her, but where's Hugo?" I ask.

"Look, beside her. They don't look good."

"What? Him?"

I'm staring at an old man, crouched over, struggling to move forward. It's impossible. But that's his gear, his tan coloured hat, the trekking poles. I can't believe that resilient, well-built Hugo has been reduced to this. He powered up hills, head high and chest out, all week. The inclines never raised his breathing. The shape below has the faltering steps of a withered refugee, dragging himself from a war zone. He's one of the guides who are supposed to lead us to the summit. I don't wish to watch their last five minutes of struggle.

Hugo and Ted are in discussion away from the table. It's decided the two patients will descend; going up is not an option. They'll spend two days at a village named Pheriche to recover, or longer if necessary. Their descent should take two hours from here. Looking at Hugo, no one could imagine him scaling Everest. Nadia's shot at Island Peak has been blown apart. I can continue, but only a delusional fool could picture me reaching the summit. And so the team divides.

Greg and I turn to face the incline that's behind our lunch stop.

"Man, that looks steep," Greg says. "You're ok to tackle it?"

"I'm still walking."

"Can you remember from last time? How high is that?"

"It's almost a full day's acclimatisation in itself." I lift up my pack. "It goes up about two hundred and fifty metres in one go. It twists through the boulders. The top is the bit you can see just there." I point. "See you at the far side, but not any time soon."

The rest of the team disappear among the rocks. I settle into a measured pace. Every fifteen minutes I sit on a rock for a five minute break. My breathing slows. Excess exertion may eject the coconut chocolate treat that comprised lunch. I keep an eye on the altimeter and note I'm over 4,750 metres. The oxygen hides from my lungs. It's odd to just sit on a rock for five minutes and stare down a valley, motionless. I care not for nature's panorama. The team has already cleared the challenge. I'm not worried about delaying anyone. Getting to Lobuche before sunset is all that matters. Not throwing up is what concerns me.

Rest over, another quarter hour of disciplined, uphill drudgery commences.

In my own world, I complete each fifteen minute section and drag in the top. The climb has belted me. But this morning, I didn't expect to see what was beyond it. With my breathing still under control, I push around the topmost boulder. I see the team just ahead, beneath prayer flags at a graveyard.

A few groups mill around to read inscriptions on the memorials. If a climber dies in these mountains, they can expect a chisel to etch out their name here in rock. Five died on Everest last year. Eleven lost their lives in 2006. I'm aiming for a Dublin epitaph, and not in this decade.

Clouds have dropped down on us. I zip up my fleece as the wind grabs the prayer flags. We had the same weather conditions the last time I was here. The mist grips these memorial rocks and dampens and depresses the surrounding mood. Not wishing to get cold, I keep walking. Greg joins me, and the two of us press on.

"You're looking a bit better," Greg says.

"Yeah, not too bad, I'll make Lobuche."

We trek through the upper valley along the banks of a small stream. The slight gradient asks few questions, and we make decent progress. Several hundred metres to our left, we see a neat collection of at least twenty tents.

"Whose tents are those I wonder?" Greg asks.

"It's the middle of nowhere, just at the base of a mountain," I say.

"Russian brides," I hear Ang Nama say.

"What? Russian brides? Let's get right over there," I say.

"No, no," Ang Nama says. "Russell Brice, not Russian brides. The tents belong to his Himex team."

"Oh, that's a disappointment. What are they doing here?"

"The Icefall is dangerous, very dangerous. Some teams do acclimatisation rotations elsewhere. Lobuche peak, just there." Ang Nama points up to the mountain on our left. "Same height as Camp 1, six thousand one hundred metres. They'll acclimatise up there, short time in Icefall."

It sounds like a clever strategy. They'll still have to do at least one rotation up to Camp 3 before attempting a summit push. But from what I've heard, the less time spent in the Icefall the better. Three Sherpas died at its hands on the same day in 1982. Six were taken in a moment back in the early seventies. Ice avalanches, falling seracs, and a tumble into a crevasse pose a constant danger.

Greg and I start the final stretch into Lobuche. Despite illness, I'm in better condition than at this point six months ago. I can remember pounding along this section with my head throbbing. Chatting with Greg, the metres disappear behind us into the weak afternoon sun. An hour later, we turn a corner to be greeted by the sight of tonight's village at 4,900 metres.

"I see standards drop as we get higher," Greg says.

"You can write off the comforts of home here."

We see half a dozen stone lodges and not much else. A small stream that trickles through provides the drinking water. We'll experience freezing conditions here tonight. I remember my last visit here: a cold damp room, so-so food, and a hole in the ground for a toilet. I read a sign requesting that the toilet door be shut to seal in the smell. That's all well and good, unless of course you're inside suffocating.

We find the lodge where the team is staying. Greg and I settle into a room barely wider than the two single beds within and only half a metre longer. It's not as bad as I'd recalled. A sheet of plywood separates each bedroom from the next. I'll be glad to lie down later. After a night of horrors and a trek with no food, I'm more than happy with our lodgings.

We head back to the mess for tea and biscuits. On the way I spot the trekker who'd been ill at lunch. She's sitting on a bed in her room, her face white as a sheet. Hopefully she'll improve, but I suspect her rough afternoon will be trumped by a harrowing night.

"You're looking much better," Martin says as I approach the table.

"My appetite's back anyway. Pass me down that flask will you?"

Angel gets up from the group and does a tour of the rooms to make sure no one's lying down. Being horizontal is thought to increase blood around the brain and contribute further to altitude sickness. I'll set up my mattress tonight to make sure my head is well raised.

As the sun sets, a pack of cards appears. We spend the evening eating, sipping tea, playing cards, and chatting. One by one we head off to bed and leave this room for the Sherpas to sleep in.

Back in our room by 9:30pm, Greg and I are stretching out our sleeping bags. Ice on the small window distorts what lies beyond in the dark, but these bags will have us cosy in no time.

"Take a Cipro," Greg says, "and another one tomorrow morning. Then you should be ok."

"Thanks. I'll open this window a little."

"What? Are you mad? It's freezing out there."

"Last time I was here, I'd a killer headache," I say. "These rooms are tiny. The little oxygen that's here will be gone in no time. By the time I tried to open the window in the middle of the night last time, it had frozen solid."

"Ok, just an inch."

I push it open a crack. The momentary touch of the glass chills my fingers. We've ascended far above the night time freezing level. Every metre above here will deliver yet colder evenings. On a single day in the mid-eighties, four Indian climbers succumbed to exposure near the summit and froze to death. Next month I might reminisce on tonight with warm, fond memories.

"Hugo was in bad shape today." I reach for the light switch. "Will he make it back?"

"He'd better. If we're down a guide, we're seriously compromised."

"Let's hope no one else falls before Base Camp."

After a distressing twenty-four hours, I consider the positive as I wait to drift off. Last time in Lobuche, I'd been one of those lying on a bed mid-afternoon, struggling to stand. I'd taken paracetamol but to no effect. And that night, I'd woken up for about two hours. Sitting on the bed, I'd thought my head would explode. I'd convinced myself that the small room was almost airtight and the oxygen in it had been used up. This evening, at most, I feel a slight dullness.

I'm on track. If I can stay healthy tomorrow morning, I'll reach Base Camp fit by early afternoon. When we set out from Lukla a week ago, I expected more than a few dints in the armour. As Greg says, just keep drinking and peeing to stay strong. Although maybe not right now; this is my sleeping bag for the next seven weeks.

APRIL 8

Trek from Lobuche (4,900m) to

Base Camp (5,350m)

One day to Base Camp. My illness from two days ago has vanished.

"That's too bad about Blake." Greg steps out into the cold morning air.

"Blake? What happened to him?" I'm pulling on my skinny gloves.

"He's out –"

"What?"

"He's out. His heart was racing over one twenty all night, same problem this morning. Ted says it's too high. The only safe option is to go down."

"No Island Peak for him?" I ask.

"His lips were blue when I examined him. I guess if he recovers down low, he can try. Maybe he could catch up with the others. Just skip the Base Camp visit."

"That sounds like a long shot. That's the end of the Chuckle Brothers."

"Reckon so," Greg says.

"Damn. There's Blake now. I better go over and say something."

He looks healthy, but the spark is missing. We exchange a few words. A couple of minutes later, he descends the valley in the company of a Sherpa who'll keep an eye on him.

Des, what remains of the Chuckle Brothers, is standing at the door with Greg and me.

"I didn't count on that." Des looks down.

"It's a shame to see him go. Well, keep your spirits up. At least he's alive and well."

I'll miss Blake's jesting. The reality dawns on me as I watch him disappear; we'll probably never see each other again.

Other teams have suffered similar illnesses as us. We hear that six out of nine climbers on the Alpine Ascents squad have already picked up infections.

We stroll out of Lobuche up a gently sloping grass valley. Under the warming sun, Greg and I natter with two Canadian trekkers from the group at the rear. We debate politics, the environment, and bankers, the bad guys of the day for all nationalities. They determine that their next holiday will be focused on leisure and relaxation. They're many years older than us. This excursion has demanded more of them than they'd planned. With luck they'll experience a night at Base Camp and then descend to lower altitudes and better times.

After an hour and a half we reach the end of the valley. Greg and I stare at a boulder strewn slope in front of us.

"We'll really push into the highlands now," I say. "After that slope, it's mostly rock and dust, very little grass."

"You know the route all the way?"

"No, somewhere this afternoon it becomes glacier. That'll be all new to me."

I plod up the track and wind around the boulders. The altimeter indicates that the 5,000 metre mark has been broken. Under normal circumstances this would be the summit of something very high. Here it's just a point in the valley. As yet we haven't even started climbing. I wipe my brow. Each step stings my legs. At the top of the hill I find the team sitting on rocks. I join them, recover, and then enjoy a snack and some water.

The end of preseason approaches. Up ahead I see Pumori, now colossal. To the right of where we'll trek stands Nuptse. Just past it, Everest rises, its summit almost four kilometres above us. Resting on this rock, I can't pretend it's not there. All this effort, the training, the planning aims to get me to that peak I can now see in the sky. God, I hope I make it.

We press on. I toil up over rocks and past boulders into thinner air. Just a few hundred metres to our right I see the Khumbu glacier. It's not the glistening white the Discovery Channel leads us to believe is the preserve of all glaciers. It's a dull grey. I can't comprehend the size of its menacing presence. Jagged ridges reach up along its length. Beside them I see shadows, darkness, probably crevasses. I suspect they're huge, lethal drops, but I'm bewildered trying to interpret this alien spectacle. It doesn't look trekker-friendly. There's something sinister to this weird shape that stretches beside us. As yet there's no sign of the famous Icefall, where millions of tons of ice soar up six hundred metres towards Camp 1.

"I don't think we're last," Greg says. "And we haven't gone any faster today."

"It's everyman for himself now." I breathe deep. "I've no idea how stretched out we are. But yeah, there're a lot behind."

We turn around a rock corner.

"In the distance," a person sitting at the side of the trail says. "That's Base Camp, the coloured spots."

I strain my eyes and focus on tiny yellow dots at the base of the West Shoulder. They must be seven kilometres from where we're standing. Preseason will soon be over.

For an hour the altitude clouts me, before the village of Gorak Shep presents itself. This is the last settlement prior to Everest, probably the highest in the world. At this height of 5,200 metres stand half a dozen teahouses. Excluding people with internet satellite accounts, this is the highest point from which an email can be sent. Many climbers from Base Camp will drop down here over the next two months to stay in touch with home.

View back down the Trail
The Khumbu glacier runs down the left of the photo between the rocks and the mountain. Vegetation has ceased. Clouds cover the lower valley.

Greg and I step into one of the buildings. I drop down on a bench and lean back against the wall. I let out a long breath. Over twenty minutes I consume three mugs of tea, pretty much drinking till I can take no more. It's a welcome break to sit with the lads. Our conversation is clipped.

"Anyone got tablets? My head's killing me," one says.

"Me too," another says.

Small containers kick around the table. I root out my medical kit and offer its contents.

Greg, Doug, and I push back onto the trail for the concluding stretch. Two dozen trekkers and climbers from other groups hike across a dry lake bed. Only a hundred and fifty metres in altitude remain for us. The trail splits. I know the route to the left; an hour that way sits Pumori Base Camp. But a signpost directs us right. Black writing on a yellow metal sign reads "WAY TO M.T. EVEREST B.C.".

The Path Diverges
Last time I went left. From here on, everything is new. The lower slope of Nuptse is on the right of the photo. The glacier is hidden, but lies between me and Nuptse. A few more kilometres and we'll round Nuptse. The peak above and to the right of the signpost is the West Shoulder. Base Camp lies below it.

We trudge up onto a small ridge, and the yellow dots reappear, this time a little larger. The lack of oxygen saps my energy. Greg draws in air beside me.

"It looks like we'll follow this ridge for a mile, maybe less." Greg pushes himself over a rock. "Then we'll move onto the glacier."

"This'll be a longer day than I thought. There's still some way to those tents." I stare down at my boots, and try to keep my breathing under control.

The others have slipped back. I slog on at the steady pace that's working for me. A drop of several metres threatens me on the left. On my right and only a stone's throw away lies the glacier. Up ahead the figure of Des becomes visible. He's shuffling forward; the thin air has thrashed most of us. High altitude is classified as 1,500 – 3,500 metres, very high altitude from 3,500 – 5,500. At 5,250 metres, we're pushing our limits today. Des cuts a lonely figure without his buddy Blake. I've also never seen him close to me near the end of a day's hike.

"Hey Des." I reach the end of the ridge.

"Dude. Some day. No Greg?"

"Just behind."

Ted appears from behind a boulder. He must marshal a long string of climbers today, each trying to make it to the finish. A kilometre ahead I spy the first tent. Beyond it stretches a chain of yellow, red, and blue blobs for over a kilometre along the rock covered glacier. This is something I've only ever seen on TV. I expected glacial white, but grey-brown is the tint of the day. For white views, I must look up high to the mountains and ridges surrounding the camp.

"Hi Fergus. Ok?" Ted asks.

"Grand, thanks." I exhale. "And yourself?"

"No problems."

"Which tents are ours? How do we get there?"

"They're at the very end. Follow the moraine, and you'll come to them."

He may as well tell me to follow the North Star, or the Death Star for that matter.

"Once again, Ted. Where are they?"

"They're over there." He points towards the West Shoulder, far past the closest tents.

The moraine Ted referred to is the glacial debris of rocks and boulders that covers the surface of the glacier, hence the dull colour. He stays where he is to encourage struggling trekkers. I commence the last challenge of preseason.

"All right, Des, let's go," I say.

"Go on yourself." He shakes his head and waves me off.

The trail drops down as it crosses a scree slope. The footsteps of Sherpas have hardened a track through the rubble. Twenty metres of gravel hang above me. I've no idea what forces of anti-gravity are keeping them from collapsing.

The route turns right, and the landscape underfoot changes. I plod on. Craters ten metres wide and deep surround me. I stare into one. Only the first metre of what I'm standing on is brown rock. Underneath the rock is solid ice. Water flows beneath that. I'm treading on the Khumbu glacier.

I slog upwards and reach a flag covered boulder, around which two dozen trekkers have gathered. Mementos and messages decorate the rocks. The first camp stands just fifty metres away. This spot has been declared the entrance to Base Camp. A bottle of champagne passes from hand to hand.

I sit on a rock to get air into my lungs. The celebration irritates me. My reaction surprises me; I should be a bigger man and delight in the success of others. But I can see no reason to rejoice on reaching this spot. Drained by the lack of oxygen, I've completed no more than ten per cent of what I set out to do. This was the easy bit. Stay healthy and keep on plodding is the preseason mantra. The challenge only begins in earnest in the next few days. I face one and a half months of even less oxygen and more suffering. However, it would be sweet to celebrate something right now.

I feel like I'm wandering through a quarry. Huge boulders and rocky debris litter the glacier. The trail winds past various camps. For now these settlements are just skeletons. Over the next two weeks, an influx of climbers, tents, and equipment will arrive. I have to retrace my footsteps when I stray off the track into danger.

I hike for forty minutes on the glacier, moving closer to the last tents. I search for a familiar face that will declare the next camp as ours. Not this one, not this one. Gasping, I step up over another rock. I want the next base to be ours, but I know the closer it is to the Icefall, the less trekking we must do in and out, once we start our acclimatisation rotations. The stretch to the finish drains me.

The mountain looms in my face. The brown pyramid lump that is the summit of Everest hides behind the West Shoulder. The next time I see the peak, I'll be up there much closer or down the valley much further away having quit. My lungs get nothing from the air. Each step hurts me.

It's been a longer drag today than I'd expected, but there it is. Forty metres ahead I spy our tents.

I am here. Preseason is over. This is Base Camp. This is now home for the greatest adventure of my life.

APRIL 8

Into Base Camp (5,350m)

This is a big set-up. The Sherpas have been busy for over a week. I see a large mess tent, a kitchen tent, and several smaller ones. All around await sites, the size of large kitchen tables, which have been levelled out in preparation for our personal sleeping tents. Rough stone steps have been fashioned to join the different levels of camp together.

I do a quick gauge of my health compared to this stage on the Pumori trip. Back then I'd a headache that would have flattened an elephant. I remember trying to pitch my tent. I'd been dazed and nauseous, incapable of binding the poles and clips together. I'd to ask Ang Nama to help me. I'd popped into the toilet tent, was walloped by the odour, stumbled out, and threw up. The lads watching had been doubled over in laughter. I'd been a sight: holding a towel in front of my manly bits in a hopeless attempt to preserve some dignity. It had been presumed the puking was from food poisoning in Lobuche, but I suspect it was just altitude sickness. That memory bares no relationship to my current state.

I recognise some of the Sherpas from Pumori; although, their names stretch beyond my reach. They fill the air with chatter. They'll have a chance to show off their skills over the next six weeks. We chat as I take on water.

"You can put your tent where you like," one says. "No person here."

I stroll around and settle on a location. Rocks to the rear and right protect it from wind. A ridge twenty metres from the front will also offer some shelter. It's not too close to the latrines; they're sure to have visitors at all hours of the night. A level path leads back to the mess. That'll minimise tripping or slipping on ice after the sun sets. This will do nicely. The view down the Khumbu Valley isn't too shabby either.

"The duffle bags are here." A Sherpa points to a plastic covered pile.

I rummage underneath it.

"This one's mine." I pull it out of the heap. "And here's the other. Great stuff, no problems with the yaks I see."

"Two? I carry one." He takes it out of my hand, and lugs it to my chosen site.

No sooner have I exposed the tent's stuff-sack, than three Sherpas take it from me. It's a Mountain Hardware Trango, standard fare up here. Their speed at this altitude amazes me.

"I've a ground sheet. Give me a second." I haul it from my bag and spread it out.

I could pitch the tent myself, but I'd be messing about for twenty minutes getting everything just so. These lads have it up in five. We secure it to rocks, and it's ready to go. I crawl inside.

It feels good to be here again, like revisiting a holiday house. This will be my residence for several weeks, best get it sorted out. I drag in stuff from the duffel bags and backpack, and set up my home from home. I shove the bits and pieces I'll need into the little pockets along the inside of the tent: toiletries, medicine, tiny MP3 and earphones, penknife, sun block, head torch, chocolate bars for the next five days, and so on. I stick my shades and hat into the pouch on the ceiling. Underneath me, I've placed a dense foam mattress which one of the Sherpas carried from the storage tent. It's comfy and will provide great insulation. Beside the mattress I position the clothes I'll wear for the next few days. I place my large, red -20C sleeping bag on top of it. I pack everything else, such as climbing gear we won't require till we venture above Base Camp, back into the duffel bags. I carry them over to the storage tent.

I wriggle back into the tent, lie down on the snug pad, and relax.

In dribs and drabs the rest of the team arrive. I hear Greg's voice outside.

"Hey buddy. You got yourself set-up?" I stick my head out into the sunshine.

"Those last two hours were the toughest this week," Greg says. "But we're here. Well done."

"Thanks, and yourself. We've a few rest days ahead, plenty of time to acclimatise and recover."

"Great," Greg says. "So that's preseason over."

"Over indeed, I didn't expect to arrive here in such good shape," I say. "Thanks for the help."

"Not at all. Now get yourself ready for the season proper."

A dinner of roasted chicken legs comes and goes. I opt for seconds of the white meat. But the carbohydrate-packing rice has me beaten. Most have retired before 9pm.

I've been looking forward to crashing out in my tent. But after a near perfect trip up the valley, sleep now deserts me. It's crucial to performance. It's a vital part of the recovery and acclimatisation process, but it will not be rushed or forced. The hours pass. At least I'm not cold; the bag and sleeping mat are protecting me from the glacier underneath.

I expected a deep slumber, but by 2am it hasn't happened. Altitude plays havoc on sleep and, ironically, just at a time when the body needs it more than ever. My heart races to get oxygen to where it's needed. My mind plays out the coming weeks in minute detail. In the small hours of the morning, I have to recognise that the mountain is the master here.

APRIL 9 – APRIL 12

Settling into Base Camp

've settled into camp life. The main activities are breakfast, lunch, and dinner. Outside of that, we're free to do whatever we want.

The large mess tent sits about twenty at a squeeze. In the evenings we wear insulated pants, down jackets, and hats for dinner. We fire up a gas heater about 5pm when the temperature drops. The last person out of the tent at night, around 10pm, switches it off. Ted has a second heater in reserve. It'll be moved in once the trekkers and Island Peak climbers have left Base Camp and there's space.

Beside the mess stands the large kitchen tent, where the cook prepares meals and the Sherpas hang out. They also eat their dinners there rather than with us. I don't know why this is. While we're already crammed around our table, and I hear they favour a different diet, I think perhaps they prefer it this way. Not all of them speak English. Excitable, fast Nepalese flows from their shelter. I can't say for certain if they appreciate our presence or view us as a necessary evil. Many of the foreigners on this glacier live to climb. They've honed mountain skills over decades. But plenty of us might be viewed as inept individuals, who've confused the value of hard-earned experience with the ease of fast-won cash. Our tourist dollars may inject life into the economy, but that doesn't mean the locals have to like it.

A small storage tent contains equipment. A provisions tent, adjacent to the kitchen, bulges with enough food to feed forty odd people for the next seven weeks. Two buckets with taps sit outside the mess. One is always filled with drinking water. The other, with the bar of soap beside it, allows us wash our hands before eating. My rudimentary cleanse is nothing compared to Surgeon Greg's meticulous five minute scrub. I'm surprised there's any skin left on his hands. Having observed him, I've expanded my simplistic rub into something more thorough.

Three toilet tents tolerate the necessities, each of which is a metre square and two and a half metres high. Beneath each lurks a bucket. The Sherpas followed a clever stonework design to ensure reasonable ventilation, but I shudder on entering. A man's got to do what a man's got to do. Even still, I'd swap my kingdom for a flushable loo.

Lastly, there's the shower tent, about two metres square. A wash is best taken around noon when the weather's warmest. To arrange one, we ask the chef in the kitchen for hot water. He fills a three gallon plastic bladder, which has a nozzle on its underside. We hang the bladder from a hook inside the shower tent, and gravity does the rest. The flow of water is feeble, but under the circumstances it's splendid.

Our personal tents sit around these team fixtures. We have sixteen for the mountaineers, three for the guides, tents for the Sherpas, and a few temporary ones for the trekkers and Island Peak climbers. A similar scene will repeat itself for every squad stretched out for a kilometre behind us along the rock-covered glacier.

Over twenty camps are being constructed. Some two hundred and fifty climbers will call this home. All are aiming for the favourable weather window in May, when the high altitude winds abate for a few days each year. With each afternoon, more coloured tents hide grey rock. I've heard that Himex, one of the largest and best known commercial teams, has brought three hundred tents with them. It seems a huge number. But adding up what will be needed at Base Camp, up on the mountain, and back at their Lobuche acclimatisation site, then perhaps there's truth in the rumour.

Our own camp is still taking shape. We're fashioning modifications and improvements in these early days. Ted and Matthew, a tall Australian who trained with Ted two years ago, have bound multiple solar panels of varying models together. I watched them channel the resulting power into car-style batteries. They spliced cables with ease and synchronised currents and amps to solve problems I never knew existed. Matthew must have been an electrician in a previous life, or perhaps electronics was part of his training in the Australian Special Forces.

Greg pitched his green tent just to the left of mine. In front sit the tents of the two Turks. To the right, Roger lives in a circular style tent with lots of space inside. That's the model I'd go for in future. He has ample freedom to sit upright and get dressed into bulky, climbing equipment. A little further in front and to the right is where Ade, Martin and Doug sleep. They look like a mini-team with their matching orange homes in a neat row.

Sitting on a rock in the morning sun, either brushing my teeth or shaving, there's usually another doing likewise or organising gear. Testing my harness one afternoon, Doug joined me, and we discussed various configurations that might come in useful. Being a fireman, he knows a thing or two about ropes. I explained how I've set up my kit for the mountain. He demonstrated some knots that'll come in handy if my abseiling gear was to become damaged up high. I've studied and practiced knots over and over; although as yet, I've used few in a real life situation.

Doug and I did as much fooling around and laughing as we did learning. Pete, a tall American, who'd been listening from his tent, came out to join us. He was impressed by what he'd heard and commented that I knew my stuff. If only he knew that most of my knot-work is limited to practicing on the leg of a table in the TV room back home. If anyone needs help to lower a TV through the Icefall later this month, I'm your man.

I'm still getting a feel for how colossal the Icefall might be. Anyone who heads for the summit from Nepal on this southern side, as we are, has to fight their way up through it and back again. There's no skipping around it. From here it looks like a pile of popcorn. The white, irregular shaped glacier funnels upwards, with the West Shoulder to its left and flanked by Nuptse on its right. It's hard to tell how far away the top is or how large these white lumps are. No doubt, those heading up the North Face from Tibet will confront their own set of hurdles.

View of the Icefall from Base Camp
1: Personal sleeping tents, 2: The shower tent
3: The next camp
4: The Icefall rises up 600 metres (Empire State Building is 380 metres)
5: The West Shoulder (this hides the summit of Everest)
6: Nuptse,
7: The peak of Lhotse in the distance, more than three kilometres above this point.

This morning I received an eye-opener. While we chatted outside the tents, someone spotted two Sherpas in the Icefall and pointed them out. I squinted and strained but couldn't see them. It took over a minute, following an outstretched finger and instructions, to see the Sherpas. These guys were in the lower third of the Icefall, nowhere near the top. From here they were two black specs in a sea of white. Towering, apartment-sized blocks of ice and snow surrounded them. That put matters into perspective; this vertical glacier is enormous. Witnessing it justifies all the stories I've heard about it. Many have turned back in there. I can only hope my climb does not bomb out at the first hurdle after Base Camp.

The ice doctors began exploring routes through the Icefall two weeks ago. Only the most experienced Sherpas gain entry to that squad. I think there are about ten of them in their team. The Everest National Park employs them. A tiny portion of our ten thousand US dollar climbing permit each covers their wages. On this moving glacier, they're tasked with creating a new passage through the danger and up to Camp 1 each year. As crevasses widen and ice boulders tumble down, they must then maintain and re-route the track until May 31. After that date, this southern route becomes impassable.

Last week they anchored the first of the ropes and ladders along their chosen path. On all but the flattest sections from here to the summit, a series of ropes known as the "fixed rope" will be laid along the trail. In the event of a slip, it'll prevent a connected climber falling to their death. On April 9th the doctors declared the channel through the Icefall to Camp 1 open. They secured over thirty ladders into the glacier with metal ice-screws to make our passage safer and easier. They would have hauled those aluminium ladders up there on their backs.

We, however, cannot venture in until a traditional ceremony has taken place for our team. This ritual, known as a Puja, is scheduled for April 12th. The climbers, Sherpas, and their equipment will be blessed. The Sherpas will not budge until it has taken place. So we sit and wait until the 13th. But that's fine, it's all part of the acclimatisation process. Our bodies need a few days to settle into this new altitude. The only disappointment is that headaches now trouble me, particularly in the mornings.

To pass time waiting for Puja, I've picked up a Swedish thriller from Ted's small library in the mess. I've taken to reading the book, by Stieg Larsson, late into the night by the light of a head torch in my tent. The watch thermometer beside me drops to -7C after nightfall, never higher, never lower. TC, a Canadian woman on our team who reached Camp 2 a few years back, has a thermometer attached to the outside of her tent. It falls to -15C in the small hours. The extreme glacial conditions, however, will only commence once we start the daunting climb out of Base Camp.

The trekkers departed on April 9th. It's unlikely I'll see any of them again. The following day, Des and the remnants of the Island Peak team exited camp to start their adventure proper. Blake could not complete the second half of the Chuckle Brothers. He had to descend to Namche Bazaar a few days ago to recover. His heart rate was still dangerously elevated. Whereas his climb is over, it's now very much back on for our guide Hugo. He ascended the remainder of the valley and is back to form. He has pitched his tent close by, between Roger and Pete.

View down the Valley from Base Camp
These tents are pitched on the moraine covered glacier, just in front of my tent.
1: Roger's tent 2: Hugo's tent 3: Pete's tent
4: Martin's tent 5: Ade's tent 6: Doug's tent
7: Another camp, 8: Nuptse

This morning we had Puja. It lasted an hour and a half. A Buddhist monk led chanting and burned fragrant twigs. He'd also performed the rite at Pumori Base

Camp. He had looked like one of the oldest people in the world back then. He's not any younger now. This is no place for old men. I was told this'll be his last year presiding at the ritual. I was upset to watch the fall he took this morning, but thankfully he wasn't injured.

His chants requested good fortune from the gods and apologised for what we're about to inflict upon nature. All things being equal, I'm certain the mountain will be the clear winner. Long after we're dead and buried, it will still be here. The Sherpas rubbed white flour on our faces in the hope we'd live long enough to be wise men with silver beards. If magic hair tonic is available, then I'd rather someone rub black flour on my receding top. Upon its conclusion, the Sherpas broke out in spontaneous song.

This afternoon we exercised with ropes and harnesses for a couple of hours within the confines of Base Camp. Ted set up several metres of line and we simulated steep terrain ascents and descents.

Basic Rope Practice in Base Camp

The mountain is now open. Tomorrow we'll don crampons and walk to the edge of the Icefall. We'll practice more rope work and climbing techniques but this time on snow and ice. The danger nears.

APRIL 13

Beyond Base Camp

L ate morning we push out of Base Camp into the lower reaches of the Icefall. Today is only practice; we'll blow away the cobwebs and tune our equipment. It's the first time this year I've donned my double layered mountaineering boots.

"OK, put your crampons on here," Ted says. "That's the end of the rocks."

"Did you ever think you'd see the day?" Greg drops his crampons onto the snow.

"There was a lot that could have prevented it." I drop down on one knee.

I clip the crampons onto my boots and then pull the straps tight. They'll give me a firm grip on snow and ice. With four sharp inch long spikes on the heel, eight on the sole, and two jutting out the front, I could in theory climb up a frozen waterfall. Safe I might be, but with just over a kilogram on each of my feet, I'm far from mobile. I'd forgotten just how cumbersome the boots and crampons are.

We walk out onto the set of a science fiction film. Ridge after ridge of ice rises up five to fifteen metres. I look behind me after five minutes and cannot remember how to get out. I'm not sure how these shapes formed. The glacier pushes down the valley about a metre a day. Millions of tons of ice above us press into this flat section. I presume these creases are forced upwards with the pressure. In a month's time, these folds will have travelled thirty metres further from the mountain. For now they're close to Nuptse and hopefully out of the track of avalanches. Our group thrusts in deeper.

The Team Pushes beyond Base Camp into the Icefall
There are several of these ridges just after Base Camp.

"What's this rubbish?" Doug points at something in the snow. "Is it metal?"

"That's the remains of a helicopter," Ted says. "There've been several crashes over the years."

Helicopters strain at altitude. But whatever about flying in thin air, landing and taking off risks disaster every time. Base Camp is close to the upper limit for a chopper to touch ground. The manoeuvre requires a highly skilled pilot. We've heard that a new generation of choppers have been seen in the region and that in an emergency they could land at Camp 2. I'm not sure how often, if ever, this has been performed.

Lift is generated by the down-force of the rotors against the air's density. The higher the altitude, the less dense the air, and the less force the rotors can provide. At a certain height, there's not enough lift to counteract the weight of the chopper. In addition, the engines suffer a loss of power due to the low oxygen environment. Landings and take offs at Base Camp always threaten carnage. The pilots never stop the blades spinning. It's been calculated that if a person was transported from sea level to the summit in a helicopter, they'd die within thirty minutes due to improper acclimatisation. It looks like there's only one way to the top, and that's the hard way. Nor are there any easy tickets home.

Ted pulls equipment out of his pack.

"Watch carefully." He places the kit onto the glacier. "This is how to screw a firm anchor into ice."

He demonstrates the process and then attaches rope to the ice-screws.

"Now it's your turn. Pair up and grab some screws. Practice it for twenty or thirty minutes."

We twist ice-screws into the glacier and test them as a firm anchor point for ropes. We shouldn't need to perform this on Everest as the Sherpas will lay a fixed rope all the way to the summit. But if something goes wrong or an avalanche sweeps away the rope, then these mountain skills and all available improvisation will be called upon.

"Ok, that's plenty on the ice-screws," Ted says. "Let's get back to climbing and rope skills. I've put some ropes onto that ridge. Everyone go up it, walk along the top and then abseil down over there." He points. "Do it a few times."

It's similar to what we did in Base Camp yesterday but on a larger scale and on snow and ice. We test ourselves and our equipment. The weather contributes to make this simulation as real as possible. Clouds have rolled in, and a biting wind reminds me we're challenging nature near the roof of the world.

While ascending, we use our jumars. It's an essential piece of mountaineering kit. The metal gadget is just larger than a fist, with a rubber coated handgrip. It employs a cam that slides in one direction along a rope, the intended path of movement, but grips it when pulled in the opposite direction. It attaches to my waist harness with a piece of strong webbing about the length of my arm. While up on the mountain, we should be attached to the fixed rope at all times via our jumar. As we ascend, we slide the jumar up along the rope. This keeps us secure. If we slip and tumble backwards, the jumar mechanism locks onto the rope and arrests our fall.

Several times I ascend the hard packed snow of the ice ridge and then abseil down the far side. Angel stands at the crest, observing technique and rope work.

"Yes, that's it, just lean back," he says. "That's perfect, super. Hand by your side. All the way down. That's it. Excellent. Now back up and do it again."

He could be a commentator at the Grand National.

Hugo stands close by. He ensures no one puts themselves into danger with an ill-fitted harness or through misuse of equipment.

As a backup, we've a second piece of webbing attached to our harness, which has a simple carabiner at its end. We clip this "safety" to the fixed rope. It has no gripping mechanism; so, if we tumble we'll fall all the way back to the last knot on the rope, maybe fifty metres below. But at least we'd still be connected to the rope and might manage to grab it and slow our fall en route. But the safety serves a purpose when ascending and reaching an anchor point. This is where a rope ends and is tied to ice-screws that have been fixed into the glacier. We must disconnect the jumar at this junction as it cannot slide over a knot to the next rope. But this leaves us exposed, even if just for a few seconds. If we slip at this moment or are thumped by a piece of debris from above, it's a one way ticket down. So before disconnecting the jumar at an anchor point, we first clip the safety onto the start of the next rope. Now, even with the jumar released, we can lean backwards as we're already fastened to the next rope. In theory, a climber should never fall off Everest. The reality is more complex. More than sixty-five climbers have fallen to their death off this mountain or died at the bottom of a crevasse.

Self-Rescue Practice
This procedure simulates a rescue from a crevasse. The jumar in my right hand is connected to my waist harness. The jumar in my left is connected to a sling in which my left boot sits. The inactive safety rests just above the right jumar. Spare carabiners, a spare jumar, and an ice axe hang from gear loops on my harness. I should be able to ascend the rope without pushing off the snow face.

It's a clever technique, but it requires an understanding of the process and repetitive practice.

"In thinner air than this, the muscle memory in the hands must be automatic," Hugo says. "They must operate in the right order."

Deprived of oxygen, the mind can play terrible tricks on the body. Hugo recounts the story of an experienced climber on a previous expedition who'd unclipped himself from the rope at high altitude. He'd sat on the edge of a cliff and had declared to all and sundry that he was enjoying a row in his father's boat. He'd then planned to dive in for a quick swim. He had to be tied down until help arrived to drag him off the mountain.

Most of us are accustomed to these routines. But I'm amazed that one of the team has never been in a harness, abseiled, or had exposure to ropes and jumars. He has no understanding why procedures must be followed in a certain order, to eliminate the risk of falling off the mountain. At one point he appears to be upside down.

After three hours training we stroll back to camp. I stride with confidence in my full mountain gear. Sherpas appear from out of the Icefall. They sport similar insulated cloths to us, although years of abuse and sunrays have worn and faded them.

"The Sherpas have been busy." Greg loosens his boots. "I just heard in the mess that they got the tents up to Camp 1."

"Great stuff, everything's going to plan."

"So far so good."

While I've honed a few skills, the real progress is that I've pushed past Base Camp. It may have only been a short incursion, but beyond it nonetheless. As long as I can stay on track and stick with the program each day, then bit by bit I'll get closer to a summit push, with an increasing chance of success.

Tomorrow will be another day of small gains. We're planning to enter the Icefall proper. We'll ascend halfway to Camp 1 and gain more acclimatisation. We've no particular altitude target, just follow the climb high-sleep low rule. I'm certain I can pass such a task with honours. I'll stare these ice formations in the eye. I'll see what stands between me and the upper camps. I'll know why so many people have died in there.

Swimming togs are optional.

APRIL 14

Into the Icefall

We'll push into the Icefall at 7:30am before the sun heats it up. I've eaten breakfast. Outside my tent I'm finalising my gear. I'll carry a light pack: water bottle, a snack, chocolate, and sun block. The sun hides behind Everest in a clear, cold sky. I walk over to the mess tent, where some of the team has already left. I slot in towards the rear of the group and head out of camp.

Less than a hundred metres from the tents, we reach the ice and strap on our crampons. Now I'm pressing into the Icefall. For so long I wondered if I'd ever see this day, advancing past the trekking stage, beyond Base Camp and onto Everest proper. This is it.

The trail winds around and over the ridges we practiced in yesterday. Up five metres and down the far side, then another and then another. I pant in the thin air and remind myself to keep an even pace. I tell myself there's no point rushing and then getting stuck behind the others in a bottleneck.

I cannot imagine a more alien environment. I've never seen anything like it. Jagged white ridges stretch up in every direction. In places, the track is only the width of a person, with sharp ice protrusions reaching up to knee height on both sides. A fall onto one of them will be nasty.

Despite the climbing, we've gained no altitude; we keep descending again. All chatter has ceased. I follow Doug who's a few metres in front of me. Whoever's leading seems to be tracking the series of metre high poles that we pass every few minutes. This must be how the ice doctors mark out the best route. I can't see the fixed rope I've heard so much about. I wonder when it will appear.

Looking ahead, I can only spot three or four of the team. The next ice formation blocks my view. I look behind and see Ade, Martin, and Angel. I think they're the last.

"Heavy going, Ade."

"You said it."

Three quarters of an hour passes. I don't know how far we've pressed into the Icefall, but we've started ascending. No longer am I looking at ridges. Up above, snow-covered ice bulges. It goes up and up. Just ahead of Doug I see some of the team clipping into a rope. This must be it: the famed fixed rope. It looks so anonymous and ordinary. It's just a loose end lying on the snow. It trails alongside the climbers and then disappears behind a white block higher up. No sign reads "This way up" or "Everest straight on". There's no indication why it's here or what we're supposed to do with it. I clip in my jumar and safety as those ahead have done and keep slogging upwards.

My altimeter indicates a slow, steady gain. I feel like an ant walking up a pile of sugar cubes thirty metres tall, but without their furtive energy. White surrounds me in every direction. On all sides and extending far above our heads, large, swollen, irregular shaped formations threaten. It's as if someone filled a soccer stadium with five-metre high clumps of paper, and I have to get from the centre circle up to row Z. Problem is, these lumps aren't soft. They're hard and cold, and if they move at the wrong time, it's game over. If my fellow climbers were to disappear and take the rope with them, I'd not find my way out of here.

Doug and I tilt our heads back and stare at a vertical face. He gasps and tugs on his jumar as he ascends the sheer wall. Now it's my turn. I've clipped in my jumar, but I let my legs do the majority of the work, just using my hands for grip. Pulling with my arms would burn up energy. Yanking and levering off the jumar would exhaust the shoulders and push a climber into oxygen debt. I'll save that till when my legs might abandon me much higher up the mountain.

My hands search for grips at head height, my nose pressed against the snowy face. Below, my legs push me higher. Previous climbers have kicked in rudimentary foot holds. I pull myself over the crest, catch a few breaths, clip into the next rope, and trudge on. Doug wheezes a pace ahead of me. It's very early in the day's adventure, and I'm not sure he has much left.

We climb from anchor point to anchor point. The fixtures appear with much greater frequency than just at the end of a fifty metre rope. Since the route twists, turns, rises, and occasionally falls, the rope has to be fastened to follow the trail. In addition, the ice doctors have bolted in ice-screws at strategic locations to increase safety. At the top of each face or sheer section we usually come upon a small loop that we can clip into. If there was to be a slip, we'd not tumble back down.

These anchor points will be crucial on the return journey. The jumar has no value going downhill, as it always slides in the direction of travel. If a climber slips on a modest slope while descending, they may tumble down to the next anchor point. That's why it's so important to have a big knot at the top of each vertical face. If a climber were to go over a cliff without stopping, there'd be no recovery.

I squeeze through a narrow passage and find myself in a kind of box. It's like looking down into an apartment from the mezzanine level. We'll have to climb down into it and then walk across. And to enter, here it is: the first ladder. It's not a difficult horizontal one over a crevasse with a drop on either side, but it's my introduction to putting mountain boots and crampons onto aluminium rungs. The ladder has taken a beating from spikes all its life. I descend it and cross the room. The thin air slaps me as I climb up the face on the far side. A step ahead, Doug wanes. Behind, Ade and Martin look like me, inside their limit but only just.

We push up further. The steep gradient bashes me. Doug struggles a pace ahead. Beyond him I see no one.

The sun rises over the crest of the Icefall and blasts down on us. I didn't expect such heat. Within minutes the temperature soars from arctic chill to stifling desert. We keep climbing. I knock back water and note I'd only packed a seven hundred mil bottle, of which little remains. Sweat runs down into my eyes.

Scaling the Icefall
Doug looks back down to me. I catch my breath and give my legs a respite by kneeling.

Another steep section. Then another. And another. The heat cripples me. The climbing is ceaseless. The track rises up again. I come alongside Doug, his pace now sluggish and irregular. I'm not sure it's my place to check up on others. Compared to the mountain specialists that now inhabit this space, I'm no outdoor expert, but I can't ignore his deterioration.

A few ice boulders always block the view back to Angel, who's bringing up the tail. I have a few words with Doug. He's further gone than I'd expected. It looks like heat exhaustion; his actions have become clumsy. This mountain is giving us a beating. How on earth will we get through the Icefall to Camp 1 later this week? I turn around, wait for Angel to appear, and indicate that he must join us. He strides past Ade and Martin, and links up with Doug.

"You lads keep going," Angel says. "I'll stay here."

We trudge on. The rest of the team has disappeared into the ice structure. On turning another white corner we're met by a smiling Ted. He has waited for us here; this is the first horizontal ladder. Beneath it looms a deep, endless crevasse. It's only two metres wide, but we must treat it with respect. The ice doctors have anchored the ladder to the ice at each side. Two ropes stretch across the void.

"Ok, guys," Ted says. "Here's the drill. One at a time. Clip your safety to the rope. You'll use the ropes for balance, like a handrail."

"Does that thing even have a bottom?" Ade peers over.

"Lean forward as you cross, gripping the rope. It should be tense behind you. Slack rope ahead, tense behind. Play it through your hands as you move. If you come across a very slack rope up ahead, get your buddy to take up the play."

"And just one rung at a time?" I ask.

"Yeah, but don't place your boot on just one. Position the front protruding spikes onto a rung. Then lower the heel so it makes contact with the rung behind it. That way, the boot rests on two rungs. Once steady, move the other foot forward."

I clip in and step to the edge. I'm staring down, concentrating on the second rung. In my peripheral vision I sense a bluish darkness on either side of the ladder. My head stays centred. I'm tempted to focus on what's between the first two rungs, but I must resist it. Between them it's blurry, white, then blue, and further below dark. There is no end. I learned a long time ago there's wisdom in the advice "Don't look down." But whoever gave that guidance wasn't walking across this ladder. I have to look down to position my boot, but somehow just focus on the small metal rungs. I put an anxious right foot forward and aim the front spikes for the target. They rest on it. I drop my heel, hoping the boot is long enough. Contact, it rests on two rungs. Half my weight, half my life, relies on two little spikes that stick out the front of my boot. I take a deep breath. I repeat the process with my left foot.

"Keep leaning forward," Ted says. "Further."

My hands are far behind me. My upper body is over the next rung. The rope in front is slack, while behind, you could bounce a coin off it.

"Looking good, Fergus, nice and cool," Martin says.

I take another cautious step, then one more. I get rhythm. The end is almost within reach. I could jump from here and probably make it. I take a slow breath and remind myself to stay cool. Three calm steps and I'm there. Two steps, one more. My boots land on snow. I clip onto the next rope to free up the ladder and relax. Another small milestone: I've crossed a ladder in the Khumbu Icefall.

"Right, see you guys later." Ted clips in his jumar and disappears around the next bend.

Ade, Martin, and I press on. The heat intensifies. We reach another ladder. We need no one's advice on this occasion. Within a few minutes the three of us reach the far side. We then put a third ladder behind us. As Martin crosses, I finish the last of my water. Panting, blasted by the heat, I slog upwards. Angel catches back up with us.

"Hi men, how're we doing?" he asks.

"Ok. How's Doug?"

"He's gone back down. He recovered a little in a shady spot. We can keep going to catch the others, or stop here for lunch and then descend."

I want to catch the others and prove my worth, but my body is running on empty. We've only climbed for two hours. It feels like I've run an uphill marathon on a summer's day. Right now, discretion has to be the better part of valour. This is an acclimatisation exercise. I've gained experience of the Icefall, crossed ladders, and pushed my blood stream to a higher altitude. But I'm ashamed of my performance.

"Maybe lunch here?" I say.

"Yeah, why not," Martin says.

"Sounds good." Ade wipes sweat from his brow.

We sit down on the snow-covered ice and grab a snack. Angel has plenty of water and passes some over to me. We remain clipped into the rope, just in case the glacier moves and fires blocks of ice our direction. Climbers pass us from above and below, on the way to their targets for the day. The sun beams down. There's no hiding from it.

"Angel, am I ok to take off the helmet?" I point to the straps. "My face, I should put on sun block."

"Of course, slap it on."

After fifteen minutes we stand up, tighten our light packs on our shoulders, and get ready to descend. This was a much shorter push into the Icefall than I'd expected. Despite the slow pace, I was close to my limit. The heat has destroyed me. It will take everything I have just to get back to Base Camp. What hidden powers must I find in the next few days to scale this Icefall? I wonder if Ade and Martin are struggling with similar realisation and doubt. They're cheery, but if they're descending with me, they've also had their asses kicked this morning.

"Hey, look, just above," Ade says, "it's the others."

It heartens me to see them; they can have only been a short distance ahead, maybe thirty metres above us. I may not have achieved as much as I'd hoped, but at least I'm on track with the rest of the team. Ade, Martin, and I start the descent, so we can clear the ladder bottlenecks before the others.

We pass over them with little fanfare. That's half a dozen crossings today at different angles, various rope tensions, some wobbly, and others with beaten rungs. This morning, the thought of ladders perched across crevasses was the stuff of legends. Now they're just something lying between us and an afternoon snack.

Ade Crosses a Crevasse in the Icefall
He has clipped in two carabiners and has tensed the ropes behind him. Two ladders have been bound together to bridge the void. I look on.

We make good progress, albeit draining. Rope by rope we descend closer to camp.

We're standing at the top of the vertical face we ascended this morning. We peer over it.

"There's no climbing down that," Ade says. "Let's hook up for an abseil."

"Yeah, better safe than sorry," Martin says.

"I'll go first." Ade forms the rope into a loop. "You guys follow."

Once he's cleared the base, I'm ready to go. I put my trust in the rope as I lean far back over the edge and let the line and harness take the strain. I feed the rope through my right hand and walk down backwards. I watch my foot placement on the uneven ice face. At the bottom I unclip.

"Off the rope!"

Martin steps forward, and I move out of the way in case debris precedes him. We continue our descent down the Icefall route.

"That's the end of the fixed rope," Ade says. "Just the ridges now."

Hugo catches up with us and strides past. I up my pace to stay on his heels. As soon as we strike the ridges, he climbs up over the first one and vanishes.

"Man, he's fast," I say.

"Let's just make it to the finish. Let him go," Ade says.

Clearing each ridge exhausts us. Up, down, up, down. The thin air pushes my cardiovascular system to its threshold. I never expected the Icefall to be this taxing. The trek up the valley was a breeze by comparison. The heat maintains its assault.

Another thirty minutes brings us to the edge of camp. Crampons off, the three of us are now sitting in the mess tent gulping down water. There's only one topic of discussion: that was tough, and that was hot.

I spend the afternoon resting in my tent, sipping on water, or snacking in the mess tent while chatting with the lads.

Dinner chatter covers the events of the day. Ted tells us of a huge serac collapse in the Icefall early this morning that was off the route. It's a common occurrence on the moving glacier. The ice doctors selected a passage that's as safe as possible and away from the worst dangers. But every now and then a movement will hit their chosen path. Over the next six weeks, the doctors will repair and improve the route as the glacier thwarts their careful plans, unseats their anchor points, and buckles the ladders.

"The two Turks, Nurhan and Yener, are sleeping at Camp 1 tonight," Ted says.

This is no surprise. Nurhan will test the limits of human performance to summit without oxygen tanks. He's following a different acclimatisation schedule to us. His good friend Yener, a six foot two inch mountain rescue professional who's spent a lifetime clinging onto rock faces, will climb alongside him. Yener can't speak English. Our conversations, while lively, have lacked recognisable sentences. After two years working in Turkey, I can do little more in his language than order a beer.

"And congratulations to Linda, good climbing by her today," Ted says.

She's a Canadian with whom I've spoken little. She set off before us this morning, with her personal Sherpa and also accompanied by her friend Domhnaill from another squad. They climbed through the Icefall almost to Camp 1 and then descended all the way back to Base Camp. Here she sits at the same table, having accomplished so much more than the rest of us today. She doesn't look fatigued either. I'm a long way behind the likes of Linda, Nurhan, and Yener. When did this team split into two tiers with me sunk in the lower league?

APRIL 15

Rest Day at Base Camp

It's dull inside my tent; there must be five centimetres of snow on top of it. In no rush to go anywhere, I turn another few chapters of my book.

After breakfast I set out for Everest ER. I want the doctor to give my throat the once over. Pain's been building all week. As I nod off to sleep each night and swallow saliva, my body shudders with the pain and jolts me awake. I'm sure it's just the usual discomfort that climbers suffer at altitude but best to verify it's nothing more sinister. Cold, dry air damaging the respiratory mucosa in the throat usually causes the ache. The increased breathing rate then further aggravates the already delicate area.

I scramble over rocks and around boulders for five minutes and reach a white tent with a big red cross on it. The clinic provides medical assistance to mountaineers and Sherpas who get into difficulty during their Everest attempt. Staffed by volunteer doctors from all over the world, they treat cases on site and stabilise patients for evacuation. Ninety per cent of those assisted are climbers and their support staff. The remainder are trekkers and media. The doctor is already attending to someone inside; so, I wait outside for a few minutes. No sofas and glossy copies of Hello magazine are available out here.

"Come in," the doctor says. "What brings you to ER this morning?"

She appears in good spirits for someone who has to both live and work at this altitude. The tent is less than ten paces long and has two beds, a desk, and a chair. At the far end, a chest contains various medicines.

"My throat's killing me. Can you take a look?"

She confirms it's only as bad as might be expected in these conditions.

"How's business?" I ask.

"There's a steady flow, but climbers are still arriving into Base Camp. It'll get busier once they move above the Icefall, always does."

She hands me a dozen lozenges. They're gold dust here. I'll have to ration them over the next few days.

Cold Day at Base Camp

1: Angel's tent
2: The two Turkish tents
3: The three tents of Martin, Ade and Doug
4: The three tents of Roger, Hugo and Pete
5: My tent
6: Greg's tent

Lunch comes and goes. The altitude has thrashed my appetite. I do my best to clear boiled tinned frankfurters from my plate but only manage small bites at a time; I feel I might throw up. I do better snacking on biscuits in the mess tent mid-afternoon, McVitie's Hob Nobs a particular favourite. I relish two chocolate bars in my tent. They're easy to swallow. They pack two hundred and fifty calories each; that's five hundred a day I can count on. But on this expedition I'll incinerate close to five thousand calories a day.

"Angel, how's Doug?" I ask. "I've not seen him."

"We brought him over to ER this morning. The doctor said he'd dehydration. He's on electrolytes and water now."

That'll bring him around, but he'll face the same challenge again very soon.

I hear an update on the Island Peak team. I'm not sure if I've got the full story. Des reached the top. I think he was the only climber from the squad of six to make it.

The mess tent now has background noise. The radio has been set up, and we hear Sherpa chatter from above the Icefall. The teams have distributed the various frequencies between them. This allows us to chat uninterrupted within a team, but also listen to what else is happening on the mountain. As yet we've had no need for radios, but we'll carry them when we climb higher. The base system can reach as far as Camp 2. Once beyond it, we won't have direct transmission to here. Instead we'll broadcast a message down to Camp 2. Someone there will relay the dispatch down to here. The rules are not hard and fast. Conditions on any given day as well as battery strengths will result in greater or lesser ranges.

As we listen to the Sherpas at Camp 1, we hear of a lucky escape for the Adventure Consultants team in the Icefall. Massive ice boulders smashed onto the route close to their position. They described the horror of staring at a gigantic grinding machine racing towards them. It was only when the powder cloud cleared that they managed to count their numbers and verify no one was injured.

"The more time a climber spends in the Icefall," Ted says, "the sooner their luck will run out."

I again consider the strategy of the Himex team who are acclimatising on Lobuche, up to its peak at 6,100 metres, the same height as Camp 1. This saves them the exposure of at least one rotation through the Icefall.

"Tomorrow we'll trek down off the glacier and then hike up Kala Patthar," Ted says. "That'll keep us safe and prepare us for the push to Camp 1."

We can see Kala Patthar's apex at 5,640 metres. The dark bulge of rock stands below the south face of Pumori. Many trekkers hike up it as part of a trip to Base Camp, since Everest is not visible from here. The non-technical climb provides the most accessible view of the uppermost summit in the world. On a clear day it offers a magnificent panorama of Everest and Nuptse. For trekkers, it's the highest point they'll reach in the Himalayas, most likely the highest they'll ever be in their life, excluding perhaps a visit to Amsterdam. We'll swap our crampons for hiking boots and then walk off the glacier, most of the way back to Gorak Shep. Ascending three hundred metres above Base Camp is still solid acclimatisation. After yesterday's beating in the Icefall, I'll take any acclimatisation I can get.

APRIL 16

Acclimatisation Hike up Kala Patthar

W e trek out of Base Camp at 10am on an overcast morning.

"This place is getting busy," Greg says. "There're tents everywhere."

"I think teams are still arriving. They've loads of time till the window opens."

We meander past the other camps at an even pace. We're hiking faster than when we arrived last week, but my breathing stays relaxed. After three quarters of an hour we've left the tents behind us and have stepped off the glacier. Our group stretches out in a line along the rock and sand ridge that runs adjacent to it. Ted leads. I trek third in line but have no intention of rushing today. We've plenty of time to get to the top of Kala Patthar, spend an hour on lunch, and then return.

"I'll leave you guys here," Ted says. "Got some work to do on the internet in Gorak Shep."

"All right, team," Hugo says, "follow me this way."

We've dropped a hundred and fifty metres since leaving Base Camp. We now face a four hundred and fifty metre uphill hike.

"God, that looks steep," Ade says.

"No point in just looking at it," Martin says.

I'd been dismissive of today's trek, but looking at the grassy incline in front of us, I realise that this afternoon's acclimatisation will be no freebie. The hill is so steep it blocks our view of all that may lie beyond it. If it was much sharper we'd need ropes. At its base we survey the memorial to Rob Hall and several others who succumbed to an Everest storm in 1996.

Our neat, single line format disintegrates as each of us picks out a route. A zigzag pattern works best. My breathing increases. I ease off the pace and try to just breathe through my nose and not work up an oxygen debt. Hugo pulls away from the group. He's making this look easy. I toil up the slope alongside Ade and Martin. No one struggles behind us.

The slope levels out to a more gradual incline, and the view opens up in front of us. Further ahead I see a steep track that will take us to the peak. The top hosts an antenna and coloured prayer flags. The last fifty metres will be a scramble over boulders. The team peppers the grass in ones and twos. Hugo has almost reached the path. Dotted all the way to the summit I see other trekkers. Below to my left sits Gorak Shep and the Khumbu glacier. Behind us, Nuptse reaches up to nearly 8,000 metres.

"Relentless," Martin says. "It's got to be done though."

"I wish there was an easier way." I pull in a deep breath.

The overcast late morning air is just right for trekking. We suffer none of the scorching heat we battled in the Icefall two days ago.

Ade and Martin drift ahead of me, but I'm enjoying wandering alone in my own thoughts. I've so much to consider, so much to achieve in the next month. But each adventure continues with the next step, and I need to ensure I stay with the programme today and ascend to the top of Kala Patthar. I set a mini-target that I'll stop for a break on reaching the steep track ahead.

I turn right onto the path. The breeze tugs at my collar; it must have been behind me on the way up. I'll need shelter for my break. I push up a few steps until I find a hollow a metre high with protection on the windward side. I'll be able to hide in there. Off with my light backpack and out with the water bottle and a Mars bar. I position the pack to insulate me from the rock and enjoy the treat.

I didn't intend to go sightseeing today, and this is unexpected. Peak after peak presents itself in the distance. The snack delivers a smile to my face. I'm in no hurry to restart; the cove grants a temporary relief from the exertion. The team is far above me, but it matters not. I'll enjoy a few more minutes here in this tiny sanctuary, accompanied by my thoughts and this spectacle.

When I can put the inevitable off no longer, I force myself up the trail. The summit of Pumori stands over a kilometre from where I labour. I can see the point where we turned around six months ago at 6,300 metres. The mountain defeated us that day. As yet, we're still a long way from that altitude. What a disappointment if I don't at least get higher than that mark on this expedition. That line lies somewhere between Camp 1 and Camp 2 on Everest. Given what happened in the Icefall the other day, reaching such a height is far from certain. But I must stay positive; just keep ascending.

I'm closing in on a trekker just ahead of me.

"How're you doing?" I ask.

"Yeah," he says.

"Feeling well?" I ask.

"Yeah."

He's a New Zealander and close to spent. He shouldn't push himself any higher. I'm no expert to give a lecture on altitude. I just encourage him to go easy and rest as necessary. I continue upwards and keep an eye behind me, in case he should come to harm.

It looks like he's stopped. Let's hope he leaves it there for the day.

The rocky section awaits a hundred metres above me. I see Hugo descending through it. He's already spent thirty to sixty minutes at the top, driving his body to acclimatise to this new height. I know there'll be a short chat as we pass. I'm keen to make it evident I'm setting my own pace rather than struggling. We exchange cheery greetings. I think he's surprised there's such upbeat humour from a man so far off the pace. He bounds on down while I toil higher. I should be at the goal in twenty minutes.

I find Nigel, from our team, sitting among the rocks. His trim, fit physique disguises his sixty years. I'm concerned to find him stationary so close to the finish.

"Hey Nigel, all good?"

"Fine, fine," he says. "I've been on top of Kala Patthar before. No need to do it again."

"Ok then, no problems?" I ask.

"None."

His personal Sherpa lingers beside him; so, I climb on.

The prayer flags are no longer just a visual marker. I can hear the wind that's blowing over the summit tear at them. I scramble over a few more boulders and join the others at the finish. I shelter behind a rock.

"Another twenty minutes and I'm done," Greg says.

"I'm going to put in an hour," I say. "Head down without me."

I get busy eating lunch and chat with the lads. One by one they head down, having hit the requisite forty-five minutes at this altitude. Once I'm fed, I pull out my camera and take a few shots. With the low cloud they'll not come out great, but there's no harm in trying. Those of us with cameras try to capture Everest. The clouds, however, conspire against us. The summit appears for just a few brief seconds at a time, never long enough for a gloved hand to take a focused shot. With the world's highest peak out of sight, I can only give my camera to Khalid, who captures a few photos of a windswept me. In due course he too descends, with his personal Sherpa Jingbar.

View from Kala Patthar

1: Khumbu glacier
2: Base Camp
3: The Icefall
4: Nuptse
5: The West Shoulder
6: Clouds drift across the summit of Everest

Those of us remaining strike up a conversation with an English trekker. In his late twenties, he's travelling alone. He'll journey no higher than this in the Himalayas. Our plans for the coming weeks seem to impress him. We answer his questions about Base Camp life and what we've seen of the Icefall so far. All the time, dark clouds threaten over Pumori.

"Another ten minutes has me at the hour mark," I say.

"Sounds good to me," Doug says.

Ade and Martin pipe up, and it's agreed the four of us will return together.

At 5,640 metres, this is the highest we've reached. My body will push itself further tonight and squeeze out a few more red blood cells.

The Englishman descends. I take in my last views. Behind us, Pumori's peak disappears among menacing clouds. Eight kilometres across the valley and three kilometres above looms the summit of Everest. We've seen enough; it's time to return to Base Camp.

I skip over the boulders and bound down the track. I wait for the other three every few minutes. I'd noticed this pattern six months ago. On ascents my speed is average at best, but on descents I come into my own. My light weight must make few demands on my knees and thigh muscles.

We've turned left off the track and are hiking down the grassy slope. My legs respond and my lungs thrive on the extra oxygen compared to the top. Doug pants.

"We're going to stay in Gorak Shep for the night," Ade says nodding at Martin. "We could do with some good food and a decent bed."

"And I'd best get on the internet," Martin says. "Keep in touch with home."

"All right, lads, we'll let Base Camp know. See you tomorrow."

Doug and I turn left. We've an hour and a half trekking ahead of us and a gain of a hundred and fifty metres in altitude. I can handle the flat sections, but the inclines bite my legs. Behind me Doug struggles. A combination of thin air and a lack of calories have conspired against us.

We keep slogging. Thirty minutes pass. My head droops. My legs burn. I fish out my last reserves of the day: a chocolate bar. I break it in half and wait for Doug.

"Here, mate, try that."

"Is that all you have?" Doug's eyes are half closed.

"That's the lot."

I hope the sugar will jumpstart our muscles in about twenty minutes.

Late afternoon draws in. The simple acclimatisation hike has granted the Himalayas another chance to kick us in the ass. We drag ourselves up onto the glacier. We trudge past the official entrance to Base Camp, knowing we face another half hour to our tents, or at this pace, longer. My eyes close as I huff. Behind me Doug falters further.

The clouds thicken. Snow falls and builds on my jacket. This is far from the pleasant hike I had in mind this morning. I drain the last few drops of my water. I shuffle towards our target. Doug cannot stay with me. We'll make it, but we'll keep nothing in reserve. I visualise reaching the mess tent and gulping down a litre of warm water. Another fifteen minutes on the rocky glacier and we fall into camp. Doug slumps into his tent. I haul myself over to the mess.

Early evening finds us sitting in the mess tent for dinner and planning.

"Tomorrow, the seventeenth, will be a rest day." Ted puts down his mug. "Get yourselves ready for the first rotation. On the eighteenth, we'll climb the Icefall and spend a night at Camp 1."

"Be good to see what's up there," Roger says.

I'm just glad tomorrow's a rest day.

"Hugo and Angel will go up with you." Ted leans forward to look at them down the table. "On the nineteenth, you'll have a climb high-sleep low day to touch Camp 2. You'll spend that night back at Camp 1. Then on the twentieth, you'll descend through the Icefall back here to Base Camp."

"This is getting serious." Greg nods to Khalid. "So that'll be two nights up at Camp 1."

"What day is it?" I ask.

"Eh, Saturday," someone says.

"No, maybe Thursday," comes another offering.

There's no weekend here, no Friday night excitement or Monday morning blues. The days have a date but no name. But regardless of what we wish to call it, in two days' time, the expedition will move up a gear. For an hour and a half, a DVD of Hollywood escapism in the mess takes my mind off reality. But alone in my tent tonight, I ponder that the suffering hasn't even started.

APRIL 17

Rest Day at Base Camp

"There're a lot of teams up in the Icefall," I say. "Things have moved up a notch."

"Yeah, I heard teams setting off at three this morning," Greg says.

"Three o'clock? Stuff that. I'd prefer to be in bed at that time."

"They must know what they're doing."

The early start gives climbers a chance to outdo the heat of the day. In theory it's safer to climb through the Icefall when the sun isn't beating down on it. This lessens the chance of an ice formation creaking forward and unleashing mayhem. On the other hand, the glacier itself could move at any time, day or night; therefore, vigilance is always required.

"Well, it's less busy than yesterday," Ted says. "Almost an entire team quit and went home."

"What happened?"

"They were shook up by a scare in the Icefall. They'd had their fill of adventure."

We hear that tragedy struck a Sherpa just below Base Camp. He'd ported goods up and didn't look healthy on arrival. He'd shown signs of severe altitude sickness and was descending to recuperate. From what we understand he was travelling alone. It seems he lay down to catch his breath and didn't get up again. One person tells us the porter died; another reported that he was revived by the staff at Everest ER.

In the afternoon, the IMG squad organised a meeting of the major teams on this south side. They wanted to arrange cooperation on fixing ropes to the summit. Ted attended and reported back to us.

"There's seven thousand metres of rope at Base Camp, good rope, new stuff," Ted says. "There'll be a single rope all the way to the summit, with a double rope at bottlenecks. The Sherpas from six teams, including ours, will fix the route between Camp 2 and Camp 4. Himex will fix the ropes from there to the summit."

The Sherpas will also remove old rope from the Yellow Band and the Geneva Spur. The tripping hazard is easy to get tangled in and confuses exhausted climbers, who may follow it by mistake. They then discover they're dangerously off route. Worse, a person might connect to a dangling thirty metre length of rope with no anchor point at its end. If a lost mountaineer falls forwards descending that, they'll slide down past the loose end and into oblivion. All this talk of Yellow Bands and Geneva Spurs is as familiar to me as the Sea of Tranquillity or the Mariana Trench. I guess I'll cross those bridges when I come to them, if I come to them.

Charlene, meanwhile, is the star attraction at our camp. Three Finnish climbers from another team came to visit her. They looked very experienced in their matching red climbing gear. There was something hardcore about these men; I think they eat mountains for breakfast. A TV crew interviewed Charlene outside her tent. Media coverage back in her home country is reporting on the unfolding story here. I don't know as yet how far above Base Camp her competitor, Anne-Mari, has acclimatised.

It's late afternoon and I'm filling my backpack for tomorrow. I'll carry only the bare essentials, but in no time the pack is full. The massive -40C sleeping bag takes up half the space, even squeezed into its stuff-sack. I've crammed in provisions for three days in a hostile environment. I'll leave this mountain equipment at Camp 1 for the next rotation. I can't fit my down suit into the pack. I'll only need it above Camp 3; so, I'll lug it up on the next cycle with other necessities like mitts and over-boots. I keep lifting the pack to test its weight and convince myself it's light.

"This weighs a damn tonne," I call over to Ade.

"Join the club." He looks at a bulging pack outside his tent.

"This is going to hurt."

At dinner I eat what I can, but I struggle. I'm not eating as much as I need for what's ahead, but it's all I can hold down.

Night has fallen and I'm lying in my tent. My watch thermometer reads -7C. Outside the temperature is plummeting to -15C. The alarm on the watch is set for 5am. There are nerves. There is doubt. I hope there will be sleep.

APRIL 18

Climb Up from Base Camp
(5,350m) to Camp 1 (6,050m)

oday we go big. Up to now we've achieved what many trekkers have: made it to Base Camp. On top of that, we'd a brief foray into the Icefall. It delivered a taste of what life up high promises. It's brutal. And that was without a load. Today I must climb to the crest of the Icefall and lug a sleeping bag, mat, food, and other essentials. My pack sits in the vestibule. It's huge and it's heavy.

I pull on my mountain gear in the tent by the light of a head torch at 5am, and then crawl out. All around, people prepare for what awaits above us. I eat a small breakfast in the mess tent, take on a few mugs of warm water, and fill my bottle. At 6am, Greg and I thrust into the darkness towards the Icefall.

"That's the end of the rocks. Let's put on the crampons," Greg says.

For half an hour we trudge up and then down the far side of each ridge. My breathing does not recover between them. My legs struggle to ascend the ice and snow steps. The mountain hits me much harder than our climb into the Icefall a few days ago; the pack causes the difference. My thighs sting as I descend. Again, it's the pack. Its size and weight unbalance me and reduce my mobility. This will be a long day.

Ade and Martin slurp in air beside me. Chatter has long died. Doug labours behind somewhere. The others have disappeared into the twists and turns of the Icefall. Those ahead, with the exception of Pete, Matthew, and TC, are assisted by a personal Sherpa. The lads close to me are all carrying their own gear.

We've put two hours behind us. Darkness has passed. I resign myself to just lifting one foot in front of the next. The trio of Ade, Martin, and I look out for each other.

"Looking good, Fergus, easy does it," Ade says as I cross a ladder.

I recognise the spot where we halted a few days ago. Above here, I push into new territory. After the holding cycle of the past week, I should be delighted to climb into fresh terrain. But the mountain has stolen my energy. Every step bites into my legs. Thin air, a heavy pack, and a lack of sugar in the blood stream inflict the reality of high altitude climbing.

A white maze surrounds me. Bulges of ice and snow press against us. The wall of the West Shoulder blocks our escape to the left. The sheer face of Nuptse soars up on our right. I focus on what's in between; that's the route to the top.

We ascend into the mound of popcorn. That's what it looks like from a distance, but up close, these irregular shaped blocks of ice threaten our very existence. A lump the size of a car dangles above us. Puffing and panting, we climb across a block as big as a house. I've no idea where this ends. Looking up at an angle of forty-five degrees, I see only ice and snow. A similar view if I tilt my head back to sixty degrees. If I look straight up, I see blue sky.

I can't measure progress in here. Staring to my left, I line up our position against formations in the West Shoulder. I set small targets for myself. Keep going till I'm in line with the black mark in the Shoulder. Keep climbing till I reach that crack in the rock. Push on till I pass that hollow of snow. Glancing at my altimeter, I can see we're gaining altitude, but the achievements are tiny.

Below me, the Khumbu Valley has opened up. A panorama of each tent of every team in Base Camp presents itself. Orange, red, and yellow dots stretch for over a kilometre. Not many ever see this sight. It cries out to be captured on film, but I won't root out my camera here. I've only put two hundred metres of this monster beneath me. Every muscle in my body wants to quit. I must keep ascending.

A terrible sense of foreboding creeps over me. I reckoned a 6am start would be a decent compromise: leave too early and climb in the frozen morning darkness, or leave too late and be ensnared in the searing, energy sapping rays. Both are our enemy. The strategy was to put most of the Icefall behind us before the sun climbed high enough to find us. I remember how hot it was here a few days ago, so blistering that I saw no point in continuing and decided the day's lesson was over. We've only driven a touch higher than that marker. This time I must reach the top, and with a full pack. It's 8:30am. A glaring whiteness is tinging the edge of the West Shoulder.

"Martin, I think the sun will be here in twenty minutes," I say.

"God no," he says. "We've a long way to go yet."

We push on. It locates us. Light and heat bounces off every white surface. We keep climbing for fifteen minutes.

"Jesus, this is scorching," I say to Ade.

Staring down, he shakes his head. I've no clue how far up the climb the others are, but I've not seen them since just after Base Camp. I flick up the ear covers on my hat that's underneath my helmet. It brings some relief.

The heat becomes cruel.

"I've got to stop and strip," I say.

I take off my pack and clip it to the fixed rope, so it doesn't slide away. I tie my jacket to the top of it; there's no room inside. Ade and Martin remove a layer.

We restart. The Icefall becomes a furnace. The mountain toys with us for another ten minutes.

"This heat's killing me." Ade wipes sweat from his face.

The altimeter places us less than three hundred metres above Base Camp. Seven hundred metres above it sits Camp 1. We've not even scraped to the halfway point. Sweat runs down my cheek. I lean forward under the weight of the pack. Dehydration is a certainty. I won't make it in this condition. I need a major wardrobe adjustment. Much of what we're wearing must come off.

Chunks of ice weighing tonnes intimidate us. The sun beats down on their surface. At some stage, they'll move.

"Screw it, let's stop here and get this stuff off," Martin says.

I whip off my hat and fleece jacket. Cooling air touches my body. I must strip off the over-pants that are above my insulated trousers. I push the harness down over my boots and crampons. I'm now sitting in the Icefall, not connected to the fixed rope. If the glacier moves, rescuers will find my harness attached to the rope but not me. And they might also discover a pair of over-pants floating in the wind. What a force of nature, what a way to go, would be the headline. I get the pants off.

"That's better," Ade says. "Let's get back to it."

We plod on. The top-heavy pack imbalances me further. We cross half a dozen crevasses via ladders. What water I packed is spent. I keep looking up to see an indication that the finish is near, but I see none. I'm not sure what I'm expecting to find, just anything to indicate that this torture will come to an end soon.

Another hour of toil passes. Ice and snow press against my nose as we snake our way up, over and around the Icefall's obstacles.

The route opens out onto a flat, white section, half the size of football field. Just ahead I spy Angel, a friendly face at last. He's standing fifty metres away in the middle of the level patch. I trudge up the slight slope towards him and collapse on the snow at his feet. I draw in air, my legs glad of the respite.

"How're you doing?" he asks.

"Tough. Hot." I roll into a sitting position.

He doesn't say how long he's been waiting. Ade and Martin remain hidden in the maze; so, I can catch my breath without hindering progress. The top must be close. It can't come soon enough.

Sitting here, despite the exhaustion and encroaching dehydration, I can't ignore the vista that's laid out in front of me. The midmorning sun reflects off the brilliant white. The tents of Base Camp have become dots. For several kilometres, the glacier extends out beneath us. It turns left down the Khumbu Valley and out of sight. Straight across the valley stand Himalayan peaks and the bold 7,150 metre Pumori. I can see the route we took up it and the point where we retreated. I'm slumped at about 5,700 metres. If all goes to plan I'll reach a personal high tomorrow, but right now that's a long way away. Priority A is to slog on and make it to Camp 1.

To our right, Ade and Martin emerge from the ice corridors. They lumber over.

"Ok, let's go," Angel says. "Follow my pace."

We grind up a smooth drag. It doesn't look steep, but at this altitude, anything more than level murders us. I place one boot forward, take a full breath in and out, and then lift the other boot past it. Almost five seconds elapse between each step, but we can go no faster.

Colossal ice boulders look down on us, the smaller ones the size of houses. The thought that one might roll and crush me is neither scary nor dramatic. I'm in too much pain to be bothered about events that may or may not happen. Looking over my shoulder, I suspect Ade and Martin are equally disinterested in the dangers around us. They too must be in their own personal torment: grafting hard with a bulging pack.

We return to the claustrophobic surroundings of ice and snow. It reminds me of Superman's home in the Arctic Circle. His kryptonite is my lack of oxygen. Each step tears at my legs. The pack pushes down on my shoulders. The sun maintains its assault.

"Look, there's Matthew." Angel points to a climber, just ahead, who's sitting on an ice shelf.

He departed Base Camp before us. We've made pitiful progress. He must be shattered. Like us, he's lugging a full load. We pause, and he then joins the back of our train, led by Angel.

Five hours have passed since Base Camp. The heat cripples me. Sweat runs into my eyes. My blood must be less like liquid and more like treacle.

"Let's take five minutes," Angel says. "Just there in the shade."

I plant my bum on a snow sill and take off my helmet. I scoop up a lump of snow, place it on my head and press down on it. My eyes close as I relish its cooling effect, just above what's left of my brain. If only I could jump into a bath of ice water. Two more handfuls of coolant on my head, and we then rise to our feet. Up above I spot colourful prayer flags. The top is within reach, perhaps thirty minutes further.

Up and up. We cross another ladder. We force ourselves over and around white boulders. We squeeze through gaps between blocks of ice. Struggling for breath, I jump across crevasses that open half a metre wide. I keep lifting one slow foot up in front of the other. My eyes close as my lungs search for oxygen. We reach the prayer flags. This is not the end. Why on earth someone hung decorations here is beyond me. They mark nothing. Overhead, all I see is more Icefall. We must continue.

Climbing the Icefall

The six hour mark flips past us. Angel maintains the slow, steady pace. I trudge right behind him, on my last legs. Thrashed as I am, I think the other three are even worse. They've left a gap to us they cannot close. It's hard to imagine how anyone could be more exhausted than me and stay upright.

It looks like what we've climbed through was the easy bit. We now confront near vertical faces. I lever off the jumar to pull myself up. If it were not for the fixed rope, the weight of my pack would pull me straight off these walls. Seasoned mountaineers would look away in dismay at how I manhandle, scrape and scramble my way up these steep sections. My arms throb. I falter under the pack. It's slaying me.

I ascend a vertical ladder anchored to a wall of snow. I must remember the procedure. I must slow down my breathing. I cannot take a lazy shortcut. One slip will deliver broken bones and worse. I'm still panting. This is hell. This is endless. This is endless hell.

We set off seven hours ago. The sequence is automatic, unquestioning: left foot, a pause, right foot. Repeat and repeat and repeat. More obstacles overcome. More crevasses crossed. Clouds drift in and rescue us from the solar attack.

Finally, we see the top. We must climb around a few more ice blocks and then ascend one last vertical face. I reach the bottom of the wall with Angel. We're in bad shape, when someone in my state is near the head of affairs rather than in a stretcher.

"I'll go up and tell you what I see," I call out. "Camp 1 should be close."

The last climb drains what's left of me. I've no one to blame only myself. I chose this. I knew it would be tough, but the drudgery of the challenge overwhelms me. There's no glamour, no glory. It's just relentless oxygen debt. Every second dispenses exhaustion. Each breath hurts. No cell escapes the suffering. I haul myself over the crest of the face. First just a forearm, then both elbows, then my stomach, and at last my legs follow. I look up from my hands and knees. I could cry. I have no words. The mountain wins again. This is not the top.

The route turns left and descends into the mother of all crevasses. We must climb down into it. Mini-crevasses loom within it. We'll have to cross those fissures on ladders and then ascend the far side on a seventy degree slope. After that waits a vertical face, which is about a hundred metres from where I'm slumped. It looks like three ladders have been tied together on it, one above the other. It'll be like scaling the side of a house. This obstacle will consume at least thirty minutes.

The Monster
Climbers struggle to clear the last crevasse of the Icefall. The man at the top stands above three vertical ladders and peeps over the crest. Below him, climbers negotiate two ladders at uneven angles over mini-crevasses. Truck-sized boulders of ice have tumbled down on the left. Glacial ice can be seen under the snow in the bottom right corner. The drop beneath this is endless.

"Can you see the camp?" I hear from below.

I cannot answer them. I cannot put together a sentence to describe what stuns my vision. It would be too cruel to tell them their ordeal is not over. The only saving grace is that there'll be no more false hopes; I can see the Cwm Valley on the far side of the monster crevasse. I look down over the edge at the lads and beckon them to climb up and join me. I ignore their calls to report what I see.

One by one the lads crawl over the crest. Angel looks strong, having spent so many years in the mountains. But for the others, the realisation that this is not the top must be another kick in the teeth. I can only stare at Ade and then shake my stooped head. Any words spoken are colourful.

We penetrate down into the crevasse just before 2pm. The early wisps of cloud have turned into soup. Sahara desert becomes Arctic chill. I wrap up in my fleece jacket and hat.

Nature has not short changed us. The Icefall furnishes an epic finish. It calls for one last push, and once again the suspension of fear. We inch down and step along a narrow ridge with a bottomless fall on both sides. No one has to remind me to clip into the rope. We descend another ladder to the mini-crevasses, which this morning I'd have referred to as full-on crevasses. I try not to look into them. But while crossing, they lie in wait, if a little out of focus, in my field of vision. Below me lurks sinister blue ice. It disappears down and down, deep down into a dark, deathly, frozen nothingness.

I climb up the far side, with Angel just behind. The Icefall's final demands are almost beyond me. I push myself up each laboured step, the snow only a foot from my face. The next mini-target is the final three ladder combo. I've seen mountaineers ascend it over the last twenty minutes; so, I know it's well fastened to ice-screws and can be mastered.

Inside the Monster
I inch across the upper crevasse on a ladder. I think it is Martin who climbs over the lower crevasse. His ladder is anchored to a melting ice boulder, which appears to be balanced on the edge of the crevasse on this moving glacier.

"You go first," Angel says. "I'll make sure the others get through and then follow."

My legs and arms quiver with tiredness. The thin air and heavy pack do not want me to see what lies beyond these rungs. The third ladder wobbles under my weight, but I place my trust in it. Going back is no longer an option. Spend several hours retreating to Base Camp? I wouldn't make it. I have no choice. In Macbeth's words: "I am in blood stepped in so far that should I wade no more, returning were as tedious as go o'er."

I heave myself over the edge. I've made it through the Icefall. Slumped on the snow, I wheeze. A metre ahead of me, a narrow crevasse plunges down. It's as if I'm atop a slim iceberg rather than a glacier. Drops surround me on all sides. On the far wing of that fissure the landscape levels off. My breathing slows. One by one the others haul themselves out of the beast.

We traversed some thirty ladders down there. Most crevasses were dispatched with a single ladder. The wider gaps required two bound together. We've toiled for eight and a half hours. This was never on the cards. When we met Angel, I thought we were near the top; we were only halfway.

"Let's keep moving; it's not safe here," Angel says.

Freezing clouds envelop us. Visibility reduces to a few hundred metres. I strain my eyes to see the orange blobs that would mark Camp 1.

"Ade, can you see anything?" I point to the grey-white nothingness up ahead.

He has no answer. He just shakes his head. We must keep going. We put a first boot forward and follow Angel.

I can hold the slow pace that Angel sets, but it crucifies me. The minor slope works against us. I feel every step. We zigzag around crevasses. We press forward, but are still not far from the top of the Icefall. I only follow Angel because I've no alternative. No one has caught sight of Camp 1.

I've nothing left within me with which to keep going. But quitting is more than just not summiting. We've pushed high into the clouds at 6,000 metres. Base Camp lies far away behind us. A night of -20C encroaches. Somewhere up ahead wait tents where we can shelter and endure that night. I know what stopping entails. The survival book described how all techniques come second to the most important and basic: the will to live. That propels me to keep putting one foot in front of the next.

"March or die," Ade says.

Maybe not as loquacious as Macbeth the general, but the ex-paratrooper's words have summed up the situation better.

We reach another crevasse. We can't walk around this one. Just to gain a few metres in distance, we must climb down into it, cross a ladder, and then ascend the far side. Several minutes of energy must be wasted to secure a handful of metres.

I'm almost numb to pain as I haul myself up the ladder on the far side. I think back to Linda's description of the route a few days ago. Leaving aside the admiration I now have for that feat, I recall what she observed at the top. She travelled for a while beyond the Icefall. Then she estimated Camp 1 at another thirty minutes. That means it's an hour from the crest of the Icefall to the tents, for a fit mountaineer.

Looking behind, Ade and Martin are slogging towards the crevasse. Matthew has dropped back further. Angel has taken it upon himself to ensure the four of us get to Camp 1, or at least are not alone if we don't.

"Keep going!" he shouts over to me.

I cannot help anyone. It'll be as much as I can do to drag myself to the finish. The fixed rope ends. I check my watch and altimeter. We've been on our feet over nine hours. At just over 6,000 metres, Camp 1 should be here somewhere. In every direction I see cloud.

The gradient almost levels. I can see ahead about a hundred metres. I follow what appear to be the footprints of previous climbers. If it was snowing on these tracks, I'd be lost in no time and playing Russian roulette with hidden crevasses. With a body and mind this tired and a blood stream struggling to get oxygen to my brain, I know it'll be easy to stray off course. I pay special attention that I'm following recent imprints, but it's far from obvious where I should aim.

I stare behind and perceive the shape of the next person in our team. When they disappear, I wait a minute for thinner cloud to breeze through so they've something to follow. There's no point being useless to the lads.

We've slogged for over nine and a half hours. The altimeter puts me at 6,050 metres, a gain of seven hundred metres. It's a massive gain for one day. That alone is putting a huge strain on my system. I concentrate on my left boot and then the right. I force myself forward. Based on everything I know and Linda's estimate, the tents must be here. But to the left and right, I can make out nothing. I must plod on.

I see something in the mist. It's not orange or yellow, but black. It must be related to Camp 1; there's nothing else out here but snow. I head for it. As I get closer, it takes the shape of a human figure on a ridge. He's not walking towards me or away from me. He's just standing there. He's tall.

"Fergus!" he roars.

It's Pete. Good man, Pete. He knows there's no rope on this section and the clouds have closed in. He stood out here to give us something to aim for.

"Pete!" I call back. "Camp 1?"

"This is it."

This nightmare will soon be over.

I close the last fifty metres. A final effort to join him on the ridge ends my suffering. There were moments in the Icefall when I thought this challenge might be beyond me. There were times at the top when I thought life might be beyond me.

"We were giving up hope," he says.

He looks fresh. He arrived hours ago and has long since got himself fed and watered. He points out camp. Down the ridge to the right, I see at least thirty tents in two neat rows, just as yellow and orange as I had imagined.

"What about the others?" he asks.

"Ade, Martin, and Matthew are back a bit. Angel's bringing them in. Maybe ten minutes. Maybe a little longer to Matthew."

"What about Doug?" Pete asks.

"Jesus, I haven't seen him since we set off. I don't know."

We wait a few minutes. Several hundred metres back, a ghostly shape materialises through the clouds.

"Head in and get rested," Pete says. "I'll take it from here."

"Thanks."

I walk along the ridge to the tents. We're pitched at the end of the line. As I pass the other teams, I see Hugo standing outside ours. Chin up, chest out I remind myself. We took much longer than this climb should have taken, all in all some ten hours. Hugo, as a guide, will observe our progress and look for weak links. He can't have anyone on the mountain who's a danger to themselves or others.

"Hi Hugo. All's good up here?"

"What?" he says. "Yeah, all's fine. What about you guys?"

"All good, little delay today."

"And the others?" he asks.

"Just behind."

"Ok," he says. "You're in a tent with Greg. The second last one, it's just there. I'm in the one after it. Start boiling water. We'll leave tomorrow at seven."

I've not had a drink in about seven hours. My blood must be close to jelly.

"Sounds good. A drink would be nice. Later."

I walk to what will be home for the next two days. I must stay upright while Hugo watches. How will I recover for tomorrow's push to Camp 2? Three tents to go, two tents to go, this is the one. I peal the pack off my back and it drops on the snow. I could float away. Greg shoves his head out of the tent.

"Get in here, Fergus. I'll take your pack. Where on earth were you guys?"

APRIL 18

Camp 1 (6,050m)

Greg's been here for hours. He has a litre of warm water ready for me and more on the boil.

"Get this into you." He hands me a bottle.

This is not a sporting event where I can come off the field and put a bad game behind me. It's more like the Tour de France. Tomorrow's stage demands my attention. I must begin the recovery process. I gulp down half a litre and hope the water will start its magic. That'll make a huge difference. If Greg wasn't here, I'd have to go back out and fill a sack with snow. Then I'd have to spend forty minutes tending a stove, to get less than a litre of water.

"I'm in good shape," he says. "I'll look after the water for the day. Get yourself set-up."

"Thanks man."

There's no obligation on Greg to do this. I hope I can return the favour later.

I'll freeze if I stay slumped on the tent floor. It offers no insulation to the snow-covered glacier. Panting, I inflate my mat. It becomes plump in less than five minutes. I pull out the other gear I'll need: the massive -40C sleeping bag, down jacket, head torch, water bottle, flask, food, hand sanitizer, a mug, and a fork. Kit lies everywhere in the three-man tent, but we organise ourselves with an imaginary line running through the middle.

"That's the first bottle inside me," I say.

"There's another one on the way."

Greg had been busy before my arrival. He'd walked out of camp to fill a bag with clean snow. Ice is better as it's dense; snow melts down into nothing. Unfortunately there's no ice near here. On returning, he'd set up the small stove in the vestibule, between the inner tent and the outer covering at the front. That area has no groundsheet. Its snowy base is perfect for storing wet equipment and firing up a gas canister on a level footing. If the pot had been anything other than even, it would have toppled once the water started to boil. He had to block all the gaps along the edge of the vestibule with boots and whatever gear came to hand; wind affects the flame and reduces the stove's heating capacity.

"We'll leave a little water in the bottom of the pot for the next boil," Greg says. "If the snow sits directly on the base, it'll burn."

"Sounds like you're on top of it."

"I've had some practice today."

The fluffy snow melts to a fraction of its initial size. He keeps adding lumps to the pot, for about fifteen minutes, till it's full of melted water. Then he keeps an eye on it for another twenty as it comes to the boil. During the process, we cannot get in or out of the tent. Sudden movements near the vestibule are out of the question.

"Good stuff, it's starting to boil," he says. "We'll give it another three minutes, kill bacteria."

Greg pulls on gloves to hold the scalding pot that's almost full to the brim.

"I wish this had a handle." He picks it up by the rim in both hands.

I'm holding a water bottle in the vestibule as he fills it.

"Shit, that's hot." I let go as trickles of boiling water spill down my fingers.

We retry and manage to get most of the water into the container.

Through trial and error, we learn to dig a five centimetres deep hole in the snow, the same circumference as the bottle, and wedge it in. This eliminates the possibility of a dropped container. After a few boils we've to throw away the debris laden base water.

We need four litres each per day to fight altitude sickness and keep our systems ticking over. Excluding what we drank this morning and on the ascent, we require nearly three litres each to rehydrate and get us through the night. As soon as Greg fills a bottle, I seal it, as if containing liquid gold. We enjoy a moment of relaxation and relief once it's deposited to one side. Then the process restarts. He never shuts off the gas. Each boil renders about eight hundred mils of water in thirty minutes. Without liquid, there will be no summit. For me there would be no progress above here.

Even small movements within the tent strain me. After ten hours of punishment today, I'm in dire need of liquid, food, and rest.

Two sealed foil packages sit in a pot of water over the stove in the vestibule. These MRE's (Meal Ready to Eat) form the basis of mountaineering and army rations. One of them has the words "BBQ Chicken" stamped on it. They start to bounce as the water comes to the boil.

"Give that chicken another few minutes," I say. "Let's hope it's good."

I last peed at 5am this morning. It's now after 5pm, and nothing stirs downstairs. I must get hydrated to thin my blood. After today's gain of seven hundred metres, I have to pee out the alkaline that's poisoning my body. The measurements on the side of the bottles make it easy to record how much we've drunk. Greg will keep boiling until we've both got two litres inside us, and a full bottle for the night. It's as well Greg is stepping up to the mark; if I went outside to collect snow, I'd be lucky to return.

Once I start peeing, my recovery will begin. After sunset, such a performance must take place inside the tent. Stepping out into -20C darkness would be asking for trouble. I'd have to put on clothes and boots that are close to -10C. Body heat and the warmth of the sleeping bag would be lost. A blast of icy air and perhaps snow would enter the tent. Instead, I'll pee into a bottle that's marked and kept for that purpose only. Some climbers place thick masking tape around such a container, so that even in the dark they'll know by touch which to use. I'd a six hundred and fifty mil bottle for the function on Pumori. I discovered the hard way that my bladder is larger. I now possess a one litre vessel for the activity.

If nature calls again later in the night, there'd be a problem. That's where Hugo's tip from a few days ago will assist. On settling into a tent, he advises crafting a hole about five centimetres wide and ten centimetres deep in the snow in the rear vestibule. Fill a pee bottle as required. Then pour the contents into the hollow. The warm liquid will melt a narrow vertical channel, that'll go down over a metre. Done correctly, it's clean and odourless.

"I've already made that hole in the back," Greg says. "And it works."

"I'm getting the gold star treatment I see."

Greg eats his dinner. I struggle with mine; it tastes so bad. I force it down. I must live on this for the next month. If I can't get sufficient calories into me each day I will crash out of the team. I manage a few smaller snacks. It's probably not just the altitude. Dehydration thrashes the digestive system.

"Try soup, it might go down better," Greg says. "Mix this packet in a mug of hot water."

My body can only take half a mug before it rebels against me. I open the rear inner zip in time to throw up into Hugo's disposal system. The soupy barf disappears to become a part of the Khumbu glacier. The few solids I'd eaten remain in my stomach. At least there'll be some source of energy for tomorrow.

"Man, you're a mess," Greg says.

"I've got to keep trying. A few sweets might stay down."

Darkness has crept upon us, and our head torches light the tent.

"Goodnight lads!" Hugo says from next door. "Up at six tomorrow and leave for Camp 2 at seven."

"Any word on Doug?" Greg asks.

"He turned back in the Icefall. He's at Base Camp."

"All right. Thanks. See you then."

It's after 6pm. We realise there's not a lot to do in a tent by the light of a torch in subzero temperatures. It's best to copy Hugo's example and get wrapped up in our sleeping bags. Greg has turned off the stove. We each have a bottle for the night. We slide into our bags. I pack some gear under my head and shoulders to keep me raised while I sleep. I set the alarm for 6am and clip my watch to a clothes line that stretches just above me. That'll allow me to check the inside air temperature during the small hours.

The mountain destroyed me, but I gain some relief lying flat. I've had plenty of liquid in the last two hours and will sip more during the night. The sleeping bag warms up. The inflatable down mattress does its job; coldness does not penetrate from below. Greg, however, has a problem. He carried up a thinner air-mat that's not down filled. It's much lighter to transport, but not as good an insulator. He suspects it's leaking. The frigid glacier chills him from beneath. There's not much we can do other than hope sleep arrives soon.

Lying in the silent dark, I reflect upon the events of the day. Who would have thought that when we met Angel our troubles were only beginning? We were not even halfway to Camp 1. How are Ade, Martin, and Matthew? It's unlikely they'd anyone to make water for them. In what condition are the others? Pete looked like he'd strolled to the shops to buy the newspapers. How can I recover from this? What demands will the climb to Camp 2 make? The altitude gain will be about four hundred metres. Perhaps I can make it.

A sensation below brings me back to the physical world; my bladder makes itself known. I consider the next move, uncertain. The experts can fill a pee bottle in their sleeping bag. This is to play with a loaded gun; too much can go wrong. Others zip the bag down, open it a crack, lie on their side with the container just outside, and perform the necessary manoeuvre. At least if it slips, it can be retrieved and the bag is kept dry. I'm more of an amateur. I prefer to zip it open halfway, kneel up with my lower legs still warm inside, pee, and close the lid. I'll lose a little heat, but it keeps risk to a minimum. In a shared tent, I'll keep my back to my climbing buddy; I don't want to show off.

"Eh, I must pee."

Greg lies centimetres from me. We've not gone through the protocol in any great depth, and I'm about to unzip more than just my sleeping bag.

"Sorry about the light. I don't want to mess this up."

I kneel on the mat and turn my back to Greg. I score a perfect ten: no stage fright, no overflowing, and no spillage.

I replace the top with care. I hold it up in front of the head torch for examination, like it's the most natural thing in the world.

"Four hundred mills and pretty clear."

Greg emits an encouraging noise. I test out Hugo's disposal system in the rear vestibule. The contents vanish into a colder world below. I drink more water and then get wrapped back up into the monstrous bag. My only hope of passing this acclimatisation rotation is constant hydration and peeing. At least that process has started. Camp 2 sits at 6,450 metres. The highest I've climbed before is 6,300 metres. Maybe tomorrow I'll ascend higher than that. Perhaps I'll make it all the way to Camp 2? What if I don't?

Despite exhaustion, the possibilities of this new environment flood my mind. This is our first night above Base Camp. We're on Everest proper.

APRIL 19

*Acclimatisation Climb from Camp
1 (6,050m) to touch Camp 2
(6,450m)*

The cold found its way into Greg's bag. He's cuddled up to my left shoulder. I've squeezed over a touch on my mat to make room for him, but it's only the width of my shoulders; so, there's not much I can do. Darkness surrounds. I can't fall back to sleep. I check my watch, but the digital readout displays garbage. Time, temperature, alarm; everything has folded. I'd put in a new battery last month. This is the Suunto Core, the outdoor man's outdoor watch. I'm astounded it has bombed. Perhaps the battery or LCD has frozen over, and it'll recover once warmed up. I hope so; I've no spare.

An hour passes. I hear a noise from the tent on our right.

"Hey Linda, what time is it?"

"5am."

"Thanks."

I gave the pee disposal system another test during the night. The quantity and clarity analysis reassured me. The litres I drank in the tent have made a big difference to my health.

Sleep will not visit me; so, I decide to get up and start boiling water. Even though we face a short acclimatisation climb today, we still plan to kick off early at 7am. Once the sun rises high, a blazing heat can engulf the Cwm Valley. Rays reflect off the ice and snow of the West Shoulder to the north and off the white sides of Nuptse on our southern side. A solar oven develops in between. It can reach +35C on a windless day. Of course, if clouds fill the sky, the temperature can drop to subzero in a matter of minutes.

The flame from the stove flickers. I can hold my hand a little above it. Ted had warned us they're inefficient when the gas is cold, but I didn't expect them to be this hopeless. Warming up the metal jam jar sized canister in my hands is out of the question; I'd stick to it. I watch as the reflected heat of the tiny fire defrosts the container. For fifteen minutes, the snow in the pot ignores my attempts to melt it. We need a better arrangement.

I hear Greg stir behind me.

"God, I was freezing all night. Be glad to get a hot drink," he says.

"I should have something ready soon."

We eat a small breakfast and enjoy a warm drink.

"We should have a bottle each in an hour. They won't be full, but close enough," I say. "That flame was useless earlier. We've got to figure a way to keep that gas warm for later."

Geared up and bottles filled, we crawl out into an ice cold morning under a clear blue-black sky. The sun won't peek over the mountain crest for another two hours. I turn around and absorb my first view of the Cwm Valley.

I'm staring up a broad, gently undulating glacial valley. Also called the Valley of Silence, it was carved out by the Khumbu Glacier, which starts at the base of the Lhotse peak. Massive lateral crevasses cut the central section. We're pitched on the far right of the lower valley, beneath Nuptse. Dead ahead of us, maybe five kilometres away, stands the Lhotse Face.

"God, that's steep. It looks like a wall," I say. "I think Camp 3 will be pitched up there somewhere."

"Yeah, we've got to get up that to summit," Greg says.

"That's another day's problem," I say.

To the left, between us and the face, Everest asserts its gigantic grandeur. I haven't seen it since Kala Patthar, and I've never seen it from so close. The huge, brown pyramid rises up to the sky, the tip still hidden from view.

Mountains hem us in on three sides. To the left and north, the West Shoulder and Everest stand. Lhotse blocks our progress some eight kilometres ahead to the east. On our immediate right, the snowy flanks of Nuptse soar up just short of 8,000 metres. Only behind us can we find an escape route. That's back down through the Icefall, some getaway plan that is.

Some of the others appear from their tents. All around, crampons are tightened and helmets are clipped on. Climbers from different teams stride past us.

"You guys ready?" Hugo sticks his head out of his tent.

"I will be in two minutes, just working on this harness," I say.

I know I must re-prove myself after yesterday's fiasco. I overhear mention of TC, but I'm not certain if she made it here or not.

"There's no point in standing here getting cold," Greg says. "It's just before seven. Let's go."

The two of us and Sherpa Penba push out, hoping to touch Camp 2 and then return.

My breathing labours on the pull up out of camp, but the light backpack is incomparable to what I lugged in yesterday's ordeal. Within the first hour we negotiate four crevasses. The drag up from each extracts its toll. We follow footprints up the white valley. They lead us from the right edge, where we started, towards the valley's upper left side. A gap has opened to Penba, who's ahead. Greg walks a pace behind me on the gentle slope. There's no fixed rope; if a climber stumbles here, they're not going to roll away.

My shoulders, in the freezing air, hunch down. My head droops. I've little in the tank. I concentrate on lifting my left foot and then the right. I'm certain Greg could go faster, but I'm just glad to be moving in the right direction and to be ahead of the posse. I can't see the rest of the team behind us. So far we've beaten the sun; although, I'd be glad of a little heat right now.

"I think Camp 2 is in those rocks. Up at the end on the left," Greg says.

I watch the dark specs of mountaineers dotted along the trail up ahead. They seem to disappear into the boulders in the distance.

"Yeah, looks like it's up there somewhere."

"Take bigger steps," Greg says over my shoulder. "A wider stride. Your pace is fine, but you still think you're on yesterday's climb. You're letting the crampons pull your feet down too early."

"Eh, I'll try it."

I stretch out my legs further in each stride. I thrust my heal spikes half a dozen centimetres further forward, before they meet the snow. Within a minute, I adjust to the new stride. It's brisker and takes no extra effort. To my astonishment, Greg drifts back off my shoulder a few metres.

The improved walking style lifts my spirits. The rocks up ahead grow larger. If Camp 2 is somewhere within those stones, then I'm certain I'll make it. That'll place me over 6,400 metres, which reminds me to check my watch. My body heat appears to have thawed out the battery or LCD. It'll stay on my wrist from now on. We've been out two hours and are over 6,300 metres. I've never been this high. I look back down the valley and stare over to Pumori. I'm level with the point where we retreated on that aborted attempt. Every step from here will carry me to a new height.

We cross a few simple crevasses. Ladders bridge the wider ones. Metre high flagpoles alert the unwary to the very narrow ones. In front of these, we first catch our breath and then leap across.

We come upon strange ice formations, half metre high mushrooms. I don't know what wind or glacial phenomenon has created these shapes near the roof of the world, but they look like seats. We stop for a rest.

"Probably an hour from here," Greg says.

"This can be done." I take a swig from my bottle. "It's not all that far away, if you're telling me that camp is somewhere within those rocks."

"It's a big turnaround from yesterday for you."

Too right.

I pull out a bar of chocolate and munch on it. Sitting down, we watch a few climbers pass us. My breathing calms.

"Set?" Greg asks.

"Let's get back to it."

My new found legs carry me to the start of the rocks, but we've more to do. The trail rises alongside the boulders for several hundred metres in front of us. The route then veers left into them and away from any crevasses. Penba urges us to follow him. Panting, I press upwards.

We reach the general area of Camp 2 but not where our tents will be pitched. Our crampons scratch over the rocks. We remove them, tie them to the side of our packs, and hike upwards through the scree. Each step guts my legs.

The sun appears over the Lhotse Face. The predictions of frying an egg on a stone have been off the mark. I relish its rays on my cheeks, a big change from yesterday when it was our enemy. I'm amazed to have done so well this morning, but that doesn't make this steep pull up any easier.

"God, why can't we stop here?" I ask. "It's just more bloody rocks. Where's Penba?"

"Somewhere up there. He must know where camp is," Greg says. "We'll keep going till we find him."

"You sure?"

"Come on."

Up and up, acclimatisation the hard way. Few tents have been pitched. I notice a few bits of old, rusted equipment lying about. Up to here, the route has been spotless. I think we're off to the side of the glacier; so, any rubbish doesn't get pushed down the valley. In recent years, the Sherpas have been paid by the kilo to lug rubbish off the mountain; therefore, these few items may also soon disappear. In addition, each team now pays a hefty deposit to the Everest National Park. The authorities only return it once they verify that, on the balance of probability, the team has left no trace at or above Base Camp. I'd heard Everest referred to as a rubbish tip in the sky. Whoever came up with that description has never been to a city in the early hours of a Saturday morning.

"Those lengths of ropes, cordoning things off, that must be where teams have marked their territory," Greg says.

"How do we know one of these is not ours?"

"Nice try, keep moving."

We push on and rise further above Camp 1.

"There he is, sitting on that rock." I point to a lone figure. "Is that the end?"

We close the gap. I drop down beside Penba. My breathing returns to normal. Visually, there's nothing special about the rock under my backside. But it means the world to me. Our Camp 2 will be pitched here. We've climbed four hundred metres in under three hours. This is 6,450 metres, the highest I've ever been. A little slower yesterday, and Angel might have turned me back. A touch faster, and I would have fallen over. But now at this spot, my expedition is again on track.

"Great stuff, Greg. Job done."

The last drag warmed me up. I throw off my upper layers to expose just the base layer. Munching on a Mars bar and knocking back water, I revel in today's early success.

Pete appears out of the boulders and strides over to us. I'm not sure if he'd been ahead or behind us on the trail.

"Good to see you, Pete."

"Looking good, guys. That was a short one today," he says.

"There were a few tough sections though."

Chatting amongst the rubble, I suspect there'll be few acclimatisation days as easy as this again. The sun's rays are penetrating my top and tickling my back. Greg has not warmed up after his miserable night. He's huddled in heavy layers.

"Take off your jacket, Greg. It'll be hotter without it," I say.

"Are you mad?" he asks.

"Serious, it feels great, nice and toasty."

"Ok, I'll try it. But I still think you're mad."

He peels off his outer layers on this still morning. Within five minutes, the smile returns to his face. Safe, warm and triumphant, these are the moments I could only dream would come our way. Many make it to Base Camp. Few see Camp 1. Less again taste Camp 2. I enjoy the views of the encircling peaks and the occasion. A trickle of climbers passes by. One joins us; it's Hugo, panting after the stinging finish.

In due course he joins the banter. I don't think he expected me here before him. There're no hooplas or high-fives from him. He mentions my recovery rate and sends a few dignified words of approval my direction. I appreciate the comments. I am back.

Penba captures a photo of us, with the lower slopes of Lhotse in the background. On such a bright day, it should be a good one. I'll have a memento of this morning in the mountains.

Back on Track after Reaching the Camp 2 Site
From left to right: Me, Greg, Pete

Greg's burst mattress becomes the brief topic of conversation.

"Shove stuff under it," Hugo says. "Empty backpack, clothes, gloves, stuff-sacks, whatever insulation comes to hand."

Clever advice, it's always so obvious after the fact.

Hugo points out what lies ahead in the coming weeks. Two obstacles that I've heard much about have come into focus: the Yellow Band and the Geneva Spur. From this distance, I can't figure out how we'll overcome them. The former appears as a long ridge of light coloured rock that stretches across our intended path. The later,

127

dark brown, looks like a mountain in its own right. Snow has slid off their steep sides. They'll be no picnic. I'll cross those bridges when I come to them. Will I even reach them? How many of us will be left at that stage?

"Where's everyone else?" I ask.

"Angel will turn anyone who doesn't make it here soon," Hugo says. "There's no point pushing upwards once the valley turns into an oven."

Charlene and her personal Sherpa, Mingmar, emerge from the rocks and close off the last few metres. She needs a minute to catch her breath but otherwise looks strong. Swapping tales of the climb to Camp 2 with Mingmar, I grasp that his morning has not been taxing. Easy going and relaxed, he outclasses all of us at this altitude. This man has summited Everest multiple times and reached the top of Pumori; I doubt making it to Camp 2 means as much to him as it does to me.

"We'll give it twenty more minutes here and then return to camp," Hugo says. "Charlene, was there anyone near you on the way up?"

"I didn't see anyone. Mingmar?"

"No one from the team," Mingmar says.

The gain of four hundred metres and an hour's rest at this new altitude will push our bodies and stimulate the creation of more red blood cells. We're sitting one kilometre above Base Camp. We've driven ourselves as far as is safe at this phase of the venture. It's time to retreat.

We hike down through the boulders. The light pack makes no demands on my legs. We refit our crampons and step back onto the smooth, snow-covered glacier. I use the new wider stride, and Camp 2 disappears from view. The sun is not the demon we expected, but instead a pleasant sensation on the back of my neck. Greg marches just behind me. The others stretch out for a hundred metres ahead and behind. We bound over small crevasses with ease. Moving at this pace, it's hard not to feel smug that my climb is back on course.

Within an hour, we tackle the large crevasses just above Camp 1. I spot Khalid and Roger on the far side of them. I don't know how far they, or the rest of the team, progressed up the valley.

"Man." I force myself up the far side of a crevasse. "These still hurt."

"Nothing for free up here," Greg says.

This is as good a day as I might hope to have on the mountain. As we climb up out of a crevasse, Camp 1 comes into view. What a difference from yesterday when, for hours, I peered in vain to catch sight of it. Today, it's presented itself on a platter. Before the noonday sun wanes, Greg and I are dragging our packs into the tent.

Camp 1
We just negotiated the crevasses behind the tents, having descended the valley in the background.

"Let's get that stove going," Greg says.

"Here's the lighter. The gas should be warm. It was a pain in the ass this morning."

My performance today was due to the massive quantity of water that Greg boiled yesterday. Rather than the heated boil-in-the-bag MRE's, I opt for cold ready-to-eat chicken from a sealed foil pouch. From the first bite, I know this will not be a struggle like yesterday. Then I try cold salmon branded Chicken of the Sea. The proteins and oils should give my physique a kick.

"This's pretty good." I take another forkful. "It says here the Omega 3 will make my brain grow."

"There's plenty of space up there. I'll stick with the hot foods." Greg wolfs down an MRE.

As the hot versus cold food debate rages in our tent, we both agree that the small, individually wrapped pieces of cheese are the clear winner. All the time, a flame heats the underneath of the pot.

Clouds close in mid-afternoon.

"I'll stretch my legs for fifteen minutes," I say. "We might have to batten down the hatches soon. It's already getting cold."

I take a few photos in every direction, hoping that one turns out decent.

View of the Lhotse Face from Camp 1
Three of our tents sit in front of the large crevasses that cut across the Cwm Valley glacier. The mountain to the left is Everest. Nuptse stands to the right. The white Lhotse Face soars up at the top of the valley, to the fourth highest mountain in the world.

Roger hears me and pops out to catch some air.

"Hey Roger, how're things?"

"Good."

"You're all set for tomorrow?" I ask.

"Yeah, I'm looking forward to it. Be easier going down."

"Let's see if this camera can make you look pretty."

I switch the camera to black and white mode and take a shot of Roger, looking rugged in the gloom. Snowflakes drift across his dark shape. The Cwm Valley forms the backdrop. An ice axe, crampons, and helmet lie at his feet. As we chat, the light fades behind thickening clouds.

"I think that's the last of the sun we'll see today," he says.

"Yeah, you're right. Be bloody cold soon. Let's get back in. See you tomorrow."

"Sleep well."

Various Team Tents sit on the Glacial Ridge that is Camp 1

Back in the tent, our routine has taken shape. We boil water and fill bottles and flasks nonstop. We don't quibble over who heats what. We each need four litres a day and keep going till we hit that target. We scald fewer fingers; we spill less liquid. The water in which the MRE's are boiled is poured into containers; nothing is wasted. We've blocked out all gaps in the vestibule through which a draught might interfere with the flame.

As one gas canister provides a flame, we test methods to warm up the next, so it'll burn hot and efficient when needed. We've placed the next cold canister on a sealed, upturned bottle of hot water, which is leaning against a backpack. This warms up the gas. It also brings the liquid in the bottle down to a drinking temperature quicker.

We've become adept at moving in the tent, eating, and tending to the stove simultaneously. The peeing routine is now just that: a routine. We validate all deliveries for quantity and clarity; we're in good health. It's not everyone who shares a tent six kilometres above sea level with a urology surgeon.

The light in the tent has all but disappeared by 6pm. From next door, Hugo calls out that he's settling in for the night. He has the right idea. It's best to set up the bedding arrangements before the temperature plunges and while the sleeping bags still have a little heat from the daytime warmth. We tuck ourselves up for the night ahead. Greg has placed everything he owns under his mat.

Twenty-four hours ago I was a vomiting shell. I wondered if my climb might be over. Now I'm relaxing in a sleeping bag. My mind postpones sleep as it runs over the events of the day. Good recollections entertain me tonight.

APRIL 20

Climb Down from Camp 1 to Base Camp

"How'd it go last night, Greg?"

"Better, I wasn't cold like yesterday. And you?"

"That was a decent sleep. I feel a bit groggy but nothing a warm drink won't fix. It'll be good to get back down and put this rotation behind us."

Food and liquid taken and backpack sorted, I face the first challenge of the day. The sleeping bag has been fantastic but stuffing it into its waterproof sack is like wrestling an anaconda. If I hadn't witnessed it in there before, I'd bet any money it'll not fit. I wait till Greg has left the tent as there may be friendly fire in the upcoming man v anaconda encounter. With fist after fist I shove the bag into the sack. It expands back out. Three minutes brawling leaves me panting. I sit on it to keep my gains in place. I catch my breath and force in the last bulging belly of the beast. It does not want to be imprisoned. Puffing, I tighten the draw cord.

I crawl out and look up to see a clear morning. I deposit the sack, the compressed mattress, and a few other items in the gear tent. I won't have to haul those objects up through the Icefall again.

"What time is it, Fergus?" Greg asks.

"Seven."

"Some of the guys have left already. We may as well get going."

"That sounds good." I tighten my crampons. "Who's here?"

"There's Ade and Martin; they're almost ready. And Angel's beside his tent. I think that's it."

We stroll over to them with our packs strapped on.

"How was the night, lads?" I ask.

"Splendid," Ade says, his height and broad shoulders more pronounced in full mountain gear. "The food's better than at Base Camp."

"Too right," Martin says. "We'd a nice brew last night. It's not Camp 1 here; it's Café One."

"I'd have killed for a bit more of that cheese," Ade says. "But we ran a good kitchen last night. It was the Bimble Brothers' Café."

The five of us join up and push out of camp. We head for the Icefall. This passage should be easier; we'll be descending and with light packs. Angel sets a steady pace on the slight downhill slope. As we get close to the abyss, crevasses surrounded us.

"Clip into the rope," Angel says. "It doesn't matter that it's flat; stumble on a crampon and it's a long way down. Even where there's no crevasse, the ground could still give way."

We weave around and over them. At the widest point, they extend a few metres across. At their narrowest, they taper to perhaps half a metre. The rope leads us to the slimmest gap, where a leap puts another crevasse behind us. Forty minutes after leaving Camp 1, we reach the edge of the Icefall.

In the distance below, the bright colours of Base Camp contrast against the ice and rock of the Khumbu glacier. Make it there, and I'll have the first rotation behind me. I peer straight down over the snowy edge, into the mother of all crevasses. I'm again gaping into the set of a science fiction film. I cannot believe we'll lower ourselves into it. Teams have been busy since the wee hours; a stream of mountaineers is ascending through the ice boulders. Climbers inch along narrow ledges. Small ladders wobble at awkward angles, above unfathomable horrors. Beneath their rungs stretches cold ice that plunges into darkness.

I recollect that the steepest, most demanding sections are here at the top. I'm fresh. If I can get the next hour behind me, then it should be plain sailing from there, relatively speaking.

"We must be mad," Ade says.

We'll have to abseil down the wall one at a time; it's not possible to clip in while someone below has their weight on the rope. Three climbers wait in front of us. Just beside the rope, mountaineers and Sherpas ascend the triple vertical ladder. A new face appears at our feet every three minutes.

"Ok, Greg, you're up. Let me check your set-up." Angel examines his waist area. "Ok, you're good to go."

Greg leans back and disappears over the edge. In due course, Ade and Martin follow. I observe Greg's progress through the monster. He'll benefit no one by waiting.

"Right, Fergus, the rope's free. Clip in and over you go. I'll follow," Angel says.

This's not Hollywood, where the hero flies down the side of a building in giant leaps. I consider my foot placements on the irregular ice. It could crack. Undue speed will send debris onto the climbers below or deliver a whack against the hard wall. After two minutes, I disconnect and turn around to tackle the behemoth.

"Off the rope!"

My breathing rises. Clipping in and out of ropes and placing that first foot on a ladder has become second nature. I put the monster crevasse behind me. Ade, Martin, and I wait where climbers pack bottlenecks. We give way to those coming against us and step aside to let fast descending Sherpas get on with their business. The delays grant me a chance to recover. Greg has disappeared among the twists and turns below.

Some steep sections do not demand abseiling, but walking down unaided risks carnage. I attack these face first, with the rope wrapped tight around my trailing arm, feeding it through my tense, gloved hands. Known as an arm rappel, the technique stops me tumbling down these short inclines. The effort tears at my shoulder muscles; they scream for relief. But once committed to a slope, any laziness will result in broken bones. I plan every boot placement and aim for the footprints below that have formed rudimentary steps.

We reach a bottleneck at a steep drop.

"I don't think we'll see Greg again till Base Camp," I say.

"He's flying," Martin says.

"It's probably quicker descending with three rather than four anyway," Ade says.

Even still, I think we're slowing each other up. At every obstacle, such as a ladder, we can only progress one at a time. Two of us wait for the first person to get clear. Then at the far side of the hurdle, we wait again till the last man rejoins. It's not a problem, but the clear, blue sky will provide no protection. We expect the rays to find us about 9am. We want to descend as low as possible before that happens.

"Ok, Fergus, that rope is free. Should be good to go now, nice and handy," Ade says.

We push down for another half hour. I'm panting with every step, but we've made good gains in this cool air. All three of us had suffered, together, on the ascent two days ago. The Icefall extracted a heavy toll on my self-belief and reserves. The sun scorched us. The freezing fog chilled us. We fell into Camp 1, shells of our former selves. Doug never reached it. But now, this trio of mountaineers descends with confidence through the infamous Icefall. We've put almost half of it, the worst half, above us already. We're hustling well together this morning. This is the sort of team climbing I'd hoped for.

The sun casts shadows below us. The sheer ice structures behind keep us in the shade.

"Only a few more minutes," Martin says. "Let's get down as far as possible before it hits."

"But that was good progress this morning, gents, good progress." Ade takes a breath before another ladder.

Another obstacle negotiated. The sun dazzles off the snow just ahead. We keep striding down. It finds us.

"Right, lads, it's all coming off, and it's coming off now." I loosen a strap. "I'm not messing about with my pack again further down."

Even though the air chills, I strip down to just a base layer on my upper body and shove all superfluous clothes into the pack. Ade and Martin do likewise. We plaster sun block onto our faces. I don't need to ask anyone's permission to remove my helmet now. I'm self-assured and at home in the ice and snow. We take on water. I note mine is almost finished. Then we load up and get going.

The heat builds.

I've traversed a ladder. Behind me, Ade exhales as he prepares to cross it.

"I'll keep going, keep things moving," I say.

He gives me a wave. I walk around the next ice formation and keep moving.

On my own, I make faster progress. The altimeter positions me four hundred metres below the crest of the Icefall. The heat saps my energy. Sweat drips off my nose. I try to set a pace that will not crucify me, but which at the same time will drop me down to Base Camp and out of this sun as quick as possible.

The route falls quiet; those ascending started early this morning. They're now near the top or in the Cwm Valley. It was unthinkable just two days ago that I'd walk in a place as dangerous as this alone. From a distance, I might look like I know what I'm doing. I clip in and out of ropes, cross ladders, and jump across small gaps. All the time I'm reeling in a successful first rotation.

If the footing beneath gives way, it'll be a long time, if ever, before anyone discovers what happened. But more pressing matters occupy my mind. My water is finished, and I must hold it together for another hour and a half to get out of here. Moments of shade are offered by some of the larger ice features. Beyond them, the rays drain me.

I've stopped for a few minutes in the shade to catch my breath and cool down.

"Hey Fergus. How're you doing? It's getting hot. You're on our own? It's super here, isn't it?"

"Hi Angel."

His arrival lifts me.

"Did you pass Ade and Martin?" I ask.

"Yeah, they're just back a bit. They'll come down at their own speed. Ready to go?"

He sets the pace, and I slot in behind. I'm reassured to travel with him; although, even he can't turn down the heat.

I hear a thunderous rumble. We look behind to see an avalanche hurtling down the West Shoulder. Clouds of white powder billow out from the slope towards us.

"Do we stay clipped in?" My hand rests on the carabiner.

I don't know whether it's best to stay attached to the rope and risk getting covered, or to unclip and go with the flow. Angel says nothing. The racing cloud approaches. We remain motionless. It tracks to our right and stays on the West Shoulder. The avalanche blasts past, running out of steam before Base Camp. The Icefall escapes. We swap a glance and a raised eyebrow.

"Let's take a short break," Angel says.

The sun belts down. Angel produces a full bottle of berry flavoured water. I've no idea what else he has in the huge pack he carries, but he seems prepared for all eventualities.

"You out?" He passes me the bottle. "Take some of that. We've still a bit to go to Base Camp."

Sitting on an ice block, the two of us nibble a snack and enjoy the juice. We chat about the events of the week. The liquid sets me up for the last thrust.

We re-start. Just a little further down, the glacier rewards us with the end of the fixed rope. We're within thirty minutes of camp. A trail of metre high flagpoles leads us towards the finish, over the series of ridges. The several metres climb over each wreck me, but I know I'm close to completing the rotation. Dagger-like ice protrusions jut up beside our feet. I'm wary of putting a leg either side; one slip and the family jewels will go for half price.

We're standing beneath another ridge.

"Camp should be here." Angel looks around. "Somewhere."

We've gone off route and can't find our way out of the ice maze.

"Back that way. Can you see the marker poles?" he asks.

"No, nothing. Where was the last one we passed?"

"I can't remember."

We back track for several minutes.

"There's the stream." Angel points to a hole in the ice. "We'll follow that."

We walk along the feature for a few minutes. It leads us home.

"Welcome, guys, well done." Ted stands up at the entrance to the mess tent. "That's the first rotation behind you."

One of the kitchen Sherpas holds out a large flask of lemon tea. I sit on a rock step and gulp back liquid. The sun has again changed from enemy to friend. Its warming rays tickle my skin as I relax and chat. Only Ade and Martin have yet to arrive. Everyone else has returned safe.

It took us forty minutes to cover the ground from Camp 1 down to the top of the Icefall. Another four hours of toil delivered me here. It's not swift, but I've put down a marker. I'd be gutted if this was as far as I got, but at least I reached Camp 2, a personal high. I gaze up at the Icefall, with another full mug in my hand. I see it in a different light to last week. I've been there. I've met those popcorn lumps up close. I traversed crevasses as big as any that can be crossed. No longer is what looms above me just something from expedition videos. I've been up to my oxters in it. I've tasted what's beyond.

I stroll to my tent and check in with Greg. He's been here some time and in rude health. There's only one more ingredient needed to perfect this moment. With a bottle of gel in my hand, I strut to the shower tent to wash the mountain off me.

APRIL 21 – 24

Resting at Base Camp before Second Acclimatisation Rotation

The team breakfasts at 9am on rest days. I wait till about 10am and enjoy the heat of my tent after the cold night. The mornings fly by as I turn another few pages of the book. Once up, I head to the mess for tea and toast. I don't feel like vomiting while eating toast. Khalid advised that a hard-boiled egg with a shake of salt can be eaten no matter how poor the appetite; he's correct. During the day, I devour two chocolate bars in my tent. The book's hero moves closer to solving the mystery of the missing person.

Lunch and dinner, however, hit me hard. I force myself to clear a small plate. Afterwards, I fight to keep it down. Often outside my tent in the dark, I suffer a mini puke. My system ejects more of an acidic liquid than food. My body can't last up here forever, far from it. The clock is ticking, and I can see my bulk thinning.

Greg and Pete always put second helpings on their plate. I wish I'd their iron constitution. Hugo also has a healthy appetite; although, he's lost a lot of weight since we first met in Kathmandu. His week of illness took its toll, and it's impossible to rebuild up here. Doug, however, cannot stomach what's put in front of him. Even the bowl of soup that starts his dinner goes back to the kitchen tent.

Most days, an avalanche tears down Nuptse or the West Shoulder. The rumble of tons of snow and ice crashing into rock reverberates around Base Camp. If I'm outside, I take in the forceful show of nature and enjoy the spectacle. If I'm reading in my tent, I pay attention for a few seconds to ascertain nothing will hit us. At most, the camp receives a dusting. We're pitched as close as possible to the Icefall, yet outside the reach of these behemoths.

An Avalanche Races down Nuptse towards Base Camp
The top of Angel's tent is in the foreground.

Aside from reading, I pass the days chatting in the mess tent, organising my equipment for the next rotation or relaxing in the late morning sun. Often I sit on a rock outside Ade's tent, shooting the breeze with him and Martin.

We hear that an American, on the north side in Tibet, is attempting to become the youngest climber to summit Everest. A fifteen year old Nepalese girl set the current record back in 2003. The lower slopes almost wiped me out. I can't grasp how someone that young has done it. The authorities on this side no longer issue climbing permits to under-sixteen's, on the grounds of safety. This forced the American to try his luck on a Chinese license. He'll need all the luck he can muster up. When I became a teenager, I was proud to climb up onto an adult's bicycle. This thirteen year old from the States is aiming somewhat higher.

Some of the team trek down to Gorak Shep, a two hour hike each way, to send emails and check in with home. I prefer not to expend such energy.

Pete displays his crafting skills with a pen knife. He forages around Base Camp and the lower Icefall for shards of wood and other material that he can fashion into a small animal or other curiosity. He returns with fragments from expeditions that took place decades earlier. I gaze on as he chips and scrapes in this near forgotten art, a throwback to days gone by.

On one of Pete's scavenging trips he makes a macabre find, one on which he'll not hone his skills. He reports back that he discovered a body near the start of the Icefall. Two of the others march out with him to examine the site and verify his discovery. I decline the offer. There are plenty of bodies out there and I'll leave them where they lie. The information is passed on to the authorities who'll ensure protocol is followed.

Darkness sets in before 7pm. Early evening, we usually play a DVD on a small portable player. Half a dozen of us crowd around it and a gas heater. We favour a comedy or something light. 9pm is a late night and we retire to our personal tents at that stage.

I often absorb the sky for a few minutes before bedtime, despite the -10C temperature. I'm not normally one for such romance, but the night-time heavens here amaze. Light pollution and noise can be found far away in cities. The silhouettes of the West Shoulder, Nuptse, Pumori, and the peaks further down the Khumbu Valley contrast against the blue-black above. An endless spectacle of stars, constellations, and galaxies, whose names I shall never know, paint the roof. Up over the Icefall and into Tibetan aerospace, lights dance in the sky. Perhaps they're lightning storms in the distance, but there's no thunder. Maybe next month as we voyage through the night to the summit, I'll look across to Tibet and discover what causes this lightshow.

After gazing at the Himalayan night sky, I crawl into my home. For such an inhospitable place, the tent is not as cold as it looks. The way I've got it set-up insulates me from the glacier:

I wear long johns, a base layer, fleece top, hat, skinny gloves, socks, and insulated booties.

A sleeping bag that is good to -20C engulfs me.

The bag lies on a soft foam pad eight centimetres thick.

The soft pad sits on a hard foam mat one centimetre thick.

The hard mat rests on the thin tent floor.

The tent is pitched on a double plastic ground sheet.

But I must still keep the draw strings tight on the sleeping bag. If the cords are slack and I judder, warm air races from the bag. By the light of my head torch in -7C, I can now read a book, turn pages, and stay warm, while it plunges to -15C outside.

With the novel illuminated by a small triangle of light, I forget my physical surroundings. It transports me to Sweden and a world of mystery and intrigue. But the sound of coughing pulls me back to reality. It's the dreaded Khumbu cough. At times it sounds like we're in a hospital ward. The low humidity and subzero temperatures cause it. The exertion of climbing leads to an increased breathing rate, which exposes the delicate lung lining to a mass of cold, dry air. Dried out membranes and damaged bronchi result. The extreme irritation manifests as a dry, persistent cough. It can be so violent that it tears chest muscles or breaks ribs. I've a rasping pain in my throat, no more than that. But Greg and Nigel have the affliction. By now I recognise their individual styles. In the distance, I hear as yet unidentified victims.

Charlene has picked up a cold. She descended the valley to Pheriche, which is a kilometre lower. She remains there, hoping the increased oxygen will help her shake the illness. We understand that her competitor, Anne-Mari, is thriving.

I paid a second visit to Everest ER, to verify there's nothing untoward affecting my nose and throat. My nose now bleeds with the slightest blow. The doctor performed a quick examination and assured me that all is well. Welcome to Hell; this is the norm here. He dispensed a handful of lozenges and a few tablets for my nose. I can't remember what they're supposed to do, but I'll take them anyway. I add them to my list: a Brufen morning and evening, Motilium before dinner, and paracetamol to ease the headaches that start the day.

Having trekked up the trail to Base Camp without head problems, I'd hoped they'd not visit me here. It seems I've not acclimatised to this altitude. It could be that my head is cold at night, so I wore a hat. Maybe the hat was too tight, so I wear a loose neck gaiter on my crown instead. Perhaps my bonce is not raised enough, so I shoved more spare clothes under the foam mattress. Maybe my breathing slows down while sleeping and the reduced oxygen causes the trouble. There's little I can do about that.

As regards climbing, favourable weather aided the rope fixing progress along the route. By April 21st, the Sherpas had passed the Bergschrund. Word reached us on the 22nd that they'd anchored the trail all the way to Camp 3. Our Sherpas are now lugging oxygen tanks up to Camp 2. The two Turks, Nurhan and Yener, shadowed close on the tail of the rope fixing squad. They're following a separate schedule to us, as Nurhan will later try to summit without tanks. They're planning to spend a night at Camp 3 as a part of their acclimatisation, whereas we'll only touch it. We hear that the track to the summit should open by May 10th.

We'll divide into two teams for the summit push. As yet no names have been matched to either. The stronger climbers will ascend first, led by Hugo. Angel will captain the second group a day later. I think Pete belongs to Team 1, always so strong. The Turks are top class mountaineers, but have their own schedule. Outside of those three, everyone else looks human. I'm certain not all these faces around me will qualify for the summit push. It would be insensitive to say it, naïve not to realise it. I hope my face finds a place in one of those groups.

During one of our team talks, Ted expressed his concern at how long we'd spent in the Icefall. I presume this speech was directed at me and the motley crew that crawled into Camp 1 after ten harrowing hours. The longer a person is among the white boulders, the longer they're exposed to danger. He demanded that the next ascent be faster. There was a suggestion that if a climber can't ascend the Icefall in a reasonable time, they've no place on the squad. I can't argue with the theory, but I'm not sure where I'll find the extra speed. Ted mentioned that we don't have to be courteous climbing through it. While there mustn't be rudeness to other mountaineers, we needn't stand back to let others come against us or overtake. At a bottleneck: just judge the fastest route through and then progress without delay.

Perhaps I should carry a very light load next time and just concentrate on a successful rotation. I can worry about porting my summit essentials when it's time for the push. It seems like robbing Peter to pay Paul, but I must knock at least an hour off my next ascent through the Icefall. Carting a heavy load and registering a slow time is not an option.

Every day we watch a trail of mountaineers and Sherpas stride past our camp, venturing into the Icefall or returning from it. I can't get the idea out of my head that they've more of a right to be here than me. They look professional, at home, and walk with confidence. I climb near my limit, particularly with a heavy load. But I surmise that viewed from a distance, even I might appear as one of them: an Everest climber. It would be something to change that title to Everest summiteer, but that label is far away right now. For a start, I must get through the Icefall twice more. Worse is to follow. Based on what I hear around me, it's only above Camp 2 that the real climbing starts.

But every journey progresses with the next step. Ted has decided we'll launch our second rotation on the 25th. He will lead. Hugo and Angel will accompany as guides. Ted has proposed that we ascend from here to Camp 2 in a single drive. That sounds impossible to me. The option was left open that some may rest at Camp 1 for the night and complete the ascent on the 26th. I've no intention of making it in one push, unless between now and then I learn to fly. But I nodded my head and agreed that the plan sounded solid.

Once at 6,450 metres, we'll acclimatise for two or three days. The team will touch Camp 3 on the 28th and return to Camp 2 that afternoon. If all goes well, we'll descend from there to Base Camp on the 29th. Nothing about this strategy surprises me; I knew it was ahead. But I now grasp how much it's going to hurt and how much it will ask of me.

It's the 24th, the day before the next trip into the unknown. The fixed line has reached the Yellow Band. Our Sherpas have pitched the Camp 3 tents. Those shelters, however, will receive one less guest than expected. I always knew the team would disintegrate. Being realistic, despite the training and preparation, I reckon most of us have far less than a fifty-fifty chance of standing on the summit. Today we lose one. Nigel handed in his guns. He cannot suffer the Khumbu cough anymore. Midmorning, he trekked out of camp and down the valley, his dream over. At sixty years of age, he may not see another attempt.

After lunch, we remain in the mess tent for a team talk. Ade is sitting next to me. Ted stands up.

"These are the masks we'll use above Camp 3." Ted distributes a mask and regulator to everyone. "Treat them with care; your life will depend on them."

Most people couldn't survive an Everest attempt without additional oxygen. By and large, the human body cannot acclimatise above 7,500 metres, that is, it can produce no more red blood cells. Some mountaineers feel that using tanks is cheating, as it makes the ascent easier. Others regard it as standard equipment, like crampons or gloves. Less than five per cent of those who've summited Everest have done so without tanks.

"The cylinders are filled with pure oxygen under pressure. You'll have five tanks each."

Nurhan explains to me the crucial benefit of oxygen. A fire cannot burn without it. Likewise, the body cannot generate heat in a low oxygen environment. It will essentially freeze from the inside out; frostbite and worse threaten.

"Familiarise yourself with the regulator." Ted holds one up in his hand. "It screws into the top of the cylinder like this." He demonstrates. "The oxygen is precious. Ration it. It's measured in litres per minute. Climbing uphill, set it between one and a half litres per minute and two. Going downhill, one and a half litres is plenty. While sleeping in Camp 4, just sip on it at half a litre a minute."

Camp 4 holds the highest tents on the mountain. Above them waits the summit. I'm familiar with scuba diving gear, but I have to start afresh with this arrangement. I think they're a novelty for all of us except Nurhan and Ade, the ex-paratrooper, who used similar on high altitude jumps.

"The mask is held over the face with these thick elastic bands. Now try them on. Get comfortable with them."

We spend ten minutes playing with the regulator and getting the fit right. I can't figure out how to breathe while wearing it.

"Ade, am I doing this right?" I ask.

"What's up, mate?"

"I don't know. As far as I can see, I'd suffocate if I wore this any longer. There's no air going in or out."

"Here, show it to me."

He fiddles with the valves.

"Yeah, this one was stuck, just there. Try it again." He passes the mask back to me. "And blow hard."

I strap the mask over my nose and mouth. I inhale and exhale a few times. I stretch it back off.

"Thanks Ade, that's it. Boy, we've got to handle these with care."

"As the man said, like your life depended on it."

Night-time on the 24th and sleep eludes me. I've finished the novel. I didn't see those last chapters coming. I try to forget what I must do tomorrow, but cannot. My mind runs over and over my preparations and what lies just hours ahead. The pack sits ready in the vestibule. My clothes are laid out in the tent. Will the Icefall hand me another beating? I'm not sure I could take it.

APRIL 25

Climb Up from Base Camp to Camp 1 or Camp 2 on Second Rotation

It's go time. Last week we touched Camp 2. Now we'll start the push to Camp 3. Nigel has surrendered. Charlene's recuperating down in Pheriche to beat a cold. Her climb persists; she'll just be a day or two behind. As ever, the two Turks have their own schedule, preparing Nurhan for an assault without oxygen tanks.

Ted expects us to climb all the way to Camp 2 today. Many climbers can scale the 1,100 metres in a single day, but I know it's beyond me. I hope to fall into Camp 1 in a reasonable time. Then I'll take it from there.

None of us has forgotten the intense heat of the Icefall, particularly Ade, Martin, Matthew, and I. Once the sun rises over the peak of Lhotse about 9am, the rays drain within minutes. We've no wish to repeat that encounter.

"You up, Greg!" I pull on my insulated pants at 3:30am by the light of a head torch.

"Just. We'll leave at four thirty as planned," Greg says from his tent.

I crawl out into the frigid darkness. Around me I hear furtive arrangements. Yellow glimmers mark the tents from where these sounds originate.

"Let's grab some breakfast," Greg says. "We'll see who's in the mess tent."

I manage a cereal bar and a little muesli. I'll burn masses of energy today. I crave the desire to eat a full hotel breakfast with all the trimmings. I've consumed fewer calories than I'll expend today; it's just a fact of life on a mountain. I knock back a litre of warm water and fill my bottle to the brim for the passage.

The other members of the team slip out of camp in ones and twos.

"Just a fleece on top for me, it'll be hot." Ted strides towards the Icefall.

"What do you think, Greg, just a fleece?" I ask.

"I think I'd die before the sun comes up."

"He's the expert, but screw it, jacket for me as well," I say.

I zip up my eight hundred fill down jacket. It weighs little and will pack up small later, but provides great insulation. Despite the solar oven beating in the Icefall last week, I'm standing in a place that's the same temperature as a household freezer. Anything could happen later.

"Right, Greg, check me over."

"Boots fastened. Crampons in your hand." He tugs my harness. "Harness tight. I see spare carabiners, a jumar, and a safety. Helmet's secure, little to protect up there. Ice axe?"

"I'll leave it here, keep the weight down. We won't need it en route. If I need one at camp, there're plenty up there."

"Your backpack is firm." He pulls the straps at the front.

I've packed light. I'd left the sleeping bag, mat, and other essentials up the mountain last time. I should lug my down suit and other summit items up there today, but a heavy load will kill me and delay my arrival. This is no time for heroics. Today is about reaching Camp 1, or Camp 2, and nothing else. I need to convince myself, if not others, that I can master the Icefall. I hope to toil through in six hours. Sherpas might laugh at such a time. But it will knock two and a half hours off my record. I examine Greg's equipment. Everything in place, we push out into the darkness.

Conversation ceases. A triangle of light from our head torches pierces the black. I'm not slayed by a heavy pack. I stretch out each stride just a little wider than before. I've more flexibility, mobility, and coordination. On the vertical and near vertical sections, there's no comparison to my previous whipping. Last time, every step was an effort, an achievement in itself. Now I lift up one boot and continue on up with the other.

Our jumars slide along the fixed rope. We traverse horizontal ladders perched above crevasses.

An hour passes and night gives way to dawn. Our vision extends beyond the snap shot the head torches provide. The Icefall displays its full brilliance. A decent portion is already below us. Few mountaineers litter the route or delay us. Our familiarity with the trail aids our momentum. Greg maintains an even speed, and I ascend a pace or two behind. I'd climb slower on my own, but I can just handle it. Ice boulders and snow press against us as we toil upwards.

We turn an ice corner and see a climber ahead. He falters. I recognise the clothing and backpack from the rear.

"It's Doug," I say.

"Oh no," Greg says.

He'd set out early to grant himself a margin of error. He'd intended to clear the Icefall before the sun hit. Looking at his gait, I can't imagine how he'll beat the beams to the top. He hasn't yet acclimatised to the Camp 1 altitude. We, on the other hand, have been as far as Camp 2. His blood is transporting less oxygen than ours.

"He's got a full pack. He has to carry everything today." I take a swig from my bottle.

We close the gap.

"Hey Doug. How's it going?" Greg asks.

"Yeah."

He reminds me of how I looked near the top last time. But in the drooped head, the stooped shoulders, the thousand yard stare, I think more than just the physical pain hurts. I suspect he knows he may not get much higher. A decision may have to be made soon, a difficult one.

He just never got his groove together near Base Camp. Like me, he found it difficult to eat. While I managed to force some food down, he rearranged it on his plate. I know how he must have felt at mealtimes. It was as much as I could do not to throw up. They were the worst times of the day for me, probably even worse for Doug.

"Just keep it steady, Doug," Greg says.

"You guys go on."

We cannot assist. We climb up around the next corner of ice, and he's no more. I wonder if I'll ever see Doug again.

The boulders release us from the claustrophobic white blocks. We trudge across a flat section of snow, half the size of a football pitch. Its presence confuses me. We've the trail to ourselves. I double check the time and altimeter on my watch. I recheck my maths. I figure out where we are.

"Greg, I can't believe it. This is where I met Angel. We're halfway. In just two hours."

"Not too shabby, Fergus. A little water and we keep going."

We slog up a snow slope in silence. I'm setting the pace, with Greg just off my shoulder. Hugo appears from behind us. He comes alongside me.

"Hi Fergus. Ok?" Hugo clips into the next rope.

"Ok, steady."

He shifts in front of me. A small gap opens. I try to stay with him. My breathing rises. My legs cry out with the effort. The brief bond breaks, and the distance widens. The Icefall has not crucified me this morning, but I'm reminded that I'm only just inside my physical limit.

Back inside the maze and crevasses, Greg again leads. We climb past the spot where, a week ago, I slumped on an ice ledge and rubbed snow into my head. I don't want to experience that ever again. But I know there'll be more days like that, and very soon.

We labour higher. Three hours have passed. The altimeter indicates less than a hundred metres to the top. During the summit push, we should ascend from Base Camp to Camp 2 in a single day. Before this morning, I didn't believe I could achieve such a feat. I've no intention of climbing past Camp 1 today, but it does at least look possible.

My nose presses against snow on a near vertical white wall. I kick in with the crampons. My legs push me up. Gloved fingers search for grip. My right arm tugs on the jumar that's attached to the fixed rope. With each foothold gained, I slide the jumar up the rope and yank on it again. Perhaps I'm cheating. This is not pure climbing. It's not man versus mountain. But it gets me up this face. There'll be plenty of time for philosophy at a later date.

Panting, I drag myself over the precipice. I can see the end of the Icefall. We'll win this race against the sun. We face one last obstacle: the massive crevasse. We must climb down twenty metres into it. Then we'll cross ladders anchored above unfathomable drops. If successful, we'll ascend a steep incline to regain the metres we gave up. Finally, we'll go vertical up three ladders that have been bound together and bolted to the ice. The last one will deliver us to the crest of the Icefall, a fitting finish to one of nature's more dangerous ascents.

The last time I saw this section, already jaded beyond use, I could have lain down and died. But now I'm just exhausted, thirsty, and breathless. I've enough strength to attack this last impediment. I descend into the monster, do what needs to be done, and get busy climbing back out.

I gasp for air on my hands and knees, and stare at the Cwm Valley. An ice cold wind scrapes my face. I check the watch. The last time through had taken eight and a half hours.

"Four hours, Greg." I suck in air. "That's some going."

We cannot savour the moment. We've escaped the ice maze, but crevasses encircle my sprawled body, the closest within reach of my fingers. The glacier shouldn't move in the next sixty seconds, but at some stage it will. The longer we loiter, the greater the risk.

"Let's go over there twenty metres, away from the edge. Take a break." I tighten my hood.

"No, let's keep going," Greg says over the wind.

"I need ten minutes, for my legs. I must take on something, and water."

"Ok."

We hunker down, bums on the snow and backs to the wind. After four hours of non-stop effort, my breathing calms for the first time since Base Camp. I munch on a small snack for what's ahead and finish my water.

"Four hours. That's a good time," Greg says.

"Super. I'm amazed. And we avoided the sun. I could do with it now though. I'm glad we wore the jackets."

"The sun should be over Lhotse within thirty minutes." Greg glances behind at the sky.

"What a place for a break." The wind blasts past me. "Angel would go nuts if he saw us here. Clipped in ...," I look at Greg, "my ass. It feels good though."

We rise to our feet and follow the rope to Camp 1. We must cross more crevasses, but otherwise we face a gentle gain of a hundred metres up to 6,050 metres. The wind gusts and tries to find a route inside my hood.

Last time, I'd no idea where the tents were located. With experience on our side, we set a pace that we expect to maintain for just over an hour.

About 9am, the sun's rays bounce off our white surroundings. On this frozen morning, I welcome its warmth on my face. Greg leads; he's stronger than me. I trudge behind.

"There's camp." Greg points to a row of about forty orange and yellow tents pitched on a ridge.

"Great stuff, about five hundred metres?"

"Yeah."

A modest slope brings us to the ridge, and we stride into the finish.

"That was an hour, five in total." I slide my sleeve back over the watch.

I've cut the ten hour climb by half, far more than I'd hoped for. The light pack and previous acclimatisation played a major part in the reduction. Improved speed at the connection points helped. I can't even estimate how much time was saved by beating the sun. But the details do not matter. I'm back on track and have proved it to myself and the team.

"I reckon we leave it here for the day. Recover, recoup our strength," I say.

"What? No way. Straight to Camp 2. From now on, this is just an emergency shelter."

"We've just gained seven hundred metres. Another four hundred is more than a kilometre. That'd be some strain on our systems."

"The plan is to go from Base to Camp 2. That's what we have to do on the summit push anyway. We should be able to."

"Yeah, but think about it," I say. "There're three acclimatisation nights at Camp 2, before we touch Camp 3. Why not sleep at this altitude and then two nights at the next? It's a lot more balanced on our bodies. We'll not lose anything."

"True."

"We could have water on the boil here within an hour and start the recovery process. And I'll tell you something, Greg." I catch my breath. "Walking on to Camp 2 is one thing. But we'll have to carry all our gear with us. That's an entirely different ball game. I could do with fresh legs before I lug a full pack."

"I suppose," he says.

"Let's ease back into this altitude today and then do the big carry tomorrow morning."

"Ok, I can't fault you. This's it for the day."

"Cool."

We drop our packs outside the same tent we were in last time. The sun sits high in the sky. The early morning coldness has passed.

"Hi guys." Hugo sticks his head out of the next tent. "Good to see you. What's your plan?"

"We'll stay here for the night. Acclimatise."

"Me too," he says. "Ted pushed on to Camp 2, just before you got here. Pete and Linda also went on."

"Ok thanks. We'll settle in. See you later," Greg says.

I stroll out forty metres to collect clean snow. On my return, I set up the stove inside the vestibule; Greg had done all the work last time. This is our third day in this tent, and we know the formula. Our mats insulate us from the glacier. Greg repaired his at Base Camp with a rubber patch and glue. It's holding up; there'll be no cuddling tonight.

"We've got six hours before the sun goes down." I position a bottle to receive the first pot of boiling water. "We need nearly three litres each?"

"Yeah, plus a bottle each for the night," Greg says.

"That's eight litres. The pot's a little smaller than a litre. It takes a half hour per pot, maybe a bit longer."

"Add in time to top up the pot. We've got to heat up the food; it's frozen solid," he says. "Five straight hours. That flame will be on the go pretty much till sundown."

A task which in a modern household takes no more than a few minutes will encompass our whole day. It frustrates me to put so much effort into such little return, but water will not appear by magic. If we'd a lump of ice half a kilo in weight, we'd get half a litre of liquid thirty minutes later. At Camp 1, the glacier is covered in a depth of snow that'd be the envy of any skier. It melts into almost nothing. To achieve a full pot of water requires constant topping up. We're tempted to drink it once warm, but to be safe we must wait till it boils. A dose of bacteria at this stage, and our climb is over.

Appetite abandons me. I force some food from a foil pouch, and some snacks, inside me. The small, individually wrapped pieces of processed white cheese taste divine. They contain fat, protein, and calcium, all packaged in a ready to eat format that needs no heating. I'm not sure how our bodies determine what they want and what to reject, but they crave this cheese.

"I'm a little off." Greg wraps his sleeping bag around him.

"What? Serious? You think you caught something?"

"Not sure, hope not."

"What is it?" I ask.

"I don't know, feel terrible."

"Just hunker down there for the day. I'll tend to the water. We've got quite a bit anyway. I'll go out and fill another bag with snow when this one's empty."

"Thanks."

"Man, that was sudden."

"Tell me about it."

The Bimble Brothers of Ade and Martin arrived some time ago. They rolled out the sleeping bags at their Café One. Khalid, and his personal Sherpa Jingbar, also split the journey to Camp 2. A few tents down, Amit and Roger decided this was far enough for today. Only Angel passed through, several hours ago, and pushed straight on to Camp 2.

I return to camp with a sack of snow over my shoulder.

"Hey Hugo. Is there any word on the others?" I ask.

"Yeah, I was on the radio to Base Camp." He pops his head out into the late afternoon light. "Doug turned back early in the Icefall. I think that's it for him."

"Yeah, we saw him. It didn't look good. Damn."

"TC and Matthew turned back as well, maybe halfway through."

"Really? What happened?"

"I don't know."

"They're still on the climb?"

"Well yeah, but they've got to get back into it. Not making it to Camp 1 at this stage, you know, it doesn't look good."

I'm tending the stove back in the tent. Clouds roll in late afternoon. The temperature plunges.

"We may as well get ourselves sorted before six, while there's still some light and heat," I say.

"I'm pretty much set for the night already," Greg says.

"Let's hope a good sleep brings you round. Let me know if you need anything."

We each have a bottle of water at our side. I leave my watch on my wrist; it died here last time. I presume it'll be about -15C in the tent tonight, but I should be snug in my bag that's rated as "Comfortable" down to -22C. I hope I don't have to test its "Transitional" capabilities, which extend down to -32C. It sounds a nice term, but I suspect the transition from comfortable to uncomfortable is anything but pleasant. I'm certain I don't want to assess the bag's "Risk" qualification that's rated all the way down to -57C. Fifteen below zero will be quite all right for the next few hours.

It's been a triumphant day. The fast ascent has put my climb back on track. If Greg recovers and the weather stays favourable, tomorrow should be a straightforward hike to Camp 2. Despite the exertions of the day, sleep doesn't come quick. Altitude maintains its relentless assault, even when lying still. My heart beats about a hundred times a minute in a vain attempt to pump sufficient oxygen around my body. Eventually I succumb and drift away to the land of Morpheus.

APRIL 26

Climb Up from Camp 1 to Camp 2 on Second Rotation

"I feel ok." Greg sits up in his bag. "Whatever it was, I think it's gone."

"Great stuff. Today shouldn't ask too much of us."

"I hope not. This one took us two and a half hours last time."

"Yeah, but this time we've got all this gear to haul up."

After breakfast we prepare ourselves. Panting, I force the huge sleeping bag into its stuff-sack. I've no choice; the only way to squeeze all the equipment into the pack is to first compress this bag down to a fraction of its normal size.

We drag our packs out into a bright morning. Hard, white snow crunches under our boots.

"We let the time get away from us. Most of the others are gone," I say.

"Yeah, we should have pushed out at eight. Those stoves are useless. What's it now?"

"Half past. The sun will be here soon." I look up the valley over Lhotse.

"There's no wind. It'll get hot."

We must gain four hundred metres today. We strap on our crampons and haul our packs onto our backs. At sea level mine would just be heavy, but up here it feels like a ship's anchor. We check each other's gear and push out.

The hundred metre rise out of camp wallops me.

"Hold on, Greg, I've got to strip." Sweat drips off my nose.

I tie the fleece top and helmet to the side of my pack. On my uppers I'm wearing a thin base layer and a sun hat.

We negotiate crevasses just above Camp 1. We climb down several metres into each and cross a ladder. The bulging pack throws my balance on the rungs. I focus on the aluminium bars, not the descent into oblivion on either side. As I ascend the far side of each, the pack tries to drag me back into Hades.

Crossing a Crevasse above Camp 1
This ladder only has one rope to grip.

"I think the next one is the last crevasse," Greg says. "Look, there's Khalid and Amit on the other side."

Amit's recording the scenery on a camcorder. Khalid's catching a few shots on his camera. I slog down to the edge, my pack threatening to push me down into the abyss. Struggling for air, I clip into the cross-over rope. I try to bring down my breathing and then place a cautious foot onto the first rung of the ladder.

I'm halfway across, leaning forward, my right hand clenching the rope. I concentrate on the next step.

"Smile," Amit says. "Say something to the camera."

I've more pressing matters on my mind. He'll edit the audio playback before a family viewing.

Now we face the long walk to the rocks. The route rises up the Cwm Valley and over to its left flank. My memory of this trail has been rose tinted. I'd been ecstatic to make it to Camp 2 last time. It'd put my climb back on track after the protracted ascent to Camp 1. As I retrace my footsteps, I remember this trek in vivid detail. Even with a light load it'd punched me. There's nothing for free at this altitude. I had to earn every step of the way a few days ago. Now I must do so again.

I gaze at the mind blowing gradient of the Lhotse Face. I determine to have a word with Ted later. If I try to lug a pack this heavy up there, in the thinner air, my legs will crumple. Today I'll concentrate on hauling myself and this oppressive load to Camp 2. By whatever means, I'll strike a deal with Ted or a Sherpa to get assistance with my sleeping bag and a few kilos above there. There's no point heaving weight up that incline and over the Yellow Band, only to fail to reach Camp 4 due to exhaustion.

It would be more virtuous to carry everything myself. Then again, it would have been even better to walk from Ireland rather than fly. It might have been nobler to lug two months of food up the trail instead of via porters. But how would the porters make a living? It might be more honourable to tow my own tent above Base Camp. But how could the climbing Sherpas make ends meet? No one travels through this life as an island; assistance is always given and received.

We trudge up and across the valley. Every few minutes, climbers stride down against us on their own rotation cycles. Occasional Sherpas march past us, hauling equipment up to Camp 2 or returning with an empty load. Camp 1 has long since disappeared from view. Behind us, the trail snakes along the glacier, punctuated by the dark specks of mountaineers that contrast against the brilliant, white snow.

"Where are Khalid and Amit?" Greg asks.

"I can't see them. None of those shapes back there are them."

"They set out before us. They can't be slower than us?"

"No one could be slower than us." I swig from my bottle.

"They were full of beans back at the crevasse."

"They must be shooting a feature film."

We reach the boulders.

"That's two and a half hours," I say.

"Not too far now," Greg says.

"Damn." I'm still looking at my watch. "The altimeter puts us at six three fifty. Can that be right? We've another hundred to the tents?"

"Really?"

"That's what it says."

They should be pitched at the far edge of the rubble. That'll allow us step straight onto snow once we push for Camp 3. Unfortunately, of course, it means we've to do all the hard work on the rocks today.

"Let's get to it." Greg turns to face the slope.

I remember these rocks from our first visit; they went on forever. Crampons tied to the side of the packs, we labour up. We reach tents, but they're not ours. Minutes and minutes of climbing pass, they feel like hours. My legs demand for this to end. The altimeter keeps me sane. Unknown forces are not conspiring to hide our camp from view; we're still gaining altitude.

We slog around more boulders. My throat burns to get anything from this air. My legs strain to push me and the pack higher. To reach our target, carrying my overnight kit and some summit gear, will be a massive achievement. My body cries out for a release from the pain. Three hours after setting off, I stumble into Camp 2.

"Mess tent? Water?"

Greg nods his head.

I free myself from the backpack. I feel a ton lighter. I give a thumbs-up to the faces inside and reach for a flask of water. In a moment I'll absorb who's here, for now I just need liquid. As the fluid fills me and my breathing calms, I can once again engage in a civilised fashion.

I'm sitting on a bench of stones, at a three metre long table built from rocks. The others relax on a similar bench on the other side. Our Sherpas have been industrious. Just beyond the table, close to a hundred orange oxygen tanks, weighing three and a half kilograms each, rest in a neat pile.

"Hi lads." I nod to Hugo and Roger. "No problems getting here?" I fill another mug.

"Fine, we're settled in," Roger says. "Good to see you guys."

"You look to be enjoying yourself, Roger. I see the mountain can't hold you down."

"Take every day as it comes."

"Who's here?" Greg asks.

"Just Khalid, Amit, Ade, and Martin still to arrive," Hugo says.

"We saw Khalid and Amit. They can't be that far behind us," Greg says.

Greg and I stroll back out to pick a tent that'll be our home for the next few days. We look around and soak in Camp 2 and its environs. We're pitched at 6,450 metres, on boulders and scree at the left edge of the Cwm Valley. Behind camp, a wall reaches up to the summit of Everest, more than two kilometres above. The jagged, sheer face holds no snow. Rock avalanches must rip down it; that's what's produced the surface on which our tents sit. Boulders must smash and explode outward to where we're standing. We'd be unlucky to be struck, but the material under our feet came from somewhere.

On the other side of camp, just a few paces away, serrated ice ridges rise up several metres. Beyond them lies the snow of the Cwm Valley. On the far side of the gorge, Nuptse soars to a height of 7,850 metres. A route to its summit twists upwards in front of my eyes, but I cannot pick it out. From where I'm standing it looks un-climbable. They were some men who headed into the unknown to conquer it, not knowing if such a feat was possible.

Our site is perhaps twenty metres by thirty. Just above it the scree ends. After that stand more ice formations and then the snow trail that heads for the Lhotse Face. We can see several camps around ours. Judging by the equipment that's arriving, more tents will be pitched soon.

Our large, circular mess tent will be for eating and team meetings. One could also say it's for relaxing; although, that might be too choice a word. Even the midday sun did not heat it. A kitchen tent is pitched beside it. A few Sherpas are chatting inside there. The gastronomy will take the form of boiling something in a big pot that sits on a gas stove.

Through the middle of camp runs a small, icy stream less than a metre wide. We see roughly ten sleeping tents. A catalogue might describe them as three-man, but two climbers and equipment will cram them. At both ends of camp stands a toilet tent, about a metre square each. Inside them, the bucket awaits. Abandon hope all ye who enter there.

"What about those three tents together, just over the stream?" Greg asks.

"They look good." I leap over the water. "Hugo's stuff is in this one. We'll take the one on the right."

We know the drill. We inflate our sleeping mats and spread out items on the floor to insulate the gaps to the cold rock. It doesn't take long to get unpacked and set-up.

At least the rock underneath won't steal the heat as quick as the snowy base at Camp 1.

Sleeping Tent – Camp 2
I settle into our new home, which has been warmed up by the late morning sun.

"I think I'll crash out for a while, Greg. This mattress feels great." I let out a long, deep breath.

The strains of the climb slide from my body, my legs weightless. My shoulders delight, liberated from the backpack. My eyes close, no longer alert and searching for a hidden crevasse. My mind drifts away.

Late afternoon, I walk back into the mess tent. Khalid tells me that Amit struggled to ascend. They arrived long after us. Khalid carried some of Amit's gear in the later stages, possibly even his harness.

"That was the hardest thing I've ever done," Amit says.

Perhaps it was just a bad day. He must know this is nothing compared to what lies ahead. In the world above Base Camp in which we now live, today was a stroll in the park. The day after tomorrow, we've to climb the wall that is the Lhotse Face.

Other teams also struggled in the Cwm Valley. Some people toiled for six hours to cover the ground from Camp 1 to Camp 2. But one mountaineer who's experiencing no such delay is the Nordic, Anne-Mari. Her contest with our Charlene rages. We hear she touched Camp 3 two days ago. Charlene, who's a day behind us, has become consumed by the duel to the top. She's placed all her eggs into the one basket of being the first woman from her nation to summit Everest. For her, reaching the peak after her competitor holds no merit. Because Charlene's on our team, we're rooting for her. But Anne-Mari also has every right to ascend first. I bear her no grudges. I hope they both stand on the roof of the world, and the better climber wins the race.

If they're both as good as each other, then may fortune favour the brave.

APRIL 27

Rest Day at Camp 2

Today we'll allow our bodies adjust to the new altitude. On our last visit, we touched Camp 2 and descended. This time I'm asking a lot more of myself; I've been here almost twenty-four hours already. Nothing grows up here. A kilometre above us looms the death zone. Up there without oxygen tanks, humans cannot live. Some may survive an hour and die. Others may function for days. But the lack of oxygen to the brain has the same effect on all comers. Death is certain.

I woke up with a headache. A Brufen has dulled the throbbing, but the discomfort nags on. Mercifully, the pain is far removed from the agony I suffered on Pumori. This is the highest I've ever been. Simple chores tax me. I don't reckon I'd score too well in a test of Sudoku right now, but there'll be plenty of time for that when this is finished.

Over in the mess, Ted updates a few of us on the mountain conditions.

"The fixed rope is well above Camp 3," he says. "The weather forecast for the next few days is good, just light winds. If it holds, then the rope will reach Camp 4 at the South Col in the next few days."

We hear that the weather on the north side has tormented mountaineers. Harsh winds and extreme temperatures have blocked progress for several squads. Details are sketchy, but the Tibetan conditions have already reduced a six-man team to just two climbers.

Camp 2 – The Team Next Door
Since the draw strings on sleeping bags are pulled tight at night, perspiration cannot escape. On clear mornings, it's normal to drape the bags over the tents under the direct light of the sun. All manner of gloves, hats, and underclothes are being dried on the leftmost tents.

All day, like a magnet, the Lhotse Face draws my attention. I cannot pretend it's not there. I've heard it said that the real difficulty only starts above Camp 2. If people are going to crash and burn, then up there just ahead of me is where it'll happen. I'm gazing at it, transfixed, and contemplating that this is where any weaknesses will be exposed. Our team has already dropped one person. Other groups have suffered attrition. All but a few members of a squad turned around in the Icefall and quit last week. Two weeks ago, a porter almost died down the valley from altitude sickness. But the experienced mountaineers are telling me that the scrambling is only beginning.

My stare focuses on a precipitous, white slope that rises up one and a half kilometres. At the top of the ice, another five hundred metres of near vertical rock soars to the Lhotse's summit. Tomorrow I must ascend the first seven hundred metres of snow and ice to Camp 3. I strain my eyes and focus on a point halfway up the incline. Irregular dots must be the tents. Located on a thirty degree gradient, the tent platforms were levelled with ice axes and shovels by our Sherpas. They'll be just wide enough to permit a safe sleep.

Many climbers pit themselves against the Lhotse Face in pursuit of all fourteen summits above 8,000 metres. All mountaineers aiming for its crown, or for Everest Camp 4 at the South Col, must ascend 1,100 metres of this glacial ice and snow. The incline climbs at forty and fifty degree pitches, with intermittent eighty degree sections. Perhaps this is where people succumb? Thus far, we've progressed using a regular stride. For the most part, the full sole of our boots has been in contact with the snow underneath. Tomorrow we must front-point. In the steeper segments of hard ice and packed snow, it won't be possible to rest our full weight on the soles and heels of our footwear. It'd be like trying to stand up straight on a Disney World water slide. Instead, to get traction and progress, we'll jam the two spikes that stick out the front of our crampons into the icy face. It will be technical. It will be exhausting.

View of the Lhotse Face from Camp 2

1: Just to the right of the number, four dots are climbers ascending to the Bergschrund.
2: This ridge is the Bergschrund. The safest place to climb it is just to the right of the number. There are two specs at that point. One is a climber at the base looking up it. The other has just peeked over the top.
3: Just to the left of this number is a dark spec. It is seven hundred metres above the camera. This is Camp 3. The summit of Everest is two and a half kilometres above the tent and left of the photo.

I fix my eyes on the lower section. If I am to stand atop Everest, then I must complete this acclimatisation rotation and touch Camp 3 tomorrow. If I cannot reach it, then how can I hope to sleep there during our summit push next month? Above those tents, we'll strap oxygen tanks to our backs. I've only ever seen that in photos or on TV. I never dreamt I could be the hardened mountaineer from those old photos. It's within touching distance.

Most Sherpas refuse to spend a night at Camp 3, as it has only forty per cent of the sea level volume of oxygen. They climb from Camp 2 to Camp 4 in a single push. A gain of 1,500 metres in one day asks a lot of the body. I'll need the rest and gradual ascent. It'll put my body in an oxygen deprived state and squeeze out the last few red blood cells. Most people can produce no more above Camp 3. My sleep at 7,100 metres on the summit push will complete the acclimatisation process. Once higher than that, I'll mask-up.

Some teams plan an acclimatisation sleep at Camp 3, in addition to their summit push. But most will follow a similar strategy to us and only touch it while preparing. This approach avoids excessive wear on the body, notwithstanding that the stress itself stimulates the body to adapt. Days at a new altitude are required to fully acclimatise. Hopefully our mere contact of Camp 3 tomorrow will allow us to climb higher next month. More important, however, is that I actually reach those tents within the next twenty-four hours.

More mountaineers arrive around us. These rocks in the middle of nowhere now look more like Base Camp.

Aside from staring at the Lhotse Face, I pass the day taking photos, nibbling food, eating meals proper, and chatting with the team in the mess.

"Hey Charlene." I swing my head around to the mess tent entrance. "You got here."

"Yeah, I just got in." She sits down with her personal Sherpa Mingmar.

"Hi Mingmar."

"Hi Fergus. Good to see you."

"How's the cold, Charlene?"

"Better, I think it's gone. The time in Pheriche helped."

"What's your plan now?"

"I've got to catch up. Anne-Mari has been to Camp 3. I'm far behind her. I'll rest here tomorrow, acclimatise. You guys will touch Camp 3 tomorrow?"

"Yeah."

"I'll touch it the day after."

"Good stuff. Hot water?"

"Thanks."

The sun dips towards Pumori. I scrutinise the Lhotse Face, trying to understand it, to convince myself I can climb it.

"Hey Fergus." Hugo's head is stuck out the tent beside me. He's been staring at me. "What are you doing? What are you looking at?"

"Nothing, I mean ... the face. Trying to see it, you know, understand it for tomorrow."

"That's no problem for you. Not everyone gets up that. You'll stroll up."

Now I'm the one staring at him. I think he's genuine. This is not a meaningless pep talk. He has no doubt I'll sail through the rigors of tomorrow. What did he see over the last month to have such faith in me? He has observed something. Perhaps tomorrow will just be a matter of lifting one foot up in front of the other.

APRIL 28

Acclimatisation Climb from Camp 2 (6,450m) to touch Camp 3 (7,100m)

This is where it gets serious. Today we ascend the infamous Lhotse Face. We'll push off at 7am.

"Greg, I'm going to be fed, geared up, and ready to go at ten to seven. I don't think this is a day to bring up the rear."

"That sounds good."

"I'll travel near the front. With so many on a single rope, there'll be twenty minutes from first to last person. If I need to rest, I can let a few past and slot in halfway back."

"I'll be ready with you. How many are we?" Greg pulls on his top.

"Nine of us, plus Ted, Hugo, and Angel, that's twelve. There'll be a few personal Sherpas as well."

"Who are we missing again?"

"The two Turks are doing their own thing; they've already been to Camp 3. Nigel's finished. And three didn't get through the Icefall this time: Doug, TC, and Matthew." I squeeze into my boots. "And Charlene, she'll go up tomorrow."

"Do you think the guys in Base Camp will catch up, get back on track?" Greg asks.

"I'm not sure. I don't think you can just skip a rotation. If it was that easy, then what are we doing here?" I slide on my gloves. "Time for breakfast." I crawl out into the bitter darkness.

On cue, I slot into third place, behind Ted and Hugo. I'd intended to test out the over-boots that slip on around the mountaineering boots. The temperature of the first two hours would justify them. I'd also planned to try out the mitts. I'm unsure how much dexterity I'll have with masses of padding surrounding my fingers. But in the end I decide against experimenting and to just keep my equipment light. If I can ascend and descend in a reasonable time, I'll consider today a success. I'm wearing a down jacket over a base layer and carry little more than a snack and a water bottle in my backpack.

Ted sets a slow pace. We march behind him in a line towards the Bergschrund. No one talks. He sports a thick pair of mitts. A gigantic, red down suit covers Hugo. Khalid also wears his for the first time, a bright yellow one. We look like intrepid explorers heading into the unknown.

To my amazement, Hugo rests his bare hands in the large pockets at the front of his suit. He's treating the morning with nonchalance. He has recovered his fitness after the illness on the trek. But not everyone feels so good today. Amit suffered a crisis of confidence in his tent. I don't know the full details, but he'll not travel higher. His climb is over. He will descend.

I see no crevasses on this side of the valley. A smooth covering of hard snow surrounds us. We follow the trail that has been marked out by successive boots. Greg had advised that at altitude a climber should set a pace that can be continued till infinity. My breathing remains under control. I've no doubt I'll make it to the Bergschrund.

Just short of it, the gradient increases, and the fixed rope begins. My legs feel the demands. My breathing deepens.

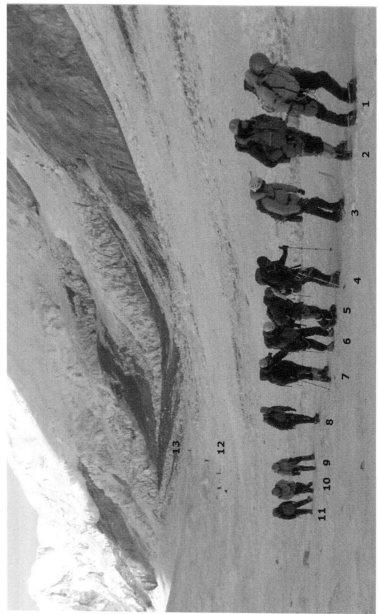

Heads Down as we Push Up to the Bergschrund
1: Ted, 2: Hugo, 3: Me, 4: Roger, 5: Roger's Personal Sherpa,
6: Pete, 7: Ade, 8: Greg, 9: Linda, 10: Khalid,
11: Sherpa, 12: Other climbers ascending, 13: Camp 2

We reach the foot of the Bergschrund. Climbers swarm around it.

"Let's stop here for a break," Ted says.

"How're you feeling?" Greg asks.

"Not too bad. Yourself?" I pull my bottle out of its holder.

"So far so good."

I glance at my watch.

"Wow, that's more than I thought. We're at six thousand seven hundred. We've already gained two hundred and fifty metres."

"That much?"

"That's what it says."

"That's a good start to the day."

The altimeter on my wrist remains a constant, silent companion. Often, when I'm down, it picks up my spirits to reveal that progress has been better than expected. Every step this morning has been a new high for me.

"There's the sun. It's either freezing or scorching in this place," I say.

Hugo has stripped off his down suit. He's stuffing it into his pack.

"I think I'll copy Hugo. There's not a cloud in the sky," I say.

I shove the down jacket into my pack.

"It'd be difficult to take it off on that slope."

On my upper body I'm just wearing a long sleeve base layer the thickness of a vest. For now the cold does not worry me. Overexertion, overheating, and dehydration do.

"Ok guys," Ted says, "let's go."

The ten metre vertical wall of ice and snow doesn't look as formidable as I'd expected. The Sherpas have anchored two ropes up it, which minimises the backlog. They've also fixed dual ropes up the Lhotse Face for at least the first hundred metres.

Our backpacks reset, Ted and Hugo ascend the wall. I follow. My cheek presses against the snow. My mouth hangs open. My feet find steps that previous climbers have kicked out. My fingers search for grip just above my head. My legs push from below. I switch my safety to the next rope. Sweat forms on my brow. I aim for the anchor point at the crest.

I pull myself over the top onto my knees. Panting, I stand up and clip into the next rope. It is behind me. I've not flunked yet. I've climbed the Bergschrund and am now about to ascend the legendary Lhotse Face.

The incline bearing down on us promises pain. My crampons scrape the ice underfoot. My leg muscles sting on the hard, slick surface. A line of climbers ahead has slowed up the pace, which suits me fine. I toil up in third place, Greg just behind.

Without crampons, it'd be impossible to stand on this slope. Even an attempt to sit still would end with a slide back down into the Bergschrund.

The Team Ascends the Lhotse Face
Hard, slick ice reflects the sun's rays.

We labour up the slope. I monitor progress on the altimeter. We should reach the 7,000 metre mark by noon.

"Six thousand, eight hundred." I turn my head back to face Greg.

He nods and breathes out.

Lhotse Face – One Step at a Time
From left to right: Ted, Hugo, Me.

Two hundred metres up the face, we scramble over two ridges. Gasping, yanking on the jumar, I pull myself over them. Apart from that, the pace has been balanced, perhaps slower than I'd expected. For the most part, my mouth has been closed. I'd anticipated more problems in this thin air near the limit where humans can survive.

"That's odd." I indicate above with my head.

Greg stands at my left shoulder.

"Yeah, I didn't expect that. What happened?" he asks.

Ten metres ahead, Ted is leaning forward, hands on his knees, face half a metre from the snow. The altitude is laying into him.

"I don't know. A bad day?"

Behind us, most of the team stands in a tight formation. We touched Kala Patthar two weeks ago without Ted. Last week, we spent two nights at Camp 1 and took a daytrip to Camp 2. Ted skipped that rotation. In addition, on this cycle, several of us broke the ascent and gave our bodies another chance to produce red blood cells during a sleep at Camp 1. Ted ascended to Camp 2 in one go, and now after three days is close to 7,000 metres. The safe formula is three hundred metre gains per day. He has thrust that schedule aside.

With a hundred and fifty metres to go, the front half dozen rest on a flat section the size of a ping pong table. The weather remains favourable. Up ahead we see orange tents. The brutal day I expected has so far been postponed. All going well, I'll reach another milestone within the hour.

We start the last push. The eleven of us, plus personal Sherpas, keep a close formation. Six hours after leaving Camp 2, we close in on the finish. A glance at the altimeter rewards me. The 7,000 metre mark has been broken. The patch of snow under me looks no different to the spot twenty metres below it. But nowhere on earth outside of the Himalayas is as high as this. If I got no further, I'd at least know I've been above the seven line. An honourable failure is within my grasp. I turn back and point to my watch.

"Greg, seven," I say.

He nods and smiles.

The last rope climbs a vertical wall of snow to the tents. Greg and I push up towards it. Ted determines that a better route for the rope is to the left, around the sheer section. He loosens the ice-screws. Hugo assists, and Angel is called up from the rear. Trying to stand stationary on the incline burns the legs, and so, one by one, each of us turns and sits on the ice, with our crampons jammed in.

Grey clouds drift across the sun. The temperature drops. I remove my backpack and clip it to the fixed rope. I pull out my jacket and get warmed up inside it. Even though I'm marvelling in the views of the valley, Pumori, and other mountains in the distance, I'd prefer to be moving. I struggle not to slide down the slope.

Angel kneels on the hard snow at my right hip.

"Don't move, Fergus."

He unties the ropes from their anchor point. If he cuts corners, Pete, Greg, and I will be clipped to an unsecured line. It might be only for a minute, but a slip would be fatal. I watch Angel untie and retie half-frozen knots as he balances on this sharp gradient. Gloves and a backpack cramp his movement. He informs Pete, Greg, and me what he's doing, where we're to move and when. He steps across the face and re-anchors the rope. I've much to learn.

We re-start. The last twenty metres deliver the slap I'd been waiting for. Maybe I got cold sitting still. Perhaps it's the usual combination of dehydration and a lack of food. The gradient increases further. My crampons scrape across the hard ice. No footholds have been kicked in up here. I wheeze, mouth wide open. Only the fixed rope prevents me tumbling off the mountain and being dumped into the Bergschrund far below. Scrambling, tugging on the jumar, I close off the last few steps. I look to my right and see our tents. We are here. This is Everest Camp 3.

Each team will pitch a camp somewhere between 7,000 and 7,400 metres. Ours lies at 7,100. Our tents sit on a ridge that runs perpendicular across the Lhotse Face. The Sherpas bashed it out further with ice axes and a shovel. It's twenty metres long and two metres wide. I step onto it. The Sherpas have planted five three-man orange tents along it.

I look along the ridge. The right side of each tent is within centimetres of the edge. A misstep there will be terminal. A small passage runs down the other side of the tents, where we can walk. To the left of that gap is a wall of packed snow. A rope trails along the walkway. To reach the last two tents requires extra caution; the line only runs to the third one.

This will be our home soon. I expected worse. It's palatial compared to our Camp 1 sleepover on Pumori. Back there, the Sherpas had pitched each tent on its own individual platform. The circumference of each had been just a few centimetres larger than the tent itself. On three sides was a vertical drop; a wall of ice had completed the fourth. We could not stand outside ours. Entering and exiting had required Houdini skills. Putting on a boot in the vestibule had risked kicking something out and down the mountain, or crueller, the boot itself. Before nodding off for the night, we'd attached a rope to our harnesses inside our sleeping bags. That rope had trailed out to a screw in the ice wall. If the ridge had collapsed or the covering blown away during the night, there'd have been no need to worry. We could have dangled in our bags in the frozen darkness, with a fatal drop beneath us.

"We'll take forty minutes to an hour for lunch," Ted says. "Then head down."

We're sitting on the snow, near the first two tents, looking down the face.

"Camp 2 is tiny from here," I say. "Isn't that it on the right of the valley?"

"Yeah, just dots." Greg chews on a snack. "And what about Camp 1? I can't see it at all."

"Nothing, I know where it is. I don't think there's anything in the way. It's just too far away to see."

"And over there where the valley narrows, the Icefall must be at the end. Somewhere below it is Base Camp."

"Yeah. That's some view."

Pumori reaches up dead ahead of us, perhaps ten kilometres away. Its peak is now only fifty metres further up in the sky. This adventure started as a trek. Bit by bit this month, I climbed closer to my highest altitude. Then step by step, I crept above it. Today, however, has been a masterstroke.

To our right, Everest has revealed more of itself. A 1,800 metre brown pyramid stands above us. We can see up as far as the South Summit, about one hundred metres from the top. I've a good view of the Geneva Spur. I still can't determine the route over that black outcrop of rock. I'll leave that problem till next month, more confident that I may reach it.

We sit for close to an hour and force our bodies to make one final acclimatisation effort. The grey clouds thicken and drop down on us. I'm not sure whether it's the coldness creeping in, hunger, thirst, the thinning air or all four, but I want out of here. My appreciation of the views diminishes. I want to descend.

This is the edge of the death zone; it must be the thin air that has dulled my senses and killed my earlier enthusiasm.

"Ok, good stuff, team," Ted says. "You can start the descent."

I'm sitting closest to the fixed rope. A dozen of us will create a queue. I've no wish to be a part of that.

With only a light backpack, I race. My left arm trails behind me horizontally. I've wrapped the rope around it. I feed it through my right hand. Rather than abseil down, I arm rappel with big strides. My grip and the friction of the rope on my left sleeve act as a brake. Breathing heavy, I eat up the distance to the Bergschrund.

Greg trails close behind. We've opened a large gap to the others. In the complex, steeper sections, I know I should ease off and abseil. But I ignore caution and manhandle myself down, grasping the rope as tight as I can with both hands. The rope scorches and stains the left sleeve of my orange jacket. The tips of two fingers on my right glove have worn away. I didn't intend that, but I can tape them up later.

In just over thirty minutes I reach the bottom of the Lhotse Face. I'd heard that Sherpas can descend from Camp 3 to Camp 2 in an hour; now I believe it. I consider arm rappelling down the Bergschrund but then think better of that plan. That's a one way ticket to the morgue. I cool my jets and calm my breathing. I connect my abseil gear to the rope and then drop over the edge.

Back down on the gentle slopes of the Cwm Valley, I walk towards Camp 2. The overcast afternoon closes in further. My legs want this day to be over. My breathing rises to keep me going. The helter-skelter descent was a little reckless, but on such an incline it would have been a shame to fight gravity's momentum. I look back up the Lhotse Face. Team members disappear up into the lowering clouds. Greg approaches the Bergschrund. I'll wait for him; there's no point walking away.

The clouds wrap around us. A light sleet lands on our jackets. We trudge in the last thirty minutes together. I struggle to close the distance to the finish.

"Man, I'm thrashed." I draw in air. "I'm running on empty. I won't recover enough this evening to make it to Base Camp tomorrow."

"Serious?"

"Yeah. I can get hydrated, no problem. But there's no way I'll eat enough, not that food. If I set out empty tomorrow, I'm in big trouble."

"Really?"

"I mean it. I'll be screwed."

"What about the day after?" Greg asks. "Charlene should touch Camp 3 tomorrow. The following day she'll head down to Base Camp. She's with Mingmar. He's top class."

"You're right. Head with them?"

"Yeah. Why not?"

"A full day here. I could nibble on biscuits or something. You're right. And buckets of water. Ok, that's what I'll do."

Back in the mess tent I gulp down warm tea. Damp clothing sticks to me and chills my body. The others arrive in ones and twos.

At dinner time, many of us just play with our food, excluding Greg and Pete who wolf it down. It stares back at me in the dim light. I force myself to take each mouthful, wash it down with liquid, and hope it stays there. What am I doing here? My head hurts. I'm shattered. This is unrelenting.

"I could do with another day here to acclimatise. I'd like to stock up before heading down. Head back with Charlene."

"Sounds good," Hugo says. "I'll be hanging on for her anyway."

"Me too," Khalid says. "I'll take an extra day here."

Ted and Angel will descend to Base Camp tomorrow with the others.

"Has anyone got Diamox?" Ted asks.

He'd lectured us before on the danger of relying on the medicine Diamox. He maintains it should only be taken where there's no alternative and should be followed by descent. It's not appropriate for someone who intends to climb further uphill and might become dependent. Slow ascent and rest, or even a temporary drop down a few hundred metres, prepares the body best.

"I've some in my kit." Linda steps up from the table.

"Once I get back to Base Camp, I'm descending to Pheriche," Hugo says. "A few days of richer oxygen will do wonders for the body."

I'd been unconvinced of the logic in descending below Base Camp to recuperate. It'd sounded like two days of wasted energy trekking there and back.

"The appetite improves. The food is better. You can take on a few decent meals and build yourself up," he says.

Slumped at a cold, grey Camp 2, pushing food around a plate, his arguments are compelling.

"The body can't mend at Base Camp. Small tears in a calf muscle, invisible things, they'll never improve there." Hugo takes another slug of tea.

I must break the daily chain of burning more energy than I consume. After many dinners I suffer a mini-vomit. There's nothing I can do to prevent it. I take Brufen morning and evening and Motilium before each meal, but their effects are limited. My body has taken as much of this mountain and food as it can handle. It wants out of here.

"The walk to Pheriche and back, the energy wasted, we'll regain it when we're there?" I ask.

"No question," Hugo says.

"Ok. Count me in." I nod to him.

Greg had previously decided that he would descend.

"Ok, I'll join you guys down there," Khalid says.

"I improved a lot down there," Charlene says. "I'm going back down too."

"When are you heading, Greg? Straight away?" I ask. "I'll be a day behind."

"No problem, I'll wait at Base Camp," Greg says. "The day after you get there, we'll trek down together."

"Thanks."

Hopefully, lower down the valley, the feel good factor will return.

APRIL 29

Recovering at Camp 2

"Ok, I'm out of here." Greg pulls on his gloves. "See you tomorrow."

"Keep it steady. See you then." I roll over; it's 6am.

I see no reason to be up and about. My head hurts. Someone has stolen my mojo. Touching the limit where most people stop acclimatising has taken a toll on my body. I can ask no more of it. If a person stays at this altitude long enough, they die. I should have gone downhill with the others. But where would I have found the energy? Lying here on this overcast morning does me no good either.

Charlene has pushed out in the other direction with Mingmar. I presume Khalid and Hugo are resting in their respective tents. The subzero temperature still holds mine in its grip.

Midmorning I eat breakfast in the mess. My body doesn't want food, but it's the one critical thing I must accomplish today. I have to munch on biscuits or something to get calories into me. I cannot underestimate tomorrow; a trip through the Icefall always requires respect, and it will need energy, lots of it. Hydrating myself with warm tea poses no challenge.

I pass the day chatting to Hugo and Khalid or resting in my tent. Simple tasks challenge me. The only possible excursion is to stroll a little along yesterday's path and then veer left. Ade mentioned that he'd gone off route on the way down from Camp 3.

"Like a big piece of smoked salmon", he'd said, his gallows humour tuned from years of active service in the army. He'd seen a human leg sticking out of the ice. I'll leave the dead to nature.

We hear breaking news from nearby Annapurna. A Spanish climber was struck by high altitude cerebral edema (HACE) and spent two nights in the open on his own at about 7,500 metres. Weather conditions prevented both Sherpa and helicopter searches from reaching him. His is another body that will be left on the mountain.

Mid-afternoon we hear Charlene arrive back from Camp 3. Her race to the summit is back on course. Mingmar steps into the tent.

"You look very fresh, Mingmar." I reach for another biscuit.

"It was a good day today. Not hot. We climbed well. Charlene is happy."

As the dim light fades further behind Nuptse and Pumori, we eat dinner and plan tomorrow.

"Fergus," Hugo says, "you and I will leave at six tomorrow. Be ready."

"Ok. Beat the heat?"

"Yeah, that's the plan." He dips a spoon back into his soup bowl. "Charlene, you'll descend with Mingmar?"

"Of course," she says.

"I thought you'd try a dash to the summit, while Anne-Mari's looking the other way," I say.

Hugo laughs.

"I wish, if only it was that easy," she says. "I've got to wait for the fixed rope. Then we'll race from Base Camp."

"Well, good luck. The acclimatisation's over now."

"And Khalid. You and Jingbar are together tomorrow?" Hugo asks.

"Yeah, no problem," Khalid says.

Before nightfall we've retired to our tents. The damp clouds never lifted today. I got no respite from the headache. I battled food for hours and mostly lost. Lying in the dark, I wish I'd left for Base Camp. But this was my decision. No one forced me to trudge up here. As long as I make it to the top, then I'll write off the troubles along the way. But if I don't make it, what a waste this all is. I keep hearing that the journey is the adventure, not the destination. I don't share that view right now. I get no pleasure from this. Bear Grylls, you can take the wonders and beauty of the wilderness and shove them where the sun don't shine; now survive that.

Get me to sleep, so I no longer suffer my body's draining fight against altitude. Pull me out of here and down the valley tomorrow, to oxygen, food, and warmth. By some means, drag myself to the summit of this mountain, so I never have to return.

APRIL 30

Climb Down from Camp 2 to Base Camp

We'll set out at 6am and put much of the Icefall behind us before the sun's assault. I rise at five. A frigid dawn breaks to reveal low clouds and falling snow. I've packed my gear and am ready on cue.

"All set Hugo!" I call out.

"Let's wait till the snow eases," he says. "Heat won't be a problem today."

"All right."

I lie back on bulging stuff-sacks. Arriving in the Himalayas, I knew if I only reached Camp 2 it'd be an achievement; it's a different world to the lower valley and far removed from trekking. Sitting at Everest Camp 3 has handed me a minor victory. I hope to climb higher, but for now I must descend into oxygen. The last twenty-four hours have flogged me. Hugo's strategy entices me: drop down a kilometre today and then escape to the green valleys a kilometre lower tomorrow.

Close to 7am I hear noises from Hugo's tent.

"Ok Fergus, that snow has eased. Let's push out in ten minutes."

"Cool."

I must cap off this cycle with a solid performance this morning. I've left my sleeping bag, mat, and other equipment in the tent. Travelling light will make matters easier. More important, I won't have to cart up that weight on my return. However, I'll store nothing at Camp 1. When we start our summit push, I'll have to ascend straight to Camp 2. If I'm exhausted, breaking the journey is no longer an option. It's a risk, but I'll take any opportunity to reduce the cargo.

We trek down through the boulders. My legs revel under the simple load. No one else stirs. Silence surrounds us in the Cwm Valley. Under the fresh snow, I cannot recognise the spot where we should move off the rocks and start the day proper.

"Let's put on the crampons here." Hugo throws his onto the snow.

I attach mine. I look up and do not see Hugo. I walk out onto the snow but cannot find him. I return to the rocks. I trek twenty metres in each direction, still no sign. Was he not crouched a few metres behind me fixing his crampons? Ten minutes pass. I daren't walk out onto the glacier and head down the valley; snow has hidden the trail. Thin crevasses lurk under a white camouflage. I feel like a fool. Hugo's a man who likes to make progress. He'll be none too impressed with this start to the day. I consider if he might have stumbled behind a boulder and been knocked unconscious.

"Hugo!" I roar out.

My voice echoes around the valley. It better not start an avalanche; that'll be my crowning moment.

Hugo reappears further down among the rubble, having back tracked. This was not the exit point onto the snow. I trek down to him and mumble an apology. The day's adventure re-commences.

I feel my crampons push down into the new snow. We're breaking trail; it'll be our prints that others follow.

"There're hidden crevasses," Hugo says. "Drop back ten metres. There's no point in us both disappearing."

Should he vanish, I'll arrange a rescue. I place my boots in his footprints to lessen the chance of discovering a fissure the hard way. It's good of Hugo to go on point.

"I'll watch our rear," I say.

"Idiot."

On the modest downhill slope we eat up the distance. Hugo spots the metre high poles that mark known, narrow crevasses and aims for them. We bound across each.

Halfway down the valley, two climbers appear out of the gloom marching against us. They look professional, breaking trail from the other direction. We exchange pleasantries. A path has now been shaped from Camp 1 to Camp 2. It'll remain till the next snow fall.

"They look like real climbers," I shout ahead.

"Of course you do," Hugo says. "We're the trail breakers today."

He's misheard what I said, but he's correct. It's early morning above 6,000 metres in the Himalayas. We're preparing for an assault on Everest. I look down at myself; harness on waist, equipment clipped in, crampons stomping on the snow. The climbers we just passed might have pegged me for an experienced mountaineer, entitled to have a shot at the summit. Maybe I've become less of a tourist. Perhaps I'm transforming from a city boy who was out of his depth in the mountains. We've several more weeks of this to go. I'll keep putting left foot after right and see where it gets me.

We negotiate the large crevasses above Camp 1 with a minimum of clipping into ropes. Hugo must be confident I won't do anything stupid. Our momentum is not broken.

Within an hour of setting off we reach Camp 1. The Bimble Brothers of Ade and Martin are crawling out of a tent. They spent the night at their Café One. We chat for a few minutes as they pack their gear.

"Let's keep moving," Hugo says. "We'll see you guys down at Base Camp."

As we approach the Icefall, we only run a loose hand along the fixed rope. Our speed amazes me. We've eliminated bending down to clip in and out every fifty metres. Fiddling with carabiners in gloved fingers is, it seems, for the prudent newbie. One and a half hours after leaving Camp 2, we touch the lip. We can see Base Camp in the distance, six hundred metres below us. We drop down over the edge.

"It's dangerous in here, more so with every day and hot afternoon," Hugo says. "Get through as quick as possible."

For a moment, I thought he was going to suggest we use caution.

On the ascent, the demands allow for nothing faster than a trudge. Now we let our momentum take us down. If we see half a gap around stationary or slow groups, we take it. We power down the vertical abseiling sections near the top. I place my full faith in the rope each time and head for oxygen.

An hour of descending delivers us to the easier lower sections of the Icefall. I feel like a pro as my swinging right arm snaps the safety carabiner onto rope after rope at each anchor point. I sometimes get too close to Hugo and interfere with the line he's on as we move over and around obstacles. Often we favour speed over vigilance and do not clip in. We only slow down for the bottomless crevasses; they still demand restraint. But mostly, we just use the line as a handrail for balance and leverage.

"For God's sake." Hugo turns back to me. "Stay off the damn rope when I'm on it."

A week ago, his speed descending the Icefall astonished me. I could do nothing to stay with him. He moves no slower today. He mentions that his knees give him trouble and he needs to watch out for them on downhill sections. Eventually I get the pacing right. I keep a connection point between us so as not to intrude on his movement. But this far into the adventure and in such an infamous place as the Icefall, I don't mind that my worst crime is going too fast.

The clouds lift to reveal a warm, bright day. We enjoy a short break for a snack and water.

Back on the move, I recognise the ladder under me as the last one. A little lower we reach the end of the rope; the danger has passed. I can't but imagine how it might feel the next time I descend through here. If I stand on the summit, then once I return to this spot I can start the celebration.

After two hours pushing through the Icefall, we stride into Base Camp. The day's descent has taken three and a half hours. I didn't think it possible. I'm starting to get a grip on this mountain.

"Congratulations." Ted stands up in front of the mess tent. "Acclimatisation complete."

"Thanks Ted." I get busy with my first mug of tea.

I'm sitting on a rock under the sun and staring up at the Icefall. I've now travelled it twice in each direction, and am on track. I refill my mug. I've climbed the Lhotse Face to over 7,000 metres, where the men get separated from the boys. So far, I'm clinging to the men's unit.

I swagger to my tent and toss down the backpack and crampons in front of it. More melt water is flowing through Base Camp than when we left; summer approaches. The Sherpas have constructed small channels to divert it down the valley. Two of the lower tents sit on their own island, surrounded by a moat. My own has sagged, the price of living on a moving glacier. I tweak the cords and shift a few rocks. It springs back up to its former shape.

Base Camp feels like a hotel compared to the Spartan conditions up higher. I stand under the shower's trickle and relish the feel of warm water on my skin. I contort myself to wet every part. A week of mountain toil runs off me and joins the stream.

I pop into clean clothes and take a short nap in my cosy tent.

Remembering how much every kilogram hurt me on the ascents, I seek out Ted. It'll be a disaster to fail in a fortnight if my legs buckle under the bulk of the pack. I'd trained on inclines with twenty-five kilograms in the pack. In hindsight, a weight of thirty-five would have better prepared me, but it's too late for that now. Ted accommodates me. We arrange for my down suit to be ported from Base Camp to Camp 2. A Sherpa will carry the sleeping bag to camps three and four on the days I need it. I'm not sure I'd make it all the way to the South Col with a full load. Now at least, I've stacked the cards in my favour.

I see the Bimble Brothers sitting on a rock outside their tents and stroll over to them. They're leaning in over Ade's transistor radio. I recognise the regal tones of the BBC World Service.

"Hi guys, well done. That's the acclimatisation behind us."

"It's good to be back," Martin says. "Well done yourself. It's all happening back in Europe." He gestures to the radio.

I'd explained the wonders of the euro to Ade only a few days ago. The broadcaster now reports on the EU's woes. The airwaves expound on the wretchedness of Greece's economy. An expert mentions the possibility of default. The currency is tanking and shedding value against sterling.

"It won't last the week," Ade says.

The three of us listen to the unfolding story and postulate on where it might end for Europe and the euro.

"It's still not too late for you Brits to join," I say.

Just beside us sits an empty stone platform; a tent has been taken down. A man who usually chats in this little group descends the valley. On his way to Lukla airport, Doug's climb has ended.

The only other news of note at Base Camp is bad news. Four days ago, a group of climbers were descending on the north side. At about 6,500 metres, an ice wall above them collapsed. It thrust them down a slope in a thirty metre wide plume of ice and debris. It ripped the fixed rope from its anchor. The force tossed one of the men into a crevasse that was then crammed with icy rubble. A search was launched. Yesterday it was called off. The mountaineer was named as Hungarian Laszlo Varkonyi. He'd planned to summit without supplementary oxygen. In a previous expedition, he'd got to within a hundred metres of the peak without a tank. The mountain takes yet another climber.

MAY 1

Trek from Base Camp down to Pheriche

This is the end of the glacier living for a while. We came here, busted ourselves for a month, and climbed higher than any mountain outside the Himalayas. We've put preseason and the main season behind us.

It feels counterintuitive to squander a day's energy trekking away from Everest. But if a fraction of what Hugo says is true, then several days down the valley with oxygen and food will reward me. A sleep in a warm, comfortable bed will do no harm either. My throat rasps, my nose often bleeds, and I've shed kilos. I need to regroup.

"We'll head off in half an hour." Greg stands up from the breakfast table.

"Excellent. What about the others?"

"Hugo's already gone. I think Charlene and Khalid are about to leave."

"What about Angel?"

"It'll be a while before he's ready. He'll follow us down."

"Cool."

We've packed light; we won't need the bulky sleeping bags. Normally for a week's holiday, I'd bring several changes of clothes. But for a week in the valley, the odd t-shirt and under items are more than adequate, added to the gear we're wearing. I don't think Pheriche will have bouncers at the nightclubs. I pull on a windproof top and skinny gloves to protect me from the cool morning.

"It's good to be out of those mountaineering boots. These feel like slippers." I point to my hiking boots.

"This's a lot easier than our last walk over this." Greg strides over a rock. "And it's not as tough as when we first came here either."

Within an hour we've climbed off the glacier and trek onwards to Gorak Shep. Another thirty minutes sees us the far side of the village. Rocks underfoot make the going tough. The altimeter puts us at much the same altitude as Base Camp.

"This'll be further than Hugo suggested," Greg says.

"I'm still waiting for all this oxygen he promised."

At the two hour mark we reach the first big drop of the day. The trail plunges a hundred metres through rocks in just a few minutes. This leads us into the short valley that heads to Lobuche. Grassy shrub covers both sides of the trail. We've broken below the 5,000 metre mark. For the first time in weeks, I walk on hard clay rather than rocks, snow, and ice. The ground is in our favour and our stride widens. The extra oxygen hits me and works its ways around my brain and muscles. No longer having to watch our every step, the chatter increases. Gone is the crouched, slogging gait of high altitude mountaineers. We seem ten years younger than this morning. The laughter flows. A small, bubbling glacial stream joins us. We leap across it as it criss-crosses the track. It reminds me of the Irish hills on a spring day. This is how it's supposed to be.

We trek into Lobuche. The village bustles with the construction of a large hostel. I don't remember these building works from our hike up here. The world may be in recession, but it's boom time for the two dozen workers around us. The walls look like a dry bond, cut slabs of rock fitted together and held in place by gravity. If there's mortar involved in this erection, it's well hidden. But the structure outclasses the surrounding dwellings. The owners will have the luxury market to themselves if they build something decent here.

"I think that's where the builders have to sleep." I point to a pile of building materials with some lean-to corrugated plastic.

"You're joking. You'd freeze in there. At night, up here?"

"Look at it. People live there."

"God, you're right."

If a tornado struck, it could do a thousand dollars' worth of improvements.

"I hope those guys are well paid for their troubles," I say. "But it's probably peanuts by world standards."

Greg and I compare what we see to the recent tales of Irish builders and developers. They got paid a fortune, but then through a series of ever greater gambles and borrowing, blew it all and ended up millions in the red. We surmise that perhaps somewhere in between the two extremes is the place to be.

We leave the village behind us and continue towards the graveyard.

"You get that?" I inhale deep through my nose. "That smells great."

"Yeah, super. What is it?"

"I don't know. It must be one of these plants. First time I've smelt anything nice in weeks."

Greg draws in a long breath.

"I think my nose might still be in shock after the toilet tent," I say. "It's nice to see a bit of colour again too."

After the graveyard, we drop two hundred and fifty metres through boulders. My legs propel me down and around the obstacles; they know what's at the bottom. Our starved bodies become the beneficiaries of some serious oxygen.

We approach Thukla, where illness struck Hugo three weeks ago. At the time, only a madman would have placed a bet on him getting back on his feet. He's most likely kicking back in Pheriche by now. He reckons the ailment was dysentery. We'll never know what it was, probably best not to.

The weather stays favourable. No longer must we confine ourselves to a narrow, dusty trail. We bound where we please on a long, grassy descent.

The vista changes and the valley opens up wide in front of us, we can see for kilometres. The Dudh Kosi River meanders through thick grasses. We identify brown specks alongside the water's edge as grazing yaks. On our right flank, a mountain soars up to a snowy peak.

"Is that it?" Greg points to a village beneath us in the distance.

"Yeah, that's Pheriche."

"About a mile away?"

"Try again, about three miles. Everything's big up here. We'll be there in an hour."

I was last here on the way down from Pumori. It had been the first day in weeks I felt energetic and enthused. That same feeling returns. Thicker, moisture laden air surrounds us. The chill of Base Camp is forgotten. Green vegetation sprouts about us. It's a different world to the harshness of glacier living. We enjoy the last of the day's walk, watching local farmers tend to their beasts of burden.

We enter the village at 4,400 metres on the flat banks of the river. Many of the locals cultivate potatoes and buckwheat, or raise yaks to earn a living. In the summer, some of its men find employment as guides and porters. We walk down the single clay street. No more than twenty stone buildings surround us. Several of them serve as hostels. We pass a small shop crammed with merchandise. In the centre of the settlement sits the Himalayan Rescue Association clinic. This will be our backdrop for the next week.

"Do you know the hostel to go for?" Greg asks.

"Yeah, the Pheriche Hotel. We'd lunch there six months ago. Everyone says it's the best. Hugo tried to stay there when he was sick but couldn't get a room."

Inside the main room we find Hugo, Charlene, Mingmar and Khalid.

"Hey guys, how's everyone?" Greg slides off his pack.

"Great," Charlene says.

"I'm afraid it's full," Hugo says. "But the owner might be able to do something."

"Let's find him," Greg says, "although, I'll settle for any bed tonight."

The owner appears and Hugo negotiates. He's a cheery man, no more than forty. A few inches shorter than me, he's eaten a few good meals in his day. The only rotund local I've ever seen in the valley.

"Sorry about tonight. You can sleep in the hostel behind. Then tomorrow, you'll get three rooms in here. Ok?"

"Perfect. We'll go there now?"

"Of course. Follow me, gentlemen."

We get three rooms upstairs. A single layer of unpainted, un-plastered plywood, with the manufacture's name printed across it, separates each room. I've two single beds in mine, each a wooden box with a thin mattress placed on top. A small window completes the decor. As ever, there's no shelf on which to place anything or a hook on which to hang something. But the spare bed spoils me for storage space.

I step out into the corridor.

"Happy days, gents, there's a real toilet."

The inbound plumbing feeds a puddle of water on the wooden floor, but importantly, the outbound sanitation looks sound.

We head back to the main hostel and join the others at a table. In the centre of the room, a stove burns yak dung and warms us. The well-stocked bar catches my eye. But given the training, sacrifice, and risk of our endeavour, I stick to my dry commitment. I want to get fat and rested. I'd love to fall into a deep sleep and wake up with an unobstructed nose, not one full of blood. A hangover won't help that process. I opt for a Coke, glad of its two hundred and fifty calories.

"How're the rooms, Khalid?" I ask.

"Very comfortable, it's a good place."

"We should be here tomorrow."

"And the food's great too." Charlene passes me a menu.

"But you've got to try the showers," Khalid says. "Unbelievable."

"Come on, Khalid, they can't be that good."

"Best ever. I feel fantastic."

The evening closes in. Even though a few electric bulbs overhead give off a faint glow, one of the young staff lights a candle on each table. Plates of food fly out of the kitchen. I feel like I'm in a restaurant. The teenager, his name is Kieron, takes orders and delivers food and drinks to the tables all night.

Well fed, we stroll to our lodgings next door and enjoy a night on a bed rather than a glacier.

A few days of this and I might just regain enough strength to climb the beast.

MAY 2 – MAY 8

Resting at Pheriche

The food is good, the egg fried noodles the highlight. I have them for breakfast each morning with a small pot of coffee, an unhurried start to my routine. I usually stroll into the dining room last and have the place to myself. Kieron looks after me, and he's always cheerful. He puts in a long day, every day. He attends to the early risers at 5am, cleans down the room about 10am, serves lunch, fires up the stove at 4pm, and doesn't finish delivering dinner and drinks till near 10pm. On top of that, he manages whatever maintenance jobs or guest requests come his way.

I've a double bed with two thick duvets, an unheard of luxury. A large window with a big sill affords a spot to store my bits and bobs. It's the first place I've seen that has a few hooks on the wall for hanging clothes. Daylight floods in through the glass and allows me to read. Even at night, I can turn a few pages by the light of the dim LED bulb. We've a whole week in which to do nothing, and I enjoy it. Breakfast, lunch, and dinner provide the main focus each day.

The shower surpasses even the highest reviews given to it by Khalid. Three US dollars cover the cost of heating the water. Two porcelain thrones facilitate the necessities. Each sits in a small, spotless tiled room. Outside them, two hand basins with running cold water and a mirror allow me enjoy the simple ablutions of the day at a leisurely pace. Since all God-fearing people are long out of bed and on their way by the time I surface each morning, I've the run of the facilities to myself each day before noon. Shit in a bucket for three weeks, and the mind refocuses life's priorities.

All week, the weather remains overcast and chilly. I usually step out for a twenty minute stroll each day. The only tourist feature stands next door. A two metres high memorial of polished steel has been fashioned into the shape of a split pyramid. A craftsman has etched two hundred plus names on it: a list of those who died on Everest. Greg and I reviewed the names and nationalities, pausing at engravings that we knew from stories and history. Some years are sparse. Others, such as 1996 (the year of the book "Into Thin Air"), are a roll call of the dead. Space has been provided for future additions. One man's name is already overdue: the climber who perished on the north side while we were acclimatising. None of us travelled here to earn a permanent inscription.

Khalid busies himself in the internet shop next door for a few hours each day. I checked my email once and rushed through a month of emails. Nothing important, the world still turns, my job continues. I didn't reply to anyone. I'd told people I'd be offline for two months and don't want to confuse that understanding now. But the messages of encouragement lifted me. Charlene spends as much time as Khalid in front of a screen; keeping in touch with home, updating her blog, and uploading photos from our adventure so far. The others spend maybe an hour a day on the net.

A few small mountaineering groups are recuperating in the hostel. A constant flow of trekkers stay a night or two. One lunchtime, I struck up a conversation with a hiker from Dublin. He understood we were climbers. Towards the end of the meal he inquired as to which summit we were attempting. He almost choked when we told him. Being wrapped up in this voyage for so long and having spent the last month on the upper slopes of Everest, I'd forgotten that we're aiming beyond the norm. For me, now, it's just something to be done.

Three hardcore Finnish mountaineers provide the entertainment at the hostel. These are the men who'd visited Charlene at Base Camp. They live it to the max. Whatever beers I've abstained from, they make up for, plus wine and anything else with alcohol. How they can train so hard and hit the booze is beyond me. Greg tells me they grab fresh air on a short hangover-cure walk each morning before I rise from bed.

They've climbed big mountains. One of them has hit the North Pole, and I hear plans for an adventure to the harsher South Pole. Two of them are aiming for Lhotse, while the third is heading for Everest. They look very professional in their matching red sponsored tops. They pack a handful of postcards: a composed photo of the three of them, fixed with unflappable stares. The chiselled looks of the youngest, and tallest, finds favour with the ladies. Greg and I should have got a few cards like that printed; although, we'd never pull off the uber-cool Nordic look. After a night or two in Pheriche, they become regulars at our table.

Hugo revels in mountain talk with other climbers. He names the various peaks in the region for curious trekkers. He's not the first Welshman to have an interest in the Himalayas. Back in 1847, the Surveyor General of India, Andrew Scott Waugh of the British Army, recorded the location of a mountaintop hidden in the nearby clouds. As a temporary measure, his department named it "Peak XV". Nepalese and Tibetan authorities forbade the surveyors to enter their countries. The closest the explorers got to the mystery mountain was a hundred and seventy-five kilometres. His team of surveyors collated trigonometry measurements of it over several years.

They took their readings from six different viewing locations, each over a hundred kilometres apart. In 1856, and after exhausting calculations, Waugh announced to the world that Peak XV was higher than all other known points on earth. Unaware of any local names for the mountain and not permitted to access the nearby villages to inquire, he struggled on a title for nine years. In 1865 he determined to call the mountain after his predecessor: the Surveyor General of India from 1830 to 1843, Welshman Sir George Everest.

Hugo makes it his personal goal to force Charlene to start writing her book. Much has been said about the novel, as yet no words have appeared on paper. She suggested that he or one of us might start it for her. I think a publishing deadline has been promised, but apart from a general Everest setting, the theme has yet to be defined. Hugo then changes tack and advises her to find a ghost writer and give up fretting about it.

Writing concerns aside, Charlene agonises about her race to the top. For us, the summit is the aim, an unequivocal success if we can climb it and return. But for her it is a duel. She has banked everything on being first. She quit her job a year ago to concentrate on training. The media back home has broadcast that one of their women will summit in May. She's planned PR events, book launches, and speeches for her return. Her competitor, Anne-Mari, is preparing up at Base Camp. Charlene worries we're too conservative in waiting for a safe weather window. Hugo spends an hour a day talking her down from the nervous edge.

Many fear that one of the contestants will jump the gun and become trapped in the jet stream near the peak. This hurricane force of over a hundred and sixty kph blasts the skies above earth between 7,000 and 10,000 metres, almost all year long. On our way up the valley from Namche, the plume of ice crystals stretching off the summit reminded us of its existence. A climbing window of a few days should open this month when the monsoon moves up over India and pushes the jet stream north above Tibet. An incorrect weather prediction will be fatal.

Hugo's words put much needed balance into the race in which Charlene has become engrossed. A small glass of red wine each evening provides the remaining equilibrium.

As the debate rages around me, I often read. The hostel owner grants a reduced rate to guests who donate a book or magazine to his small library. I thumb through a few old issues of Men's Health (Indian version) and learn everything I need to know about six packs, trendy clothes, urban chic, and chat up lines. In one issue, Hugo and I take a test on reading a woman's mind by looking at her facial expression. Should I ever find myself in Delhi, the local ladies won't have a chance.

I vanish into Michael J. Fox's novel "Always Looking Up: The Adventures of an Incurable Optimist". In bed or in the dining room, he shares his life with Parkinson's disease and describes his foundation, which is trying to find a cure. He reveals the personal philosophy that carried him through his darkest hours, and how he became a happier person by recognising the gifts of everyday life.

But beyond the reading and fooling about, our minds are on the climb. Every day we receive updates on the rope fixing progress and the weather forecast. For each prediction that the summit window will be around the 17th, someone else projects that it will not be until the 22nd, almost three weeks away. Perhaps we arrived too early. We may lose our acclimatisation by that stage. Then another estimate would arrive between those two dates, or even earlier. We can only keep on eating and resting.

On May 2nd, the fixed rope reached the South Col at nearly 8,000 metres. We hear that most teams are continuing to acclimatise and that some have spent a night at Camp 3. Our Sherpas are porting oxygen bottles, stoves, fuel, and tents up the mountain past Camp 2. The weather remains quite dry, but high winds above 7,000 metres challenge the Sherpas. We heard from Alpine Ascents:

> Today there were several big lenticular clouds over the higher mountains. Lenticular clouds are lens shaped clouds formed by high winds, and we are hoping we won't see any of them tomorrow. If the winds are blowing the team can always wait another day at Camp 2 before going up.

Apa Sherpa's team reported on May 2nd:

> We woke up this morning to 5 inches of snow at Base Camp and the same amount at Camp 2. The weather forecasts have just upped the amount of snow for the rest of the week. Apa and everyone else at Camp 2 are coming down as soon as possible.

Khalid and Angel stay up to date with the weather forecasts and predictions via the internet. We may as well relax here as be further up the mountain. Another climber, Scott Woolums, recorded what he saw:

> Last night was a bit rowdy with high winds and a lot of snow. No sunshine this morning ... Can hear huge winds up towards the summit ... Yesterday we came up from Base Camp directly to Camp 2 ... Was incredibly hot yesterday on the way up, quite a contrast to now.

And from the Adventure Consultants team we heard:

> *Last night was quite a spectacular storm and being perched on an ice ledge on the Lhotse Face was more than a little menacing. So much for trusting weather forecasts! ... Fortunately, the snow that fell blew away or was otherwise redistributed before an avalanche hazard within our path developed.*

In fresh snow, teams will achieve little progress; it's heavy going underfoot. Climbing in a blizzard risks death, unless trying to escape, in which case there's no other option. The high risk of avalanche poses a bigger threat. New snow sits above a harder layer or on ice. On a steep slope it can slide without warning. Camouflaged crevasses lurk. Rope fixing above the South Col was postponed while the surface settled.

We heard that several teams were stuck in Camp 2, unable to go up or down. But despite this, word arrived that Linda, from our team, is aiming to summit on May 6th. The news stunned Charlene. She can't understand what has led her to be down the valley, when one of our squad is shooting for the top. Hugo explained that the race is not worth an injury. The debate ebbed and flowed for days. Hugo illuminated how the mountain is bigger than all of us. He has waited years for this opportunity, as many have. Now is not the time to throw away that preparation with a rash decision. When the monsoon pushes up from India in mid-May, the real weather window will open. Some people gamble on a mini-window, just wide enough to sprint to the peak and back. The gap might exist, but if something goes wrong, there's no margin for error. The clouds will swirl back in and steal away anyone they find up high. A mountaineer on the Sky Climber team expressed his opinion on Linda's preparations:

> *To aim for the 6th of May summit feels totally insane for us. To follow the Sherpa team fixing the ropes would extend the summit day at least to 20+ hours. Even at the best of circumstances the summit would be reached way too late for it to be safe. Also, the strong winds forecasted to hit the summit on 7th May might return earlier than expected, perhaps already in the afternoon of the 6th of May. The safety margins for the 6th of May summit are way too narrow for our liking. We have decided to be patient and wait in the safety of the Base Camp for a*

> *longer weather window. Impatience rarely brings anything good but in mountaineering it can get you killed.*

Word filters to us that Alpine Ascents had to turn around on May 3rd, unable to make it to Camp 3. They'll try again when there's a break in the weather.

Then we heard what we'd been waiting for. At noon on May 5th, nine Sherpas on the rope fixing team completed the last stretch to the summit. The mountain is open for business. So what are we doing down here?

We re-examine the plan with each new development. Angel and Hugo know the difference between mountaineering in favourable weather and being trapped in a storm at altitude. It will take us a day to get from Base Camp to Camp 2, where we'll have thirty-six hours rest and re-acclimatise. Then we'll climb for a day to Camp 3 and another to Camp 4. We'll set out late that fourth evening and ascend through the night to the summit, planning to revert to the South Col on the afternoon of the fifth day. If capable, the team will continue the descent. If not, we'll spend the night there and then set out for Camp 2. Then after a night's sleep, our squad will slog amidst the Icefall for the last time. We require a straight week of clear conditions for success. Any wind or heavy snow in that window and few of us will return.

With more news of Base Camp and expected weather windows, the ER doctor joined us for lunch one day. She was trekking down the valley, having completed her sojourn at Everest ER. They'd a busy month and had attended to over two hundred and twenty people. From forecasts and based on what teams told her, she predicted a rash of summits this week. She reckons her replacement will be finished in two weeks. Charlene was agitated to hear this; her nemesis lurks above somewhere.

The oncoming storm concerns all teams. Many have descended the valley to recuperate and recharge. Here in the Pheriche Hotel, the food is good, the beds warm, the company entertaining, and the shower in a class of its own. The mountaineer Anatoli Boukreev was one of the first to popularise the approach of descending before ascending, with the words "Touching the green grass before the summit." He'd led the Mountain Madness expedition headed by Scott Fischer in May 1996. The squad was one of several attempting to summit Everest when a storm hit and killed eight climbers in a single night. In total, fifteen people died on Everest that season. Boukreev rescued a number of people stranded above Camp 4. A few suffered permanent frostbite injuries and later amputations. The Wall Street Journal described his rescue efforts as:

> *One of the most amazing rescues in mountaineering history performed single-handedly a few hours after climbing Everest without oxygen by a man some describe as the Tiger Woods of Himalayan climbing.*

But as Hugo often reminds me "There are bold climbers and there are old climbers, but there are no old, bold climbers". The organiser of Boukreev's Mountain Madness group, Scott Fischer, died that day. His body rests behind a boulder at Camp 4. Ted has advised us to take a look at it if we reach the South Col, to emphasise what can happen up there. I can't see myself heading off track for such a recap. I'm well aware how grim it may become in the next two weeks. I don't need to view a corpse of fifteen years to bring that point home. And as for the fearless Boukreev, the mountains also took him. While trying to ascend the tenth highest peak in the world the following year, the 8,100 metre Annapurna, he was swept away by an avalanche. At its base stands a memorial in his honour, on which is inscribed his quotation:

> *Mountains are not stadiums where I satisfy my ambition to achieve, they are the cathedrals where I practice my religion...I go to them as humans go to worship. From their lofty summits I view my past, dream of the future and, with an unusual acuity, am allowed to experience the present moment...my vision cleared, my strength renewed. In the mountains I celebrate creation. On each journey I am reborn.*

He had a love of mountains that is lost on me. If this is practicing a religion, then what I feel is penance and sacrifice. If I make it to the top, there'll be a moment of relief, and then an over-riding urge to get the hell out of there before my luck runs out. Boukreev's strength is renewed by altitude; mine is sapped. He celebrates creation; I colour the air with curses. He dreams of the future; I dream of escape and a friendly bar on a sandy beach. He is a real man of the mountains. I conclude I am not.

Another man of altitude, Nurhan, arrived at the hostel one lunchtime. He'd taken Boukreev's advice to heart and was descending all the way to Namche Bazaar in a single day. Over a yak burger, he explained that he needed meat; his body was craving protein. He reckoned he'd get better quality down lower, not to mention more oxygen. The amount of extra trekking this entailed horrified me, but he said it was necessary. His muscles were wasting away and he had to take decisive action. He would arrive in Namche that evening, eat as much meat as is possible in two or three days, and then ascend back to Base Camp.

Martin and Ade appeared at the hostel. They reported that the days were dragging at Base Camp. We now crowd around the dinner table each evening, and there's always someone to chat to during the day.

They attended an afternoon lecture on altitude sickness, that's held daily at the Himalayan Rescue Association clinic next door. They recounted that it's an hour well spent, and so Greg and I decided to listen to it the following day. The only dealing we'd had with the facility was a quick visit on arrival in Pheriche. I needed throat lozenges, but they were out of stock. Greg requested cough syrup for his escalating cough. They only had two of that product left and wouldn't sell it to him; it was being kept for emergencies.

The small Pheriche clinic is one of two aid posts owned and run by the Himalayan Rescue Association. The other is Everest ER, the highest hospital in the world. A wind turbine and solar panels provide energy to run lights, equipment, and an oxygen concentrator. It boasts a consulting / examination room, a small ward, three bedrooms for staff, and a day room. In addition, space has been set aside for anyone wishing to undertake research into altitude sickness.

The illness can strike without warning, even if the rules of ascent have been obeyed. It doesn't heed age or fitness. It can, and does, kill. An approachable young doctor, possibly from the USA, delivered the presentation. Greg and I learnt little new, but we were glad to have old points reinforced.

All week we picked up titbits of information on summit prospects. We learned that Linda and her friend Domhnaill were trailing the rope fixing team. On May 6th they reached Camp 4. They intend to reach the peak on the morning of the 7th, during a narrow window. Strong winds are forecast for the 8th, with near storm conditions expected up high from the 10th to the 13th.

It's May 7th, and I'm sitting behind a lone breakfast table at my usual mid-morning time and pace. Most mortals have long started their day. Greg arrives and tells me that Linda and Domhnaill summited about 6am. Their gamble has paid off, but the news bewilders me having just risen from bed in Pheriche. Had I not flown into Lukla with them five weeks ago? Did I not complete the acclimatisation phase? Regardless, I'm four and a half kilometres below the goal, with it all still to do.

We discuss the boldness of the endeavour. Angel joins us at the table and reports a problem on the descent. Details are unclear. Linda's personal Sherpa has radioed those lower on the mountain that she's unable to walk, due to fatigue or confusion. Our team has Sherpas at Camp 4 who've just dropped equipment there. A rescue team has been assembled and dispatched above the South Col.

A strange couple of hours pass. None of us know quite what to say or do, other than listen for an update. We grasp that a storm is approaching and time is not on their side. It was always the tightest of windows and a delay was never on the agenda.

At lunchtime, Angel conveys that Linda has reached Camp 4. The group will take a brief rest and then descend.

Linda has proved the mountain is open. Charlene feels she has missed an early opportunity for success. She believes the team has made the wrong choice by waiting for a safe window. Her aim is to be first. Second place holds nothing for her, better never to have started. On the other hand, better to be alive. John Furneaux, a guide for the Canada West Everest team, describes his feelings on the early shot to the summit:

> *There is no way we can climb in those conditions. We need low winds, less than 40 kilometres per hour, and hopefully clear skies. We can climb with a few clouds around, but too many clouds usually means snowfall, which will tire us out ... We need at least three days of good weather up high to be successful. For now, we're in a holding pattern.*

The hostel becomes busier as more climbers retreat from Base Camp. They've completed their acclimatisation and are following the forecasts. While it's impossible to foretell good weather, it seems predicting bad weather is a simpler affair. A storm will blast the upper mountain for the next several days. Most teams now plan a summit bid after May 19th. Kieron has stepped up his game and tends to the crowded tables. The Finns' bar tab grows.

Angel informs us that Ted has made the decision on dividing our group into two teams. The first contains the stronger climbers, not that there's much between us, with the exception of Pete. Ted has placed me on Team 2, as my sleeping bag will be carried up by a Sherpa with the excess gear of Martin and Ade. It's unlikely that the same man will carry the items for the three of us at the same time, but so be it. The logic perplexes Hugo. He leads Team 1 and had presumed both Greg and I would be with him.

The team number makes no difference to me, but it means I'll be split from Greg. On the trail in from Lukla, we trekked together most of the time. We climbed as a pair on much of the route above Base Camp. We shared a tent in an extreme environment. It's an intimate living space. We divvied up tasks as needed. If one of us was down, the other took over the snow collection, water boiling, and cooking duties. We'd an agreement on how far open to leave the tent zips at night, to get the balance right between insulation and asphyxiation. I favoured oxygen; Greg preferred warmth. It had not occurred to me that I would push for the summit without him.

On the positive side, Ade and Martin are great men on the mountain. But they'll hustle together as the Bimble Brothers. I'll have to shack up with someone else.

On the morning of May 8th I bid adieu to Hugo, Charlene, Greg, and Khalid. Their holiday has come to an end. They'll join Pete and Roger at Base Camp and get ready for their summit push within a day or two. Angel, Ade, Martin, and I will return tomorrow. We'll follow one day behind Team 1.

May 8th slips away at the hostel. The four of us know that matters are about to get very serious. We'll climb as a team. We'll be united in the death zone for a few challenging days. We enjoy our last decent meal together for some time.

The pain in my throat has eased. My nose has responded to the extra moisture in the air. The last page of this Pheriche vacation is to say farewell to Mr Michael J. Fox; I finish his last chapter and turn off the light.

MAY 9

Trek from Pheriche back up to Base Camp

"Thanks a lot, sir. Great week, beautiful place." I set some euros on the counter. "That's the right amount?"

"That's it, perfect," the owner says. "Next time we see you, you'll have climbed Everest, yes?"

"Let's hope so." I throw my pack onto my back. "We should be back in two weeks. If we make it to the top, there'll be some party here."

"Best of luck, gentlemen."

"All right, Ade, Martin. Holiday's over. It's back to the grindstone. See you Kieron. Thanks man."

"Let's get to it." Ade strides out the door.

We trek under the sun up the Dudh Kosi valley. We chat and joke as Pheriche shrinks behind us. The greenery thins as we push upwards. I'll miss it.

We stop at Thukla for a short break and a Coke.

"There's that hill again." Martin looks up at the two hundred and fifty metre incline to our left.

"After that, it's back into thinner air," Ade says. "Let's take it steady."

Our drinks finished, we labour up the rocky path to memorial hill.

"That was a lot easier than a month ago," I say.

"Have we really acclimatised that well?" Martin asks.

"I don't know, but something was different. Let's hope the rest of the day is that easy."

The temperature cools and clouds gather. We press on to Lobuche. It's no longer such a foreign village; this is my fifth time through this settlement at 4,900 metres.

"This place always looks drearier on the way up. I skipped through here with Greg last week."

"A little break, gents?" Ade says.

"Good thinking." Martin sits down on a low wall.

The conversation turns to cars. We weigh up the English Aston Martin against the Italian Maserati. Nice vehicles, but both equally useless up here.

"Lads, this's going to be a longer day than we thought." I rise to my feet. "When we first trekked to Base Camp, this was our morning starting point. We've got pretty much a full day's walk ahead of us."

"There's no going back now," Ade says.

An hour beyond Lobuche, our boots touch the rocks. Little grows at this height above 5,000 metres. The air thins and the temperature drops.

"Yeah, I remember this, a slog," Ade says.

Five hours on the trail and we reach Gorak Shep. My earlier enthusiasm has been wiped away. The altitude once again dominates me.

"Another two hours I guess," Martin says. "Let's take a final break here."

We sit down on benches in a teahouse. As the two lads chat, I recline. The thin air is hitting me harder than I expected. We just had a week of food and rest. I'm supposed to be stronger, not weaker. For ten minutes I doze and concentrate on my breathing.

"Back to it, Fergus," Ade says.

"Yeah, yeah. All good here. Ready to go." I force my body upright.

The hike into Base Camp slaps me; it's as if all my acclimatisation has been lost. Ade and Martin trudge up beside me. A month ago, I laboured over these last kilometres. Doug and I crawled along here after the trek up Kala Patthar. Maybe I've forgotten how high we are.

The trail over the rock-covered ice sucks the life out of us. I pull in the cold air. I'm glad we spent a week down the valley. Hugo was correct; the body did feel stronger in Pheriche, and my appetite returned. But from here up we tread on glacier. The holiday is over.

MAY 9 – MAY 11

At Base Camp

"Welcome back, lads," Roger says. "How was it?"

"Let me get some water first." I reach for a flask in the mess tent.

I collapse into a chair and start on the first mug. Several of the lads chat around me.

"It was a good week, Roger. Like a holiday. I hear you're on Team 1. You guys are setting off in a day or two?"

"No, it's pushed back. The –"

"What? We're not going?"

"The window around the sixteenth is too dangerous. We're going to wait till the twenty second."

"No. We could have stayed in Pheriche." I put the mug on the table. "Another week here. I don't believe it. I was starting to feel human down there."

My energy and muscles will start to degrade. I can take one final push of several days and either way, success or failure, be done.

"When was that decided?"

"I think two days ago. I heard a message was put on our blog yesterday, telling you guys to stay down the valley for a few more days."

Why would we read our own blog to find out what we've been doing? Maybe it had been agreed that messages would be sent to us this way, but this fact was lost on us down in Pheriche.

"Ok, Base Camp it is for a few days. What's new here, guys? Apart from Linda, that was a cheeky sprint."

She got back here yesterday and will be relaxing in Kathmandu before any climber can replicate her accomplishment. She encountered a few difficulties on the descent. I hear that the mask might not have been on her face at some stage.

"Guys," Ted says, "do not take your masks off up high."

In thin air, the mind can play tricks. In addition, the hose might get tangled or an adjustment may be needed. There could be a legitimate, yet limited, reason to remove it. I try to instil an extra alarm bell in my brain: even in a confused state, never pull the mask off my face.

"And if for some reason you have to take it off," Ted points at us, "for God's sake leave the oxygen running, even at a low rate. There'll be moisture on the inlet valve. It'll freeze in seconds if the oxygen's not flowing. If that happens, with gloves or mitts, you'll have some job getting the flow going again. And let's be careful up there. There've been a few injuries. A Sherpa who climbed with us on Pumori took a fall off a face. Either the rope gave way, or he lost his grip. His pack saved him from a broken back."

"Is he all right?" Greg asks.

"He's injured, but he'll climb again," Ted says. "And there was another accident in the Icefall. A ladder pulled away from its anchor. A Sherpa came down with it and broke his arm."

We must account for our own actions. But if something goes wrong, the buck stops with Ted. We might perform a foolish manoeuvre, or luck may deal us a nasty hand. It's our problem, but others will look to him to solve it. He summited Everest before and has no appetite to climb through the Icefall again this month. From here on, this is as high as he'll go. We'll be led up Everest by Hugo and Angel, neither of whom has stood on top of this mountain.

I hear that while we were gone, a body surfaced through the ice next to our camp. Only a small portion was visible. The lads in the mess tent reckon it must have lain undiscovered for fifty years, judging by the clothing that the climber was wearing: a thick tweed type material.

Before the advent of helicopters, dragging a dead climber out would have taken days. Apart from being dangerous, it was also undignified. Cremation was the most respectable exit, but a lack of timber in this unforgiving environment ruled out even such a modest farewell. Survivors usually dropped corpses into a crevasse. But as the glacier inches downhill, it deposits its cargo at Base Camp or further down the valley.

It was decided to remove the body. Pete spares me no detail in explaining how this process panned out. The cadaver had remained intact for perhaps half a century, protected in a frozen tomb as it edged lower. That silent gracious path to the next world ended this morning; the glacier didn't wish to give up its prisoner. In the end, it was more similar to hacking a lump of frozen meat from an iced-over freezer. The Sherpas loaded several parts into a bag. The last chapter will now close on the gentleman's life.

Charlene appears in the mess tent.

"These are for you, Fergus." She hands me half a dozen protein bars and a handful of energy snacks. "For the computer help last week. You said you needed protein."

"Fantastic. I didn't expect anything. You have them to spare?"

"Yeah, I got loads from my sponsor. But be warned: those protein bars are really hard to eat."

"Don't worry, I'll lash through them." I glance at the wrappers. "Forty per cent protein, cool. You wouldn't believe how thin my legs are. I'll eat all of them before I go up that hill again." I glance towards the Icefall. "One bar a day."

If I can get something into my muscles, I might just make it to the top before I fall over. Such a day cannot be too far away.

I'm sitting out under the direct rays of the sun on the morning of May 10th. On the peak, however, no one reclines. One hundred and twenty kph winds blast our target. The weather forecast predicts that the jet stream will sit above Everest until at least May 13th. Some teams are still toying with the May 16th window, but waiting till the 18th seems the safer option. Several have decided that the real summit window lies somewhere between the 20th and the 25th.

I settle back into Base Camp life and prepare for another week here. I discover the truth of what Charlene said; these protein bars taste like wood. I spend thirty-five minutes forcing one down, nibble by nibble, with gulps of water. But so be it, I take my medicine for the day.

In the mess, I'm charging up the batteries for my electric foot warmers from the solar panels. I'll place them inside my boots on summit day, when I'll need every bit of heat I can get. I expect the process to take several hours, but after twenty minutes the indicator light suggests they'll take no more juice. TC has the same heaters as me. Hers also complete much quicker than expected.

"Do you think they charged?" I hold the batteries in my hand.

"It seems a bit quick," TC says. "There's no way to know."

"There might be a voltage or amp difference between what we need and what's coming off the solar supply. The charger for my spare AA batteries didn't work off this."

"Let's hope they've something," TC says.

"Best we can do."

A dozen trekkers should join us this afternoon. They've hiked up the valley the last eight days. Angel, who'd set out after us yesterday, had bumped into them on his ascent from Pheriche. They'll spend a night or two with us and then descend. It must be quite a spectacle to reach Everest Base Camp and see climbers preparing for a summit push. It'll be very different to the normal tourist sights one might see on holidays. It strikes me as dull now, but I think back to the enthusiasm when I first got here. Several hundred mountaineers now reside here, whom, when kitted up, look like something from an apocalypse movie. We're living in a tented village on a moving glacier.

"They should be here early afternoon," Ted says. "The group's carrying a bug. Two of them have turned back. We've set up a separate mess tent for them. Keep your contact to a minimum. Be careful shaking hands. I'll tell them the same thing."

Having travelled this far, they'll now be treated as lepers. In the build-up to their trip, they must have imagined a more triumphant arrival. But a violent case of Khumbu belly at this stage will be the end of our summit push; at least, it'll lead to a very different kind of four day push.

As the sun dips and the temperatures drop, the trekkers slump into camp. Just before dinner I pop into their tent to say hello and be polite. Tired faces stare back at me. I hope they sleep tonight and can explore tomorrow. The world's elite climbers and some of the planet's greatest optimists are preparing on all sides. They're getting ready to do what they do best: take on Everest and re-test their skills, or find out the hard way if they have what it takes.

For one of the trekkers, the journey will deliver more than just tourist photos. Yvette is the mother of Guy Leveille, a Canadian climber. She'd wanted to visit the area where her son spent his last days. The nearby Cho Oyu took him two years ago. On the trek up, she and a few Sherpas built a small memorial near Namche.

After dinner in our mess tent, Linda passes around her camera. She has a few great shots of herself and her climbing buddy Domhnaill on the summit. I note she's not wearing gloves at the top, or an oxygen mask. Fumbling with focus settings in mitts is difficult. Regardless, she's sitting here among us and has lived to tell the tale.

"This is superb." I pull the camera's display screen closer. "They've got the same shot framed on the wall at the Pheriche place where we stayed. It was spectacular. I couldn't even work it out at first glance."

Taken from just below the summit, she has captured the shadow of Everest cast by the early morning low-lying sun. The light comes from the east. The silhouette is a perfect pyramid to the west. It must cover hundreds of square kilometres.

"You did pretty well to catch that, Linda." I pass the camera on.

If all goes well, the mountain will treat me to a similar view within the next two weeks. But I know how I operate. I doubt I'll stop to ruffle out a camera at that altitude. Far too much can go wrong on summit night. I'll be focused on the bare minimum: get up and get down, as quick as possible, and in one piece.

It's May 11th and I'm basking in the warmth that the morning sun delivers to my tent. The temperature has shot up from -7C just fifteen minutes ago. I've transitioned from being cocooned in a sleeping bag, to releasing the zips, to lying on top of it. A tiny MP3 player fills my ears with music. I feel weightless as the watch display approaches +30C. I pull in air in slow, deep breaths. Time waiting at Base Camp is time to be killed. This is as good as it gets here.

About 10am I head to the mess tent.

"Hey Greg, late breakfast for you today?" I sit down. "I hope you're not picking up my bad habits."

"There's not much to do, no point in making the day any longer. Try this cereal with yogurt. It tastes great."

"Really? Where did yogurt come from?"

"Beats me."

My body must be low on calcium and dairy; it slides down.

Back in my tent, I commence the half hour battle with a protein bar. I knock two minutes off my best time and count it as a small victory.

Late afternoon, I'm sitting alone at the mess table. Ted and Hugo stand near the radio. Weather forecasts have ebbed and flowed, but I sense a change of mind.

"The Icefall's becoming unstable," Ted says. "Every day it's melting. The longer we wait, the greater the risk."

"What do you reckon?" Hugo asks.

"The window for the sixteenth looks good. We'll go for it."

"Sure?"

"There're several forecasts going around, all different. I see a window. Team 1 leaves tomorrow, four AM."

"Ok. But the Turks are still on their way back up the valley. What about the teams?" Hugo asks. "They're not even now."

"We'll have to rejig them. You'll lead Team 1 as planned. The Turks are off Team 1."

"Ok," Hugo says. "So I've got Charlene, Greg, Khalid, Pete, and Roger."

"That's right. Matthew was Team 2, but he's out, urinary tract infection. He's heading down the valley. Angel will take Team 2. That's Ade, Martin, TC, Fergus, and the Turks."

"There should be one more on Team 1 then," Hugo says.

I can see where this is going. I take another sip of tea.

"You're right," Ted says.

"What about Fergus?" Hugo asks. "For Team 1."

They turn around and look down at me. A lot has happened in the last minute. I didn't want to hang about Base Camp for a week, but this development startles me. There are only a few hours left in the day. There'll be a short sleep, then a 3am alarm call for a push at Everest. After six weeks of acclimatisation and a year of preparation, the playoffs have commenced. I've qualified.

"Yeah, sounds good." I nod my head.

I've got to get my equipment ready, figure out how much food to carry, and fill my pack. The clock is ticking.

"I'll just make a few final adjustments to my gear." I stroll out of the tent.

I can't hide the smile on my face, nor can I wait to tell Greg the news.

The Route

1: Base Camp
2: The Ice Fall
3: Camp 2 is pressed against the side of Everest
4: Camp 3 is halfway up the Lhotse Face
5: The Yellow Band is the light shade of rock that we must cross
6: The Geneva Spur is the black outcrop that we must cross
7: Camp 4 at the South Col is hidden around the rear of Everest
8: We should climb the rear of Everest to the summit

207

MAY 12

Climb Up from Base Camp to Camp 2 on the Summit Push

U p to now, any of us could have a bad day and then catch up later. Any delays or illness from here on and that's it, no summit.

I picked up a few hours of sleep, on and off. I wake before my watch rings at 3am. Today I must reach Camp 2. That distance will be a first for me.

"Fergus! You up?" Greg calls from his tent.

"Getting dressed."

I crawl out into the glacial dark and shuffle to the mess tent. A triangle of light from the head torch illuminates the way. Outside of that, blackness reigns. My breath floats in the frigid air. Flickering blobs of orange and yellow reveal where other climbers are preparing.

At the table, I knock back a litre of warm water, which one of the Sherpas has ready for us. I force down a cereal bar. The rest of Team 1 appear for breakfast, fill their bottles with water, and set off. Greg arrives and eats some food. I pick up the remaining flask, intending to fill my bottle. In an automatic motion, I pass the thermos spout under my nose and take a whiff.

"I don't know about that." I frown. "Greg, does that seem ok to you? It smells odd."

He bends down over the flask.

"Seems fine."

"Sure?" I sniff it again. "I'll see if there's any more water about."

"It's grand, no worries."

I can't find any other container. Greg downs two mugs of water from the flask. That being the case, I fill my litre bottle and place it into the insulated mounting on the side of my pack. Greg does likewise and we walk out into the darkness.

Ice ridges reach up around us in the darkness. Greg has stopped.

"Any idea?" He looks left and right.

"No. Damn. It all looks the same to me. No sign of the others?"

"No, I can't see a marker stick either. I don't recognise this. Let's back track."

Thirty minutes have passed since leaving. I plod behind Greg.

"Up above. Lights, moving. Just there." Greg points. "Yeah, I know this bit. We're good."

We leave the ridges behind us. Panting, I lug my boots up each step. I can't believe a person could feel this bad and yet launch themselves into a full day's climbing. It's as if there's no oxygen in this freezing maze.

We should reach the fixed rope in a minute. The climb proper commences.

"I need a second." Greg leans over.

He hurls. I shudder watching him. My stomach spasms and I step away a few paces. He vomits again. I double over. I dry wretch. I can't remember if I drank from the ill smelling flask or not. I didn't down mugs of it like Greg. I regain my breath and stand a little taller, hands on my thighs.

"Take your time, Greg."

He throws up again.

"Are you guys ok?" I recognise Khalid's voice from up above us.

He's climbing with Jingbar and is accompanied by another personal Sherpa from one of the climbers who'd quit two weeks ago. Moving lights indicate their position.

"Not sure, sick. Greg's throwing up. I think it was the water."

"I'll be ok." Greg says from his knees.

"No rush."

We can't make out what the guys above are explaining, but get the gist that a Sherpa or two have also been struck ill. One of Khalid's personal Sherpas may be lying down vomiting in the dark.

"This is a dog show." I take my bottle from its holder and pour a litre of still warm water onto the snow. "No point in carrying that shit up the mountain."

Greg empties his bottle. Five minutes ago, we faced the prospect of a day's mountaineering in one of the most dangerous places on earth. That's become a pleasant memory. We now confront an appalling vista. Greg is nauseous. Whatever fluid was in his body has landed on the snow. Dehydration is just a matter of time. He has a litre of orange flavoured water in his pack, which he prepared from a clean source. But he can't drink it; he'll throw up again soon and waste it. I might be healthy. If I did swallow the tainted liquid, it was only a mouthful. However, I must tackle an eight hour climb or more with an empty bottle.

"What do you think, Greg?"

"Let's go on." He stands upright. "See how far we get. If I go back, it's over."

"Sure?"

"Yeah."

As plans go, it's as bad a proposal as I can imagine. I take the lead. We trudge upwards and close the gap to the lights.

Khalid is struggling to stay on his feet. He's light headed. I think he said one of his Sherpas has thrown up, but I'm unclear.

"Is there anything I can do?" I put a hand on his shoulder.

"No."

"This is a mess."

"I'll keep going, slow," Greg says. "Try to stay with me, Khalid."

"Ok."

"Onwards, I suppose." I turn and follow the rope.

Hugo, Pete, Roger, and Charlene are climbing above us in the darkness, oblivious. I plod upwards at the front. I can't figure out how I will ascend to the top of the Icefall. It's so early in the day and I have nothing left. I have to rely on Mr Jonny Walker's simple advice: keep on walking. But whatever about my problems, I can't grasp how Greg and Khalid, ten metres behind, can keep on climbing. Every few minutes I look back to check on them. They take turns throwing up or grappling to stay upright.

Two hours of torture inflicts itself upon us.

Day break arrives and we switch off our head torches. Greg has recovered more than I could have imagined was possible. We're far from strong, but we focus on reaching the top of the Icefall. Just below us, Khalid slogs upwards. Looking to my left, I measure our progress by lining our position level with landmarks in the West Shoulder. Headway is slow, but we're ascending. I expected a busier route. Perhaps many have interpreted the weather forecast different to us.

Winded, Greg and I climb up the last vertical face that marks the crest of the Icefall. We're through it.

"Five hours, Greg." I slip my watch back under the sleeve. "That's incredible. I thought you were finished down there."

"Tell me about it."

"Only an hour longer than last time. Man, we need water."

"Ok, let's get to Camp 1. We'll crack into my bottle there."

An hour later we reach Camp 1. We collapse onto the hard snow beside a tent. It's about 10am on a bright morning. Under the sun's rays, the cold cannot find us.

Charlene is resting in one of the shelters. She's been here for some time with Mingmar, having set off before 3am in her race to the summit. Hugo, Pete, and Roger had pushed on towards Camp 2 before we got here. Roger must get stronger the more this mountain throws at him. As for Pete, I don't think machines weaken.

"Let me get that water." Greg reaches into his pack.

"It was from a different flask?"

"Definitely. No question about it."

My whole being centres on the bottle. He takes a swig and passes it to me. I gulp down two mouthfuls and hand it back to him. I close my eyes. Our prospects improve. We'll get hydrated. The sun has moved high in the sky, but it won't be too hot for walking. The wind is just a breeze. I lie back, happier.

"No!" he says. "The bottle."

My back hits something. He'd placed the opened bottle behind me. I try to save it, but it's fallen down the side of the tent upside down. I strain to grab it. By the time I haul it out, the precious contents are melting the snow underneath the tent. There'll be no water.

Greg spent six hours porting a kilogram of liquid up through the Icefall to here. He waited until this moment to drink it, when he was certain he wouldn't throw up its contents. But the fluid is now a part of the Khumbu glacier. The stain of orange coloured snow devastates me.

After some silence, punctuated by obscenities, we accept that the water is gone. So be it, just another setback in an otherwise terrible day.

"Hey guys, how're you doing?" Mingmar stands above us.

We swap our stories of the day. Understanding our plight, he produces half a litre of water from somewhere and donates it to us. We thank him and start drinking. This liquid will not be spilt. Greg and I pass the bottle between us like bomb disposal experts handling a device. Finally, we have a little fluid inside us. We should be able to make it to Camp 2 in less than three hours. Once there, we'll drink our fill.

We say goodbye to Charlene and Mingmar, throw on our packs, and press on. She says she'll follow. We maintain a steady pace and negotiate the crevasses just above Camp 1.

"There's Charlene behind us, about a hundred metres back," I say.

"She's the only one else out here. Is no one else going for this window?"

"Doesn't look like it. Maybe other teams are at Camp 2 already."

After the crevasses we face the long walk across and up the valley. It's not steep, more of a false flat. The sun's rays bounce off the snow. Charlene closes the gap. She catches up and passes by in the same movement. I don't even try to match her pace. We keep on slogging, crippled by dehydration.

We've trudged for two hours since Camp 1. The noonday sun blasts down on us. The boulders that mark our target grow in size, perhaps a kilometre away. Gasping, we grind on in their direction. From there, we'll have to overcome the last one hundred metres gain on rocks to the tents.

But this last kilometre of snow will not disappear. Our steps shorten. Charlene has become a red dot, at least seven hundred metres ahead. She'll soon turn left off the snow and into the rocks. My movement becomes a dazed shuffle. It's impossible to think we might not make it from here. It's so close, but I've nothing more to give. Greg lumbers ten metres behind. Only one thought keeps me going: there's no alternative. If we stop, we're quitting and waiting for a rescue, or worse.

Greg leans down and puts a hand on my back.

"You ok, puking?"

I'd dropped to one knee; standing had asked too much of me.

"No." I search for air. "Just wrecked."

We're within touching distance of the tents and water, but I'm not certain I'll make it. We left Camp 1 three hours ago, nine since Base Camp. Two Sherpas catch up to us. I think they'd been with Khalid earlier. They know the problem we've had. If I understand what they're saying, one of these men had been sick in the Icefall.

"Slowly, slowly," one of them says.

How I could go slower is beyond me. The slope steepens as we approach the last eight hundred metres before the rocks. The pain ratchets up another notch. It's only numbed by a decrease in my senses as I start to feel less of everything.

A black speck that had appeared out of the rocks grows. It's coming towards us. It's a Sherpa. For every few paces I achieve uphill, he makes twenty going downhill.

He has closed the gap and stands just a few metres in front of me. He produces a flask and mugs and offers me a drink. I'm stunned, bewildered. What strange trick is this? Memories of the last thermos I looked into still swirl around my head, if not also my stomach.

"No." I shake my head.

A bizarre standoff ensues. Two strangers stare at each other. His presence and actions amaze me. My refusal seems to have bamboozled him.

"No problem, he is with us. Our team," one of our Sherpas says.

"What? Again? He is us?"

"Yes, yes, he –"

I give the mystery man a clumsy thumbs-up and point to a mug. My gaze locks on as he pours liquid into it. It's passed to me. Panting, I tip it down my throat. I close my eyes as I hand back the mug for a refill. I drop down on one knee in the snow.

Greg gets in on the action. Above me everyone is drinking. Another mug of warm lemon tea is delivered down to me. Chatter increases. I sip this one at a less cannibalistic rate. I piece together that Khalid or a Sherpa had got a message up to

Camp 2. The dispatch seems to have been: send down water now or send down stretchers later.

We drink and chat with the Sherpas. The fatigue will not go away, but the liquid will change today's outcome. We'll make it to Camp 2. Now it's just a matter of getting down to it.

We set off again. I fight for air with each step. On our last trip, the length of the rocky trek to the finish surprised me. I no longer expect the next cluster of tents to be ours. If I continue, then I'll stumble upon them. My body wants the penance to end. I consider every boot placement to see if it can be made easier. It cannot. The boulders go on and on. I hate the rocks just for being here. Eventually, I rise over a ridge and recognise my surroundings. Greg slumps into our sleeping tent. I stagger for the mess.

I collapse on the stone bench.

"Hey Fergus, what took you guys so long?" Hugo slides a flask in my direction. "We've been here ages."

I fill a mug. I strain to keep the flask steady. I drink liquid. I focus on Greg's advice: water makes the pain go away.

I look at Hugo.

"Nightmare. Damn nightmare." I stop for air. "I don't know how Greg got here. The water was bad."

"What? What water?"

"What we got in Base Camp was shit." I refill my mug. "Greg threw up in the Icefall, at the bottom. Had to pour away what we had." I take a mouthful. "We climbed here on nothing."

"What? You guys ok? How's Greg?"

"Tent. Alive. And Sherpas sick." I huff. "And something happened Khalid. Not sure if he threw up. But all over the place, fainting or something."

"Where's he now?"

"No idea. Sherpas with him."

"Sorry. I'd no idea."

The pain in my legs loses its intensity. My shoulders slumped, eyes half closed, I answer Hugo's questions.

Greg wobbles into the tent, his face pale.

"I can't believe what I just heard," Hugo says. "Sit here. How're you now?"

"Better. Whatever it was, I think it's gone." Greg reaches for a mug. "I should be ok, after a day's rest."

"So what was in the water?" Hugo asks.

"Don't know," I say. "Stagnant water. Water that had been used for washing?"

"Effluent?" Greg says.

"Maybe fungus in the flask, that's what it smelt like. Hold on, my bottle, I can check." I pull the container out of the pack. "Nothing, just a few drops down the bottom. Well, for what it's worth."

I open the bottle and inhale above the opening.

"Oh my God." I put my hand to my face. "Oh God. Greg, you must've been asleep when you cleared that for drinking. That'd knock over a herd of elephants."

I pass the bottle over to Hugo. Pete enters the tent.

"Do I have to?" Hugo wafts his hand over the bottle towards his nose.

His eyes water. He struggles for the right words.

"You idiots drank that?"

"Well, Greg's the doctor."

At least he'd been good enough to take the medicine he'd prescribed.

We discuss whether to destroy both bottles, lest a future generation chance upon them. However, we'll need them for the summit push.

"I've got chorine, for times like this," Pete says. "Pass me your bottles. I'll kill whatever's in them."

He disappears. A little later he declares them fit for use and returns them, smelling like a swimming pool.

We settle into our new home. This is now Base Camp. We eat food and sip tea while Pete works on a new creation. He found a piece of wood the size of a cigarette packet. In no time he fashions a closed fist with a finger pointing upwards. He scrapes the surface silky smooth. He etches the words "This way up" onto the outstretched digit. It now hangs above us in the mess tent.

Talk turns to the Bimble Brothers, Ade and Martin, who've pitched at their Café One. They prefer it to Base Camp and enjoy the MRE's. I'd have thought their time in the army and Marines would have treated them to enough of such meals to last a lifetime. They're probably settling into a brew and cheese now. They maintain it's the best part of the expedition: hot tea, a little sugar, a chance to relax, and a few laughs.

The weather forecasts occupy our thoughts. Wind is blasting the summit at a hundred and thirty kph. A reduction has been predicted around May 15th. It'll then strengthen again. Anything over fifty kph poses a risk. A climbing delay in extreme gusts will inflict frostbite, hypothermia, and worse. Several teams have refused to touch the upcoming gap in the storm. They're calculating that the correct window, when the monsoon pushes away the gales, will be between May 22nd and May 26th.

As the sun sets, the temperature in the mess tent plunges.

"Let's head back to the tent before it gets any colder," Greg says.

"Good thinking," I say. "It'll be easier to get settled in while there's still some light. It'll be dark in twenty minutes. Night lads."

We've put the first day of the big push behind us. The mountain thrashed us once again, but we made it. Might we both stand on top of Everest in four days' time on the 16th? I try to put such thoughts out of my head and get to sleep. Will we make it? How might it feel to stroll back into Base Camp, having finished the job we came here to do? What if we mistime the storm's arrival? There'll be no way down if it swallows us.

MAY 13 – MAY 14

At Camp 2 Preparing for the Summit Push

Charlene, who's been pulling on the leash for a month, set out in the early hours for Camp 3. Accompanied by Mingmar, she's shooting for the earliest possible gap. She plans to summit on May 15th, a risky venture. The winds up high are deadly now. She's gambling they'll peter out the moment she climbs over the Geneva Spur. Fortune favours the brave.

We listen to weather forecasts. They conflict. The wind beats the mess tent. We struggle to hear ourselves talk inside it. Squalls fight the cover from every angle. It's holding up, but the gusts test the makeshift patches to breaking point. Our smaller sleeping tents have better shelter, and there's no danger they'll tear.

The jet stream is blasting a plume of snow off the peak at well over a hundred kph. Picking the right summit window is crucial. A climber would be dead in minutes up there right now. The forecasts predict a small floating window from May 15th – 18th, but there may be minor storms within that gap. At that altitude, they'll be anything but minor. For Greg and me, it's a waiting game.

"My lungs are a mess," Greg says. "Look at the muck that's coming up from them."

"What's causing it? You seem worst in the mornings."

"It's probably a respiratory infection. The Khumbu cough doesn't help."

"You're still stronger than me."

"Yeah, but for how much longer?"

I force down what food I can. Linda had given me half a dozen dried figs back in Base Camp, after her adventure finished. I ate one in my tent this morning and it tasted incredible. I'd intended to ration them over the next two days, but munched another and another till they were gone. I'm glad to have quality grub in my belly, pity I didn't have more. I could eat several packets of them at this altitude.

Ade and Martin from Team 2 join us about noon.

"We stayed at Café One, broke the journey," Ade says.

"Right choice, I feel pretty good today," Martin says.

"I wish I had," I say. "Let me tell you how our trip up went."

Angel, who'll lead Team 2, arrives in the afternoon. He climbed straight from Base Camp. He assisted TC through the Icefall this morning. She doubted she'd make it. At the top, she decided to split the journey. She'll recuperate at Camp 1 and reach here tomorrow, the 14th.

The race rages between Charlene and her competitor Anne-Mari, who's chasing her to Camp 3. Both are ready to strike should half a window open. The contest has left several teams unimpressed. They feel that in light of the weather forecasts, it places unnecessary risk on all those involved. Some teams have decided that the opportunity on the 16th and 17th has now closed, the safety margin too tight. A few have had their equipment at Camp 2 decimated. Most are waiting at Base Camp.

Both teams in the Scandinavian race are keeping an eye on the actions and reports of the other. Anne-Mari appears more aware of the consequences of pitting herself against the might of an Everest storm. In such a battle, there'll be only one winner. She'd previously written on her blog:

> I don't see Charlene as my competitor ... If I am unsuccessful in mountain climbing it is possible to risk my life. But of course my goal is to be the first. My mind is very competitive and I hate losing. If we both have same day summit push of course then I try to be first on the top.

There've been suggestions of foul play, with deliberate attempts to mislead. Charlene had set out from Base Camp about 2am yesterday. Anne-Mari's Sherpa had been answering a call of nature at the time and spotted her. He woke Anne-Mari who then dashed for the Icefall. We discuss the likely outcome for them and the rest of us in the mess.

"Right," Hugo says over the noise of the flailing tent, "let's plan this out. Charlene's already at Camp 3. Team 1 leaves first thing tomorrow to summit on the sixteenth. The forecast is for strong winds on the sixteenth, lighter on the seventeenth. That's when Team 2 should reach the top."

"Should we not all wait for the seventeenth?" Nurhan asks. "It's the safer option."

"The forecast might change," Angel says.

"Greg and I overheard other team radios." I lean in onto the table. "They've written off this window completely. Many are waiting for the twenty second. But we're here now."

"What seems certain is -"

A gust blasts the tent and throws up dust. We wait.

"What seems certain is that a storm will hit on the eighteenth," Hugo says. "We need to be well below the South Col by then."

"I'll go as planned," Roger says. "I'm here, I'm ready. Let's get this done."

"Me too," Pete says.

Nothing the mountain has thrown at Pete has slowed him down. He does a morning's climbing, crafts something, cracks a few jokes, and heads to bed. Day in and day out, he's a machine.

"I'm going to wait a day," I say. "I've no idea which forecast will be the right one, but it seems the seventeenth will be quieter. I've got to go with that. Is that ok with you, Angel?"

"No problem."

The two experts huddle together and discuss the situation in Turkish.

"I'm in no rush. Safer option for me," Greg says.

"Same for me," Khalid says. "I'll go with the second group."

"We'll also wait," Nurhan says. "Safety first on the mountain."

"Ok," Hugo says. "So tomorrow, it's me with Pete and Roger."

"And the following day, everyone else with me," Angel says.

It's May 14th, and the Scandinavian race has heated up. An update from Anne-Mari's team confirms that little love has been lost on the mountain:

> Today ... Anne-Mari ... started again to climb to Camp 3 in gusty winds. We also received information from our Camp 2 team that Charlene had started her climb towards Camp 4 in the morning. This confirmed our thoughts that the information of Charlene spending two nights in Camp 3 was all along intended to mislead us.

I compare what unfolds around me to a sports event. An athlete would not reveal their strategy to a competitor in advance. But this is not a race inside a stadium. This is mountaineering. We climb to answer the challenge that nature has put in front of us. We climb, because to ignore that challenge is to fail. We climb to test ourselves. We climb because it is there. Anyone who summits this monster deserves a position on the podium. But after Hillary and Tenzing, the rest of us are all tied for second place.

I don't know if Charlene did push up from Camp 3 this morning. The winds at our altitude here are merciless. Up higher, they're lethal. But whether she tried and turned back, or never set out at all, we now know she lies low in Camp 3. She'll be stuck there another night, imprisoned by the storm. Alongside her, buffeted in her own tent, stalks Anne-Mari.

But for one woman, there'll be no more risk. TC reached us here today. Taking everything into account, she concluded her health is not strong enough to continue. She'll turn and descend tomorrow.

For the rest of us on the mountain, the concern is also safety, not speed. Any window must be long enough for all climbers on a team to descend; the top is only halfway. Scientific weather forecasts come and go, but the art is in the interpretation. Two people look at the same data and reach a different conclusion. Both agree a storm is coming. One believes it will hit Everest directly, the other that it will slip by just east of the peak. But both concur that a direct strike will kill everyone above the South Summit.

MAY 15

Climb Up from Camp 2 to Camp 3
on the Summit Push

"Time to get up, Fergus." Greg nudges me.

"Yeah, I'm onto it."

We pull on our down suits, staying inside our bags where possible to preserve heat.

"That wind has died, hasn't it? I can't hear anything," he says.

"Great stuff. It's still cold though."

Over in the mess tent I coerce down cereal and bread. It'd be easier to swallow sawdust. I stand up from the table.

"Pass me that flask, Angel, I'll fill my bottle."

As it nears 6am, colourful down suits appear next to the mess. Khalid, his wingman Jingbar, and a second Sherpa are all set.

"Ok guys, everyone ready?" Angel asks.

"Good to go." Greg zips up his massive red down suit.

"All set." Ade, in black from head to toe, gives a thumbs-up.

"Yeah." Martin nods his head.

Angel walks towards the Bergschrund in a large, red down suit, and we follow. No one talks. Two weeks ago I reached Camp 3; it was straightforward. I've a heavier pack this time, but with a steady pace, I should be fine.

Few mountaineers dot the route. A short distance out of camp a woman passes against us. I pay little attention to her. She's just another climber in what's a tougher start to the day than I expected.

"That's her," Greg says. "That was Anne-Mari."

"No way," Angel says. "She's up above Camp 3."

"I'm telling you, that was her."

"Why would she be here if Charlene's up above?" Khalid asks.

I'd not have recognised Anne-Mari under her full climbing gear.

"I don't know," Greg says, "But that was her, and she's on her way down."

We've put thirty minutes behind us. Angel sets the pace. I struggle to stay with him. He'd never set a foolish speed out of camp; he wouldn't do that anywhere on a mountain. But he's walking ten metres ahead of me and I can't close the gap. Why can I not stay with him?

One step behind me walks Ade. I can hear his balanced breathing. Normally it's more intense. I keep pacing. Angel creeps away. I glance over my right shoulder. The rest of the team are jammed on top of each other. The sun has not even risen above the Lhotse ridge. I can't be dehydrated; I've only just left the breakfast table. I didn't eat much, but we're all in that boat. Being thrashed is one thing, but delaying the lads so early in the day is another matter. I can't wiggle my toes. My feet are cold.

Ade strides past me. I slurp in air but cannot stay with him. A familiar feeling creeps over me. This was something I'd feared, something that will prevent me reaching the summit. Not a fall. Not a storm. Not an avalanche.

My sight slips away. It narrows. My head droops. Cold sweat sits on my forehead. I can't pull air into my mouth, just shallow breaths. I can keep walking, but I'll keel over in less than thirty seconds. Losing consciousness at 6,500 metres will be the end of the adventure.

I step to the side to let the others pass.

"Greg, problem, weak." I point to my head and drop down onto my hands and knees.

"What's up?"

"Don't know, fainting."

"You've got gel packs?"

"Yeah, in my backpack." I tug the chest straps loose.

He helps me get the pack off. I fumble inside it. I tear open a packet with my fingers and suck in its contents.

"How's that?" Greg looks down on me.

"Still bad. Head's gone." I try to draw in air. "Oh God, oh shit, my hands."

Pain surges into both of them. It feels like they've been plunged into icy water, only colder. I stare at them and roar expletives. I can no longer move the fingers.

"I think the blood has stopped at the wrists," I say.

Greg tries to shove on my gloves, but fails. I can't assist.

Ten minutes have elapsed since I dropped to the snow. The fainting sensation has eased, but that's no longer my concern. My body's collapsing around me.

Angel has backtracked fifty metres and stands over me. Between swearwords, I tell him my hands have stopped working; it feels like they're on fire.

"Have you got mitts?"

"Yeah, in my pack."

"Gloves are no use now." He fishes out the mitts.

My hands can generate no heat. Placing each digit in a separate finger in a glove will wrap them in a narrow, icy coffin from which they'll not recover. I groan with agony. But the curses are different. The pain does not cause the obscenities. They find voice because I know my climb is over.

Angel wraps my hands in the double mitts.

"Is that better?" he asks.

"Same." I try to move my hands but can't.

The mitts are the same temperature as the surrounding air, below -15C. The circulation has stopped at my wrists. These frigid wrappers will not help.

"The pain." I know the clock is ticking.

"Greg, keep going. There's nothing you can do," Angel says. "You'll get cold standing here."

"Ok, good luck Fergus."

He must know this is the end for me.

I'm standing in front of Angel. He holds my mitten wrapped hands. I shake my head. Curses emit.

"Jesus, it's killing me. Can't move them."

"Ok, try this." He opens his suit down to the lower chest.

He yanks the right mitt off and shoves my bare hand inside his suit, deep into his armpit. Within ten seconds I feel something.

"Yeah, yeah, it's working," I say.

The pain eases. For the first time in twenty minutes I feel hope. My breathing relaxes. The foul language reduces.

"That's almost a minute. Let's get it into the mitt quick," he says.

We make the switch. A few seconds passes.

"Shit, no," I say.

The coldness returns. Again, I cannot move my fingers. I fear I'll lose my hands.

"Ok, let's get this right hand working. Let's figure it out. Then we'll do the same on the left." He thrusts the hand back inside his armpit to steal his body heat. The left remains frozen in its mitt.

As Angel's core heat transfers to my right hand, the warmth and blood return to it.

"We'll give it two minutes," he says. "Then we'll put it into the inner liner of the mitt. Let's not lock it away in the full mitt."

"Ok, ready? Do the switch quick," he says.

"All set."

We fit my hand into the inner liner. Angel kneads and massages it as I fight against him.

"I can feel that. That's it." I move and twist my hand against his.

Within five minutes it's an equal battle. My hand strengthens. It has reignited.

"Ok, here's the outer mitt." He slides it on. "Keep moving those fingers. Don't stop for twenty minutes. Now let's sort out that left hand."

Three minutes later my left hand has robbed enough of Angel's body heat to start the recovery process. We wrestle for five minutes. I now have two limbs that work.

"Thanks, Angel." I breathe out, look down, and shake my head.

Calmness returns, but I'm weak. My climb is probably finished. Standing still is not an option. If I go up, I should reach the Bergschrund in half an hour. The sun will rise over Lhotse about the same time; that'll warm me up. Descending is the safer choice, but I'll be in the shadow of Everest for at least twenty minutes longer.

I decide to go up. It's not just the sun. I've been higher than this before. This is not new territory. I know my body can take this altitude. I know I can perform at Camp 3. How can I quit in the lowlands of 6,600 metres? Something will prevent me from summiting. It will probably occur within the next hour. But whatever it is that stops me, it will not be right now. Not at this spot.

"Angel, thanks. I was in trouble there. I'll keep going, into the sun."

What he just did was astounding: his experience, the improvisation, the quick thinking. This morning would have gone a different route if he wasn't here. The unscheduled stop has lasted forty-five minutes. I lift up a left boot, then a right. I'll keep doing it till I can do it no more.

The View Ahead
Climbers dot the route up the Lhotse Face to the tents at Camp 3.

I reach the Bergschrund. Martin stands alone.

"Hey Martin, you ok?"

"No, my hands. I'm finished," he says.

"What? No. I had the same. Angel got me going."

"They're killing me. Been like this for ages. Ade tried to help, but I sent him on. I didn't want him cold too."

"Angel helped me. He put my hands in his armpits. Let me see them. He –"

"It's no good. Go on."

How can this strike Martin too? Was it colder this morning? Is there less oxygen in the air? Are we all starting to degrade after six weeks in the mountains? There must be a link.

"Angel is just there." I point down the valley. "He'll be here in five or six minutes."

I argue with Martin that he can still recover. Angel did not give up on me. I cannot pass on by after the second chance I've received. All the time, I wiggle my fingers in the mitts. Angel draws close to us.

"Angel, it's Martin. He's got the same problem I had. His hands are frozen, been that way since before I got here."

"What? You're still ok?"

"I'm good, yeah." I show him the mitts opening and closing as I flex my hands.

"Right, you keep moving. I'll look after Martin."

"Ok. Martin. Martin." I stare at him. "You'll be fine. I'll see you up on the face."

He looks back at me. I'm not convinced.

I climb up the Bergschrund. The traffic has kicked in a few footholds.

I start the Lhotse Face. Above me looms a forty degrees slope, dead straight, all the way to Camp 3 at 7,100 metres. I'm standing at 6,700 metres. I'll climb and see how far I get.

I get into a rhythm, slow and steady. Mountaineers ascend the rope to my left at about the same speed as me. I look behind but see no sign of Angel or Martin. They'll appear over the Bergschrund in due course and catch up to me.

I think to look at my altimeter. It surprises me; I'm making progress. I'm at 6,850 metres. A hundred and fifty metres of the Lhotse Face lies beneath me. My climb might not be over. If I can reach Camp 3, take on water and food, and grab a night's sleep, I could be back on track tomorrow. I must gain two hundred and fifty metres more in altitude to fight another day. I'll have to set mini-goals to get there, but every fifty metres is too optimistic. I could achieve targets of thirty metres. I've eight sections above. The thirty metre calculations will be more complex than just adding up groups of fifty. The mathematics will keep me engaged, focus me on the job at hand, distract me from thoughts I must avoid.

Over my shoulder I search for Angel and Martin. Several climbers are ascending the two ropes below me, but I can't make out the familiar pair of white and orange helmets.

I reach another thirty metres goal. I turn around and peer down the mountain. Angel's form, crowned in white headgear, ascends. I eliminate the mountaineers one by one, all the way to the Bergschrund. The slope lacks the orange helmet of Martin. Something has gone wrong. I allow myself believe he's just delayed and will appear. But I know Angel would never leave a person to climb up alone in such circumstances. The sight saddens me.

I climb on, breathing under control. Up ahead the two ropes join. For twenty minutes I've been reeling in someone to my left. We reach the meeting point at the same time. We turn around and sit down beside each other for a break.

"Hi there. How's your day going?" I ask.

"Good." She reaches for her bottle. "And you?"

"Not too bad, not too far away now."

I'm sitting beside Bonita Norris. She's vying to be the youngest British woman to summit Everest. Gazing down the Cwm Valley, we swap a few stories and share a laugh. In a day that's been far from normal, this moment of serenity allows me escape its hardships. For a few minutes, I could be sitting in a foreign beauty spot chatting to a fellow traveller. I start to believe I'll reach Camp 3. Bonita doesn't know what a rough ride I've had. If she thinks I look like any other climber on his way to the top, then that's what I must be. Five more thirty metre goals and I can rest.

"I'm going to push on." I rise to my feet.

"I'll take a few more minutes to recover," she says.

"It was nice to meet you. Good luck." I turn my back on the valley and lift a boot forward.

Euphoria replaces exhaustion and anxiety. I cannot believe I'm still in the game. A few hours ago, it was as good as over. I imagine the look on Greg's face when he sees me slipping into Camp 3.

I put in another hour and a half of climbing and close in on the tents. The coldness has long left my body. If my muscles are tired, I'm not aware of it. I've pulled success out of nowhere. Within forty-eight hours I might even stand atop Everest.

I hit the last thirty metre section. I know the entrance to camp deceives, and it will extract another twenty minutes of slog. But I'm ready for it and pace myself into the finish, a finish I'd written off just a few hours ago.

Greg stares at me as I stride past the tents. Mountain ranges beyond Pumori paint the scenery to my right. Today's starting point lies far below.

"Didn't expect to see me?" A smile extends across my face.

"Oh my God, Fergus." He shakes my hand. "How on earth did you do that?"

"Don't ask. There were a few hairy moments this morning."

"Yeah, I think I saw them. How are the hands?"

"Fine I think. Which tent is ours?"

"Just there." He points.

"Hey Fergus, how's Martin?" I hear Ade's voice.

I turn around. He's a few metres away outside a tent. I didn't want to do this. I walk over to him.

"Ade, for the last three hours, I've been looking down the slope. He's not there. I was looking for his orange helmet, no sign. I saw Angel. He's not with him. Sorry."

"No, no." Ade puts his hand on his brow. "Oh, not Martin. This meant so much to him. He'll be devastated."

"Yeah, I know."

"Just like that." Ade looks away from me. "He was a great man to climb with."

"Yeah, it was a good team you had. You'd have lost the Bimble Brothers title anyway, with the speed you came up there today."

"Damn."

The two ex-soldiers will not make a brew together in their tent tonight.

Greg and I are melting snow in the tent and recuperating. We've another two hours of daylight. Today has taken little out of him.

"You're ok for tomorrow?" he asks.

"Yeah, I'll just take on as much food and water as I can. My hands hurt though. Look at the back of them."

"Man, they're swollen. At least the colour's ok." He takes my hands.

"I can't squeeze a fist, that's as far as I get." I force my fingers to touch my thumbs. "There's no gripping strength. And that hurts too."

"Let me see." He prods the back of my hands. "That's not good."

He mumbles something about crystals under the skin.

"There could be some dead tissue there," he says. "Do not get them cold. I'm serious. Whatever you do, you must never get those cold again until we get back to Base Camp."

"Got you."

"If that happens again, they won't recover."

"OK, got it. Warm from here on in."

Subzero temperatures surround us. In the next forty-eight hours, we'll ascend to one of the coldest places on earth. I hope I don't do anything stupid.

As for the other teams, several are huddled in twos and threes, boiling water into the night like Greg and me. But most are down at Base Camp. Jet stream winds scour the mountain above the South Col. Many squads will not touch this window.

Angel filters news to us that it was Anne-Mari who Greg had seen this morning. Her Altitude Junkies team expects high winds on the 16th and 17th. They instructed her to descend and will not support a climb in these conditions. In their words:

> ... we are glad to concede the race that has become dangerous and at times too deceptive for our liking.

MAY 16

Climb Up from Camp 3 (7,100m)

to Camp 4 (approx. 8,000m) on

the Summit Push

Greg and I drag our packs out of the tent at 7am. Just beside us, Ade and Roger ready themselves on a bright, still morning. Khalid and his two Sherpas shuffle out of their shelters. We've a clear view of the Cwm Valley below. The peak of Pumori stands less than a hundred metres higher than us. Climbing above it will be an achievement. It's a strange aim, but a target nonetheless. As I ascend, I'll observe the altimeter and glance over my shoulder. 7,200 metres should be an early boost to the day.

Roger didn't continue with Team 1 yesterday, I'm not sure why. But Hugo, Charlene, and Pete are deep into their summit push. They might even be at the top.

"Morning, Angel. Is there any word on the others, Team 1?" Greg asks.

"They didn't set out. They're at Camp 4." Angel pockets his walkie-talkie.

"What?" I say. "What happened?"

They had problems. There weren't enough working stoves. The guys couldn't get hydrated or fill their bottles for the push. Dehydration will result in frostbite, deteriorating performance, and a risky finish to a fifteen hour journey to the summit and back. In addition, there was a lack of Sherpas at Camp 4 to carry the necessary oxygen tanks. Details are hazy. It's possible the Sherpas were there, but they were too tired to assist having spent all day climbing direct from Camp 2. They only reached the South Col a short time before the push was due to begin.

"What does that mean?" I ask.

"We'll all climb tonight as one team," Angel says. "Ok, get your oxygen tanks set up."

Greg and I lift up a cylinder each, sit down on a snow ridge, and connect up the parts. I slide the tank into my backpack, leaving the regulator sticking out the top. I pull the mask over my nose and mouth and tighten the elastic cheek straps.

"Greg." I stretch the mask a centimetre from my face. "Set me on two litres."

"Turn around." He plays with the valve behind my neck.

He taps me on the shoulder and gives me a thumbs-up. Speaking isn't possible from under these masks; only an incoherent mumble escapes. I set up Greg's flow, and we double check each other. Signals and firm gestures replace words.

I can hear a faint hissing noise on the right side of the mask where the oxygen hose is connected. I think that's a good sign. I hold the plastic bottle that contains the bladder and examine it. As I breathe in hard, it deflates. As I stare at it, it expands. I satisfy myself that if the bag is inflating, the system is working.

We walk out of camp towards the fixed rope. Climbers ascending from lower tents jam it. Everyone here is aiming for the same window. We spot a small gap in the stream of mountaineers and clip in. My crampons scrape across the seventy degree gradient of hard blue ice. Whoever said the climb from Camp 2 to Camp 3 separates those who summit from those who go belly-up was never here.

Everyone is tugging on the rope. I can purchase no grip underfoot. My breathing soars. I scramble to gain a handful of steps. This is not how I'm supposed to climb. I reach a spot a pace wide, where the slope is less severe. I calm my gasping, relieved to ease the strain from my legs and right arm for a few moments. Then it's up again. In front of me, a metre from my face, a wall of ice stands. Above me, a line of climbers are wrestling the surface, almost on top of each other. Just behind and below, Greg pushes up.

I kick the spikes that jut out the front of my boots into the ice face. At times, the sole of my boot makes no contact with the smooth, near vertical wall. The jumar stops me falling off the mountain. The technique works, but despite the slow pace ahead, it exhausts me. I can't do this all day.

I push myself over a ridge. The wall of ice at my nose relents. The Lhotse Face opens up in front of me. I'm staring at a more moderate white slope, all the way up to the rocky summit of the world's fourth highest mountain. I can see what's ahead. It'll be easier than the first half hour. I also understand what's caused the delay. Fifty metres from me, an injured climber is lying on the snow.

We plod up towards the incapacitated person. He remains motionless in a bright orange and yellow jacket, bound in ropes. A cord connects him to the fixed line. I watch mountaineers, ten paces ahead, trudge past him in silence. It's clear the man is not injured. He is dead.

I'm taken aback by the man's demise. I'm not sure of the protocol. He lies here at the entrance to the death zone. I didn't expect to find a sentry guarding a checkpoint, but nor did I expect death to wave us through.

The only guidance I can take is the climber's silent warning to the rest of us: this is a treacherous undertaking. I lumber by, as the procession ahead has, and acknowledge the moment.

Greg and I are pushing up a long, steep, snowy slope. I've got into a rhythm. I take one pace with my right boot and then inhale and exhale through the mask. Then I take another full breath, in and out, and lift my left boot upwards. I'm stationary for almost ten seconds after every step. The early bunching of climbers has dissipated. Angel, Ade, and Khalid are battling somewhere below us.

"Perfect speed." Greg, behind me, slides his mask back over his mouth.

My feet are cold; I can't move the toes. This is the norm for me above Camp 1. It concerns me, but I've noticed that once the sun hits, my right foot warms up within half an hour. The left usually comes round some twenty minutes after that. I don't know why the left takes longer, but that's been the trend. A glaring white to the east indicates that the stove is about to switch on. I could do with its warming rays.

I glance at my altimeter. It reveals we're at 7,250 metres. Up ahead I see the same scene I've had for the last hour, a relentless incline that must be conquered. The mask hides my smile; I know Pumori sits below me. I half turn to my left and look over my shoulder. The view overwhelms me. We've been at altitude for a month, but always surrounded by giants. Now, a Himalayan vista of peaks and distant mountain ranges is thrust at me.

I can't guess the breadth of what's presented. Back in the Dublin hills, the Mountains of Mourne in Northern Ireland and the Welsh highlands can be seen on a clear day. It's a panorama of eighty kilometres, from a viewing point just four hundred metres above sea level. I'm now standing over seven kilometres into the heavens.

I search for Pumori. At Base Camp, it towers above us. Now, its snowy apex is camouflaged by taller, white mountains beyond. I trace out its form and its summit. It sits below us. I inhale through the mask. There's been much hardship since I set out on this path. Very few climb to the top of Pumori. I will never be one of them. But I've seen over its crown. It's a stalemate I can take to the grave. I turn back to my right and lift a boot upwards.

The sun peeks over the Lhotse ridge. Seconds later, its rays blast down onto the snow.

"Greg, one minute, sun block." The mask springs back on my face.

I rub protection on the exposed parts: the bridge of my nose, cheekbones, and a one centimetre gap between the rim of my shades and the fleece hat. I pass the tube to Greg and relax as he does the necessary.

"Oh no." I close my eyes.

I grab my exposed right hand. The pain pierces me. I think the tip of the index finger, where the cream was, is about to fall off. I stare at the limb. I can't understand how it can generate so much suffering. I can't believe I've been so stupid. A surge of foul language fills my mask. I try to warm my hand and massage it. Then I ram it back into the cold glove. I get no respite. It seems my system has decided not to return cold blood to my core and heart. It has cut off my right hand.

"You ok?" Greg asks.

"Damn hand, happened again."

I can't warm it. The torture increases. How can I bring this hand back?

"Here, try this." Greg steps closer and unzips the top of his down suit.

He shoves my right hand into his left armpit. I breathe easier. I feel the limb come back to life.

"Yeah, that's working." I stick my glove down the front of my suit to defrost it. "Thanks buddy. Can we leave my hand there another minute? Yesterday with Angel, we took it out too quick, and it got cold again."

"Sure. Dude, you've got to stop doing this. Leave those gloves on from here on in."

"Definitely, like I said last time."

We get back into a rhythm, two breaths between each step, and push up the Lhotse Face.

Stopping for a Moment on the Lhotse Face – 7,300 metres

A group of thirty climbers and Sherpas moves out onto the rope above us. Their tents sit off to the right at upper Camp 3. A mass of red, orange, and yellow suits are shuffling uphill. We let the last few members of the team onto the line ahead of us. The masks prevent a meaningful conversation. A nod of the head and a thumbs-up completes the exchange. I've never seen the fixed rope so busy.

I repeat Greg's advice to myself: the perfect high altitude pace is one that could be maintained till eternity, well, at least till the end of the day.

Looking ahead, I try to understand the route. We'll ascend another two hundred metres up the right side of the Lhotse Face. It's a consistent incline on hard snow, maybe forty-five degrees. Then we'll traverse the face, a few hundred metres in width, to the Yellow Band. That obstacle will demand vertical climbing over rock and snow. I can't see the trail past it, but somewhere beyond hides a path over the Geneva Spur. Once we get clear of that, we'll head for Camp 4 at the South Col, at close to 8,000 metres.

I've no idea what the Geneva Spur will present. It sounds daunting. I doubt a five centimetre pile of snow would be given its own name. There'll be work ahead. I'll worry about that later. I lift my boot and breathe and breathe again. Greg does the same just behind me.

I feel almost bored. I'd been told today would be harrowing. The Lhotse Face has been the end to many a climber's ascent, and not always a pretty conclusion. This pace is so even and slow, I think I could maintain it all day. I've already consumed a gooey gel packet. Perhaps my body is bathing in the flow of oxygen that's entering the mask. Everyone I've seen today has a tank. I'll enjoy the good times while they last.

My mind drifts back to the dead climber. What caused his life to end here on the snow? Many have died on this mountain over the years. Those who die lower down can be dragged back to Base Camp by a paid Sherpa team. Those who succumb up high are dropped down a crevasse or pulled a little off route, away from the public glare. At some stage in the future, the manpower and equipment may be available to carry them down to a decent burial. The glacier grinds down the valley, while millions of tons of fresh snow fall on it each year. Apart from the harsh environs above Camp 4, it doesn't disclose where the dead have lain. It will receive a few more bodies in the coming days. I consider the law of averages, presume it will be no one on our team, and lift my left boot upwards.

Even behind my shades, I see the ice and snow of the Lhotse Face glimmer in the still air. Twenty minutes above, several climbers are sitting on the white surface just before the traverse. I glance back and down at Greg. I point to the resting climbers, then to him and me, and indicate drinking a pint of beer. He returns a thumbs-up.

Our safeties remain connected to the rope. We've put four hundred metres below us today. We must dig in the crampons as we lower our backsides to the snow. Just sitting here and not sliding down the slope challenges me.

"Going well," Greg says.

"So far so good." I stretch the mask down over my chin. "Let's get a water bottle out."

Climbers Approach the Lhotse Face Traverse near 7,500 metres
1: Ade, Khalid, and Angel are in the centre of this group
2: Camp 2
3: Location of Camp 1
4: Top of the Icefall
5: The peak of Pumori is just out of shot above the number.

In between nibbles of chocolate and clipped conversation, I slide the mask over my nose to get maximum benefit from the tank on my back. The mountains of Nepal stretch out in front of us. Angel, Ade, and Khalid labour up the last thirty metres towards where we're sitting. The exertion has them doubled over.

Teammates Approach the Lhotse Face Traverse near 7,500 metres
From left to right: Unknown climber, Ade, Khalid, probably Jingbar (obscured), Angel.

Greg nudges me and points to the Yellow Band. I nod to him. We rise to our feet and traverse the Lhotse Face.

I'm watching a clump of mountaineers who've reached the Yellow Band. One by one, they climb a vertical wall several metres high. Then each catches their breath in a snowy hollow. After that, they tackle a forty degree slope of exposed, yellow smooth rock. The metal crampons will slide on that. Then the colourful shapes disappear over the top and are gone from view. I can imitate what I've seen.

Greg takes the lead at the Yellow Band. He makes short work of the vertical section.

I lack climbing grace. I shove a gloved hand or boot wherever it gets a grip and manhandle myself up the wall.

236

Gasping, my crampons tear at the smooth slab. But with each effort, there's less stone ahead.

Several climbers have bunched in the gruelling bottleneck. I straighten up and catch my breath. Greg is standing just in front of my right boot.

Standing on the Yellow Band
Camp 2 is 1,000 metres below, at my right elbow. Pumori stands in plain view, although camouflaged by the ranges behind it.

Ten metres ahead, a mountaineer appears to be sunbathing. He's lying back against the rock. Perhaps he's a guide, waiting for his group to come through. We force ourselves up a few more steps. I recognise the man.

"Hey Roger, what's up? You ok?" Greg asks.

"Fine."

"Here." Greg hands Roger a camera. "Take a shot of Fergus and me."

Greg and I at the Yellow Band

The line of climbers moves on. Greg tucks the camera away, the moment recorded.

"Ok Roger, let's move," Greg says.

"I'm fine here."

"What?" Greg looks over to Roger's Sherpa and then back at Roger. "Let's go, Camp 4."

The Sherpa is standing a few metres away.

"Roger, get moving!" Greg says. "Your Sherpa will get frostbite."

Roger rises.

Having heard so much of the infamous Yellow Band, I'm relieved to have it behind me. The fixed rope made a near impossible task into something that is just difficult. I'm back on snow and now looking at a different landscape.

Ahead of us lies a snow-filled valley. A string of climbers are moving up its centre. To our right, less than a kilometre away, the brown ridge at the top of the Lhotse Face has come into focus. The brown and white Geneva Spur stretches along our left side, five hundred metres from where we stand. I imagine at lower altitudes, this'd be a beautiful winter day's walk. The bottleneck at the Yellow Band had caused congestion. But once through it, we've freed up again.

Greg and I get back into our groove and pace ourselves along the route. I can't see the path that'll lead us over the obstacle of rock and snow. The furthest climbers ahead become smaller and smaller, until they are just a dot of colour in a sea of white. At some stage they must turn left and attack the Spur, but I cannot determine where or how. We labour on.

I strain my eyes to figure out how the trail will conquer the challenge. Once or twice, I think I see a route that could be the passage to Camp 4, but it lacks movement. I trace the ridge along the top of the brown spur where it contrasts against the sky. I search for motion. After several hundred metres plodding, I spy a rock in the distance move in front of the blue backdrop. I lock in on that position. A minute later, I spot another rock do the same thing. It moves up and over the crest of the spur. Those are climbers; that's the track. I trace down from that point and make out more movement. The path reveals itself. Like at the Yellow Band, watching others ahead boosts me. It's just a matter of putting left foot after right and not asking why.

"Over there, Greg." I point to what I've seen. "We go to the end of this valley, then turn left."

He looks and then gives me a thumbs-up.

Halfway through the gorge, we come upon boot prints that turn to the right and off the route. It's the first time in a month I've seen something not directed at the summit of Everest. They disappear up a steep incline that ends at jagged, near vertical walls of rock, about half a kilometre high.

"To summit Lhotse." Greg holds his mask away from his face. "The Finns will go that way."

It looks like a death trap, or as the Finns might say: breakfast.

We reach the end of the valley, turn left, and follow the rope up the Spur.

"We've gained a lot of height since the Yellow Band," Greg says.

"Yeah." I look up. "Should be less than a hundred to the top. Not too far now."

"Just follow the rope."

"We can do this."

I'm standing at the base of the Geneva Spur, with the expectation that I'll have scaled it within the hour. In days gone by, with lesser equipment and support, this was the end of many a climb.

My legs hurt as I push up the narrow trail. A lifestyle of good food, comfortable beds, cars, central heating, and safety has long been flushed from my body. Anything which is bearable is considered a minor comfort. A barrier of rock and snow presses at my right shoulder. A drop into oblivion expands on the left. The mask hinders the view of where I'm placing my boots. But this fifty centimetre wide snaking path, marked by a rope, is all I need for now.

Two lines have been anchored on the final, near vertical section. I opt for the one with the faster moving climbers. I put a gloved finger wherever I can feel a grip and pull myself up. My legs give what they can. Where this is not enough, I lever off the jumar and inch up the fixed rope.

My knee pressed against the mask, my face in the snow, I drag myself over an outcrop. Within a few minutes, I'm half-climbing, half-crawling over the crest of the spur. I'm now one of the shifting rocks I'd seen a couple of hours ago. I'm standing above the Geneva Spur.

I try to regain my breath on a rock at close to 8,000 metres. At my two o'clock, I'm staring straight over Nuptse at everything that lies behind it. Mountains, peaks, and ranges stretch beneath blue sky. At my ten o'clock, ridges disappear into the distance. The jagged crest of Lhotse stands to my left and blocks the view beyond. I gaze down into the Cwm Valley, one and a half kilometres below me. I could reach Camp 2 via the express route in less than a minute.

Just over my right shoulder is the reason I'm heaving into this mask. Few people see it from so close. A massive brown pyramid imposes on the sky above me. Will I stand on top of it in less than twenty-four hours?

It's 2pm, and I've no idea how far it is to Camp 4. Once there, we must recover, boil snow, eat, drink, and fill our bottles. Then we'll step out into the night at 10pm for the summit push. Without water, there'll be no attempt tonight. I'll press on, Greg will catch up.

I'm following the near level route, over broken slate, along the crest of the Geneva Spur. As I round each crag, I look ahead for Camp 4. I'm tired, but functioning. We'll receive only a few hours break before pushing out tonight, and I'm anxious that it comes into view. After thirty minutes, I walk past a protrusion and spy coloured tents a few hundred metres further. The settlement is sitting on a flat bed of rock and snow that extends for several hundred square metres. I expected something more testing, worse than Camp 3, shelters carved into a steep incline.

I find our tents and unstrap my crampons. Hugo sticks his face out from behind a zip. The play offs are over. This is the final.

MAY 16

Camp 4

"Hi Fergus, you made it," Hugo says. "Where are the others?"

"Greg should be here in a few minutes." I bend down on one knee to hear him. "The others are behind. I've not seen them since the Lhotse Face."

"Ok. Change of plan. There's a storm forecast for tomorrow afternoon. We've got to be down from the upper slopes and back here by early afternoon tomorrow, at the latest. We'll push off at six."

"What?" I look at my watch.

"Six. That's when we leave. Collect ice and start boiling water. Pete and Charlene are in here with me. We'll be ready."

That's only three hours away. We're up against the clock.

I take an axe to the ice at the edge of camp. It just throws shards up in the air. The effort exhausts me. I'm not wearing crampons. As I bring down the tool, I slide away with an equal and opposite force. Eventually, I've half-filled the sack. I've done my duty.

I set up my equipment in a tent and start up the stove.

"You in there, Fergus?"

"Hey Greg, yeah." I open the zip. "Watch the stove. What was the delay?"

"I got stuck behind a climber for forty minutes near the top of the spur." He crawls into the tent. "I had to talk her through it. In the end, a Sherpa had to physically push her up, by her arse."

"Could do without that. Bad news: we leave at six."

"What? You're kidding?"

"No, Hugo said so. Storm's coming in tomorrow. Can't risk getting stuck in it." I place the mask back over my face.

"That's two and a half hours away. That's not enough time to make water."

"I know. Well, let's boil as much as we can and see where it gets us."

"Damn. How's the boiling going?"

"Hopeless. Those zips are damaged. There's wind all over the vestibule. The flame's tiny; the air's so damn thin. The canisters are frozen, and the ice is far below zero to start with."

"Ok, let's do what we can and prepare."

The mask and connected oxygen tank complicate simple movements. We melt ice for an hour but have little to show for our efforts. The temperature is dropping and the wind is picking up.

"Guys, I'm coming in." We hear Ade's voice.

"Cool, be careful. Mind the water." Greg picks up the pot. "Let me move it first."

Ade crawls in and drags his equipment with him. He squeezes in between the two of us.

"Damn. I can't believe it. Bloody six o'clock. An hour and a half away," Ade says.

"You were talking to Hugo?" I ask.

"Damn right. That's it, finished for me. It's not possible to rehydrate. We need two bottles for the push. And we need food and water now. I'd to tell Hugo I'm out."

"Man, you sure?" Greg asks.

"What choice do I have? I'll never recover in an hour and a half."

"Sorry Ade," I say. "After all that, I can't believe it's come to this."

Whatever water we boil must now be split three ways. There're no other stoves; therefore, boiling up two lots at once is not possible.

"Let's try moving the stove inside here with us. It's a waste of time in the vestibule."

"Anything at this stage," Greg says.

"This's the same shit that happened here yesterday, that's what Angel said this morning. The lads couldn't go for the summit because they'd no water."

From the limited communication we have with the other tents, we piece together that we may also be suffering from a lack of manpower.

"There's still no sign of Penba," Greg says. "He's got our gear. No one knows where he is. He set out early this morning from Camp 2, but that's all that's known."

"Can you go without that gear?" I ask.

"Not really. And his job is to carry the spare tanks." Greg shakes his head. "Even if he does get here now, he'll not be in any condition to continue."

"Same as yesterday."

"One of Khalid's Sherpas has also not made it yet."

The wind rattles the tent cover. The eight hour climb today has dehydrated me. We've not poured any water into our bottles for the journey. The sun dips lower in the sky. The push starts in sixty minutes.

"What do you think, Greg?"

"We have a problem."

I hold the mask a few centimetres from my face while talking, and then press it against my nose and mouth while listening.

"A disaster on the mountain isn't caused by one big incident." Greg says. "It's a build-up of small screw-ups, little things, all going in the wrong direction. None of them big enough to cause anyone to say stop."

"Yeah?"

"A series of small failures, compounded by poor judgement."

"We're short on water." I check the pot on the stove. "Equipment is missing. Sherpas aren't here. The wind's picking up. A storm's forecast for tomorrow."

It's decision time. Ade sits silent between us.

"What about the window on the twenty second?" I ask. "Every other window has been up and down. That one never moved. Every forecast said that's the real gap. That's when the monsoon moves up."

"Go back down? Try again?" Greg puts his mask back over his face.

"Other teams are going for it. I think we know what could happen if we go up tonight. I'm parched. We might reach the summit, but after that?" I say.

"Camp 4 is the point of no return. I don't know of many who retreat from here and try again," Greg says.

"Nor I. Do we have a choice? Plan A is in pieces. What if I talk to the others? What if one of the guides will support us?"

"That would change everything," Greg says. "Go back to Camp 2 tomorrow and try again in a few days. If a guide is with us, it's the best option we have."

"OK, I'll go to the other tents and see if I can persuade Hugo or Angel. If they say yes, we go down. If they say no, we've to make a decision."

"I don't want to have to make that decision." Greg looks at me.

"I'll give it everything I've got. Ade, if we go back down, then you're back on."

"That'd be something." Ade sits upright. "I could do with that."

"Wish me luck." I drag my tank behind me out of the tent.

The wind scours my face. We've less than an hour of daylight. I shuffle to the tent of Angel, Nurhan, and Yener.

"Hi guys." I stick my head in through their tent zip.

In clipped words I sum up the situation. Nurhan translates for Yener. Immediate agreement is achieved. With Angel and the two Turks on board, Ade's climb restarts. Greg and I have been saved from having to make a terrible decision.

"Be ready to descend early tomorrow," Angel says.

Others may wish to join the train. I explain what's unfolding to Roger, Khalid, and Jingbar from their vestibule. They tell me that the full team cannot try for the summit; the support is not here. They'll descend in the morning.

I crouch down outside the entrance to Hugo's tent. Battling the wind, I explain to him what's taking place.

"You're not going to try?" he asks.

"Can't."

"We're ok." He looks back to Charlene and Pete. "We spent the day in the tent hydrating. We've had food and our bottles are full."

"You're going to go for it?"

He turns to the others, then back to me.

"There are enough-" the wind blasts across his words.

"There are enough Sherpas to support a push by us three. You won't try with us?"

"Sorry Hugo. I don't mind taking crazy risks. I know that's what it needs. But this one I can't take. It just feels like suicide. I mean .... Sorry, I don't mean to say that."

"No problem."

"Best of luck. Go big." I give him a thumbs-up and escape from the wind.

Back in the tent, we're preparing for a night at the South Col. The last few days have been a waste of energy and oxygen. On the positive side, we now know the route to Camp 4 and may gain a small acclimatisation advantage.

The light fades. Above the wind, we hear Hugo, Charlene, and Pete outside our tent making final preparations.

"I must get another tank." Greg crawls over Ade's legs to the exit. "I'll wish the guys luck as well."

A blast of icy air hits Ade and me as he exits.

"Oh shit. Get it," I say.

The pot of water, which had almost come to the boil, tips off the stove.

"I don't believe it," Ade says.

A pool of water collects where Greg had been.

"Get a lump of snow from the vestibule, Fergus. That'll soak it up."

"I don't know how that happened. Let's wait till Greg's back before starting another pot."

Several minutes later, Greg wriggles into the tent.

"That took a long time," Ade says.

"That was some mess out there." Greg jams back in on the far side of Ade. "As far as I could tell, some of the Sherpas didn't want to go. And some refused to carry tanks. There should be four Sherpas: one for each, plus Mingmar for Charlene."

"What happened?" I ask.

"In the end, Hugo demanded to see the other three Sherpas standing in front of him. And he insisted on seeing the correct number of tanks on the ground where he stood. He wouldn't set off until he saw them."

"You're kidding me?"

"There was a huge argument between the Sherpas. A fight broke out."

"No way," Ade says. "Was this not all trashed out a long time ago?"

"I thought this is what these guys did for a living. What the hell are they doing here if they don't want to climb and assist? At the very least, I thought this crap would have been sorted out after yesterday. Nothing has been bloody learned." I press the mask back over my mouth and nose.

"I don't know who's in charge," Greg says. "Hugo's a stud. He was having none of it and wasn't leaving without his shit."

"Well, someone paid these guys for a month's work. This is a fine time to discover they're unhappy."

We hear our guys depart for the summit. Over the next hour we listen, as team after team walks past our tent. With each group's passing, I contemplate that I'm not a part of it. We keep boiling water.

The wind buffets the tent. The temperature has plunged. We daren't move for fear of knocking over the stove. Outside would be little worse. Should we have risked it? To have gone through so much to end up in this situation; no words give solace.

"All that matters," I lift the mask from my face, "is that we get to the top. Then this gets put behind us. It'll be irrelevant. Whatever suffering it takes, so be it."

"Sounds good," Ade says. "What matters now is that we get reset for a push on the twenty second."

"Agreed," Greg says.

"But man ... this is really starting to piss me off." I clamp my mask back on my face.

The plod of boots passing our tent ceases. However, we cannot close off the day yet. We still have a teammate unaccounted for on the mountain. It's agreed that Penba is neither an experienced climber nor survival expert. He left Camp 2 about 4am. It's now close to 8pm. A mini-rescue party of our Sherpas sets out to try and find him.

The wind fades. We start to settle down.

"My eyes are at me," Ade says. "Stinging."

"Let me see." Greg turns and examines him by the light of his head torch. "Snow blindness."

"What? Are you sure? I'd my shades on, like every other day."

"It was the mask, Ade," I say. "I remember now when we met you at the traverse; your shades were pushed down a little on your nose. The strap had interfered with them."

"God, you're right." Ade puts his fist against his forehead.

The UV rays have burnt his corneas.

"Sun was overhead. It found the small gap. Is it bad?" I ask.

"I'll live."

Ade has dozed off. Greg tries to switch oxygen tanks; the one he had today has run out.

"I can't get this nut off the fresh tank. Can you try?" he asks.

I try but cannot turn it. It's frozen solid. We have a stab with everything we can think of, but it will not budge.

"I need this. I can't just go to sleep with no oxygen, not up here."

"Let's keep trying, but no bare flesh," I say. "Can we warm it up? Use a lighter?"

Greg holds a lighter under the nut.

"Guys, stop, stop." Ade sits bolt upright. "No fire, no fire. You'll kill the lot of us."

We stare at Ade. We explain the problem.

"Let me find my penknife." Ade rummages in his pack. "That's pressurised oxygen. On high altitude parachute jumps, we weren't even allowed lip balm; the oil in it was considered an ignition source. That tank has hundreds of litres of pure oxygen. Ok, here's that penknife. Try the screwdriver, Greg."

Greg makes the switch.

About 9pm, one of the Sherpas pokes in his head to say that Penba has been found. He was near the Geneva Spur and struggling. He was helped up to camp. He should recover.

In full down suits with hoods up, we tighten our sleeping bags around us. The oxygen mask hisses on my face. I switch off the head torch for a night in the death zone.

MAY 17

Climb Down from Camp 4 to Camp 2

'd a rough night. We were packed in like three sardines. I'd carried up Greg's spare mat yesterday, as it's light and perfect for sitting on. But its thin, three quarter length design isn't for a sleep at the South Col. My freezing feet woke me every hour. Each time, I spent fifteen minutes pulling them up off the tent base and massaging them inside my bag. It did some good, but the pain soon returned.

The scene in the tent reminded me of a ship that had strayed into Antarctica and got wedged there for a month. A layer of ice or frozen condensation encrusted everything: the sleeping bags, the tent material, the oxygen tanks, and the equipment. It was hard to believe Ade and Greg were alive under it. It would have made for a great photo, but I wouldn't disturb the lads with a flash camera. That image, like so many others, will fade with memory.

"That was a cold one. It felt like I was sleeping on ice." Greg sits up.

"Don't ask." I unzip my bag. "God, I feel groggy."

"I'd a great sleep, one of the best so far," Ade says. "I'd the mask beside my face, rather than on it. I just let the oxygen drift by me."

"I saw that, good thinking," I say. "The mask was hard to fall asleep in. Condensation kept running out of it and down my neck. My hands were locked in the bag; so, I couldn't wipe it away. I didn't want to lose any heat. But I didn't want the water to freeze on me either."

"So what did you do?"

"Just had a lousy night."

We're standing outside the tent. Our breaths hang in the air. My watch would go pear-shaped before I even loosened the strap. Up near the South Summit, seven hundred metres above, we can see a line of insects. They're not far from the top.

"I just heard on the radio there've been summits," Angel says.

Those black dots are climbers. And us here, we're just campers. What set of events led this to happen? We laboured for six weeks and dragged ourselves to this frigid death zone eight kilometres up in the sky, only to stand here and watch others summit. There's no point in dwelling on the last twenty-four hours any longer.

"Ok guys, gather round." Angel holds a radio in his gloved hand. "Everyone, Sherpas as well." He waits a moment. "I've been onto Base Camp. Here's the latest forecast." He looks at the circle of a dozen that has formed. "As expected, there'll be a storm this afternoon. It might not be as bad as predicted. We could sit it out in the tents."

Nurhan whispers in Yener's ear.

"A gap in the weather is predicted for tonight. A summit bid is possible."

I nudge Greg and raise an eyebrow.

"However, a huge storm is predicted for tomorrow. If we're back down by noon, we should be ok. We can try again tonight or descend and wait for the window on the twenty second."

"Angel, will you support us for either bid?" I ask.

"I will."

"Ok guys, let's go with a majority decision, but try for unanimous. Does that make sense?" I ask.

Heads nod.

"Look, I'll shoot first," I say. "We're here. We've done the hard work. We can hydrate today. If the Sherpas can support us," I look over to Teshi, "then I say: let's go tonight. Teshi, what's your position? You and the Sherpas, will you speak for all of them?"

Teshi represents them and confesses they're not in a position to support a push tonight for the full team. There's a lack of food and manpower, the same problem as last night. His preference is to descend, regroup, and acquire supplies from Base Camp. I hear no doubt in his voice. His vote carries a lot of weight.

"Nurhan, you're the most experienced. What's your opinion? And can you speak for Yener also?" I ask.

"Summits of this nature are undertaken during a weather window, not a gap in a storm. The weather window is May twenty-two / twenty-three. It has been for some time. Trying to summit tonight is an unnecessary risk. We should descend and retry. That is mountaineering."

"Right gents, I'm changing my mind, sorry. Based on what I've heard, I'm now voting to descend."

It kills me to be so close and yet leave with nothing. Precious energy has been wasted. Climbers are standing on the summit behind us as we speak. Some are making the return journey.

Everyone expresses their feelings, concerns, and disappointment. Each makes a free choice. But within a few minutes, Greg, Khalid, Ade, and Roger have all declared that we must wait for another day.

"All right, let's pack up and get out of here to Camp 2 as quick as possible," Angel says. "We'll take down the tents and cover them to protect them from the storm."

Ade and I drag everything out of our tent. Inside we find sheets of ice where Greg had slept. It seems I'd not soaked up all the spillage last night.

The Sherpas protect the flattened tents with rocks. My pack bulges with the addition of the mountain sleeping bag. I've not had any water or food this morning, I doubt Greg and Ade have either. Nor do I have anything in my bottle. The emphasis is on escape. Going downhill should not be too testing.

"Angel, I'm out of oxygen. Can I get a tank?" I ask.

"Here's one. It should do. The needle's at five." He hands me a tank.

"Five? Twenty-five is a full tank."

"Yeah, but we can't waste them. Now we're making a second attempt, we must preserve them. We need to leave the full tanks up here. That should be enough to get you close to Camp 3."

"Sure?"

"Yeah, from there you can make it without oxygen."

I haul the heavy pack onto my back and set off with Greg. The two of us make good progress along the Geneva Spur slate ridge; it's in our favour.

We're walking in single file. Greg moves past a slower mountaineer on spotting an opportunity. The man plods in front of me. The gap to Greg grows. I cannot pass the climber. To the right, a rock slope and a kilometre and a half tumble down to Camp 2 threatens. My safety slides along the horizontal rope on the left. The man has not clipped himself in. He's just running a hand over the line. His feet look unsteady. He's not wearing an oxygen mask. I'm walking two metres behind him. He's unaware of my presence.

He strolls to the right and off the edge. The rope stays trapped under his armpit as he falls down the broken slate. I've tied myself to the ship's anchor. His momentum yanks the line and slingshots me over the verge. I'm not sure if the connection point will hold the weight of two flailing men.

My crampons scrape the rocks. We judder to a halt.

We climb back up to the trail. He trudges on, still oblivious to my existence.

Greg's waiting in line at the bottleneck at the top of the abseil section. We sit down on a snow ledge for ten minutes. Conversation is a casualty of the masks.

Greg then clips in, leans back over the edge, and disappears. I'm up next. I'm connecting the fixed rope to my harness. The climber without the oxygen tank crouches down beside me. He's untying the anchor point.

"Hey, hold on, stop that," I say.

He continues to fumble with the knot.

"Hey, stop. What are you doing?"

"These ropes are wrong, the knots are wrong. They should be the other way." He tries to undo our route out of the South Col.

"Jesus, stop. They're fine. I just watched five people descend on this rope. So did you."

"They're in the wrong place. They should be over there." He points to a rock three metres away.

I'm connected to the rope with a twenty metre sheer drop behind me. I've nothing with which to help the man; I've limited oxygen in my tank and no water. Nor can I go over the edge. He may be moments away from reaching for a saw knife.

"Hi Fergus, everything ok?" Khalid arrives with Jingbar.

I explain the situation to them.

"Ok, you go down. We'll keep him away from the rope," Khalid says. "I've got spare water. We'll get him down this section. It's easier after that."

I make fast progress through the white valley, passing Greg, and scramble down the Yellow Band. I traverse the Lhotse Face and then turn right to look straight down its slope.

I'm lugging a heavy pack. The sun has risen into the clear, blue sky. My legs cannot answer the demands I make on them. What I thought would be a simple stroll downhill is anything but.

At each connection point I rest to calm my breathing. The sun is beating down on me. Sweat rolls off my brow. My thighs scream for release.

I'm sitting, my left forearm on the snow and my face centimetres from its cooling effect. I stare down at Camp 2, a kilometre below. I could give up. There'd be no sense of dishonour. I think back over the last month, over last night. It was a rotten evening, disappointing. But we lived on the edge. I've been near the 8,000 metre mark.

For the last year I'd trained with a backpack, its model name: "South Col". If that bag could have spoken, it would have mocked me. Filled with dumb bells, I'd exercised in a city of four million people in the Middle East. But yesterday, stuffed with an oxygen tank, I took her home. I carried her and me to her namesake. It's a place where few have trod. I've had adventure, astounding altitude. I lived a night of drama at Everest Camp 4. I've pushed myself as far as I can. But now I'm exhausted. I've done enough. If I had to go home now, I could say I'd had my fill.

But I'm not quitting.

The pack murders me. My face boils under the mask. I stretch it outwards to suck in cooling air. My legs are struggling to keep me upright. Greg catches up and strides past. At each connection point, one or two other climbers catch their breath as I fight for mine. The sun's rays bounce off the white surroundings.

I must drink water. Setting out on an empty stomach I can handle, but not dehydration. I'll stop at Camp 3, two hundred metres lower, and boil snow. I descended from there to Camp 2 in just over an hour when we acclimatised; it'll take longer today. I set mini-targets to make it from one connection point to the next, maybe fifty metres in length. My legs wobble. A misstep will shoot me down the fixed rope. A cut to a calf muscle from a crampon must be avoided. I wipe sweat out of my eyes.

I look back. Some of the guys now descending the Yellow Band may be climbers or Sherpas who summited at dawn. For them it's almost over. The realisation sickens me. I have to ascend and do it all again.

An icy fog has rolled in over the upper few hundred metres of Everest. It'll be a whiteout up there, probably windy. If I'm exhausted here, there may be several worse above me.

We were warned yesterday to be back at Camp 4 by noon. I wonder how low trouble might drop. I'd convinced myself that I'm in the lowlands; that I'd descended into safe, oxygen-laden air. But it only takes a glance in front to realise this is not the case. I've been on airplanes lower than this. I can see over the peak of Pumori. Six months ago, I'd gazed up to it and considered it the most dangerous place I'd ever seen. Now I'm looking down on it, shattered and out of water, while a blizzard approaches. The hiss of oxygen in my mask has ceased.

Close to Camp 3 I fight hard ice as I descend. Panting, I arm rappel to stop myself falling forward. Where it's too steep for that I abseil. My crampons scratch over the surface. I search ahead and to the left for our tents. The clouds reach down to me.

About 1pm I stumble into Camp 3. I peel off the pack and drop onto a snow shelf. My head droops. For a minute I do nothing, just stare at my boots, puffing. Greg taps me on the shoulder.

"Fergus, I'm just about to leave."

"Ok, see you later."

"Come over here, Fergus." Khalid beckons me to join him in a tent.

I clamber down into it; half a metre of fresh snow surrounds it.

"Khalid, where do you keep getting all this water from?" I stare at a pot that's just coming to the boil.

He pours half a litre into my bottle. I gulp it back.

"Hey guys, any water in there?" Roger calls in from above the entrance.

"Pass in a bottle, Roger," Khalid says.

My day should be finished. I'm drained from lugging a full pack after a night at the South Col. But we're at 7,100 metres and a storm approaches.

"Let's get out of here in ten minutes," Khalid says.

"Man, I could do with a rest and more water. But you're right," I say. "We need to be off this mountain."

"Roger, we'll head in a few minutes," Khalid says.

"No, I'll stay here," Roger says.

"What?" Khalid looks out to him. "We've got to get out. There's a storm coming."

"No, this's great here. I'll stay, at least half an hour."

"Roger, we need to get moving. It's not safe here," I say.

"I'm enjoying it here."

"Roger! We're all out of here in a few minutes," I say. "Khalid, where's his Sherpa? And thanks for the water."

I haul the pack back up and tighten the chest straps. If I lose the race against the snowstorm, it contains the sleeping bag and mat I'll need to bivouac. Roger moves out to the fixed rope. I follow.

Just below camp, Roger is struggling to switch his safety to the next rope. It should take less than five seconds. His personal Sherpa gives directions. They're talking, but the swap is not made. I can't see the problem; climbers further down have passed through this point. I think Roger's unhappy with how the rope is connected to the ice-screw. The Sherpa knows more about such matters than me.

"Guys, I'm coming past. Stay still." I stretch my right arm around them, slap my safety onto the next rope, and walk on downwards.

Snow under my feet eases the passage. Clouds shroud Everest above and the valley below. The route becomes quiet, the air still. The break and water has postponed my collapse. I count each anchor point as an achievement.

I reach the Bergschrund, the last challenge of the day. My head falls forward between breaths. The damp rope has iced over. My damaged hands fight to make a loop in it and hold it there. Standing on a ridge centimetres wide, I wrestle it into the carabiner on my harness. A jagged bone breaker looms beneath me. There's no one in sight if this goes wrong.

Below the Bergschrund, visibility drops to forty metres. There's no guiding rope. Crevasses lurk off-route. I stop and kneel on the snow. Jingbar, who accompanies Khalid, will lead me to safety. I got from here to Camp 2 in thirty minutes last time. It'll take twice that in my current condition.

After fifteen minutes, Khalid and Jingbar materialise through the clouds. They abseil down the wall.

"Hi guys." I exhale. "Thought it best to wait. The route's hidden."

"How're you doing?" Khalid looks down on me.

"Shattered."

"Jingbar will take some of your stuff."

"No way, he's got a full pack."

"Come on, it's best, a few kilos," Khalid says.

"No problem," Jingbar says.

"No way."

Khalid grabs my upper body and holds me face down in the snow.

"Jingbar, quick. Take some stuff," he says.

Jingbar opens my pack and ransacks it. I've little left with which to battle. An Omani sits on top of me in a whiteout as a Himalayan storm approaches. Meanwhile, a Nepalese man does me a favour and steals my belongings. He gets one or two items before laughter gets the better of the three of us.

We follow Jingbar's yellow jacket through the wet, soupy cloud. I see a boulder up ahead, the only landmark. I'm just about lifting one foot in front of the other. Dehydration and a lack of salt and food have flogged me. Beside the rock stands a person, the first we've seen in almost an hour. We get closer. The Sherpa's holding a flask. I stop, my eyes close. I let out a long breath.

"He's one of ours." I point.

"I know," Khalid says. "He's also with me. At Camp 3 I asked him to shoot down and bring up a flask to meet us. I knew it'd be a hard finish."

"Winner."

The Sherpa produces three camp mugs and fills them. Slumped against the rock, I open my eyes to direct the mug to my lips, take a mouthful, and let my eyelids fall again. Warm lemon tea runs down my throat.

I follow them to camp. I strain to lift my boots above the snow. Jingbar looks strong. My body hurts trying to hang onto their coattails. We cross a trickle of melt water where there'd been ice and snow a few days ago. The Icefall will become unstable. I presume I'll descend it one more time. Will I do so, knowing I reached the summit and take whatever it throws at me once more? Or will I trudge down, despondent, regretting having ever come here?

MAY 17 – MAY 19

Back at Camp 2

We're sitting in the mess tent around the stone table. The last three days have been a waste. Few words are said. The food has all but run out.

We learn over the radio that Hugo, Charlene, and Pete reached the summit this morning. They'll recover at Camp 4 tonight and descend to here tomorrow. They've shown it can be done. Charlene has succeeded in her quest to become the first woman from her country to summit Everest, but she's far from safety.

We're aiming to summit on the morning of the 23rd. That means we'll push up from Camp 4 at 6pm on the 22nd. None of us trust the stoves to boil enough snow for the night time assault; therefore, we'll spend the night before at the South Col. That'll give us all day on the 22nd to get hydrated and fill two bottles each. We'll set off from here to Camp 3 on the 20th.

Angel has been outside on the walkie-talkie to Base Camp. He comes back in. We need a resolution on the food situation.

"Ted says we've to go down to Base Camp and bring up food." Angel looks at us.

"What the fuck? How can we do that and summit?" I ask. "It'll take us a day to descend, which is tomorrow, the eighteenth. That'll burn up energy."

"Not the damn Icefall again," someone says.

Voices rise. Angel has the radio in his hand; the anger focuses on him.

"Then we'll have to climb up through the Icefall the next day with a load. That'll waste more energy. Then the following day, we'll start straight into the summit push and ascend to Camp 3."

"Look, that's what I was told," Angel says.

There is near mutiny.

"Well, that's bollox. We're thrashed. We've no food. How in God's name will we get through the Icefall twice and then try for the summit?" I ask. "We just spent a night at the South Col."

"After all this training, to crash out because of no food, that doesn't make sense," someone says. "There's loads of food down in Base Camp."

"Angel, get on the radio and tell Ted to send up a Sherpa with food. This is ridiculous."

Angel steps outside. He comes back in. He hesitates.

"Ted says that if the Sherpas bring up food, they'll be too tired to assist a summit push."

Someone shouts at Angel. Ade shakes his head and mumbles something.

"Angel, this is beyond a joke," I say. "If the climbers are tired, there's no damn summit for anyone. What in God's name are we keeping the Sherpas fresh for? If a Sherpa who carries a load through the Icefall is no longer able to reach the top, then the same must be true of us. The purpose of the expedition is to get the climbers to the peak, not the Sherpas. If us lads sitting here can't climb, then nobody goes to the summit."

"Look guys, I'm on your side," Angel says.

"Angel, about three hundred climbers arrived in Base Camp, right?"

"Yes."

"Forty summited last night. Probably twice that number has already quit. Correct?"

"More or less."

"The season's almost over. There must be dozens of Sherpas down at Base Camp who've nothing to do. They'd be delighted to get an extra carry. That's what they do for a living. That's why they're here. They get paid a pittance to haul rubbish off this mountain. I'm sure we can offer above the going rate for one of them to bring food up to hungry climbers."

"Well, I'm not sure what arrangements have been made," Angel says.

"Angel, tell Ted to send the damn food up here or we'll arrange it ourselves." I turn to the faces around the table. "Lads, we can have a word with Teshi or one of the others. They understand business; they're not fools. We'll come to an arrangement with them and they'll sort out someone they know to bring up the food. If Teshi makes a few dollars on the side, that's fine by me. He deserves it. I've busted my ass too far to throw it away over a few lousy dollars."

"That's the spirit," Ade says.

"And another thing. I don't see why the damn Sherpa who carries the food has to be the same one who goes to the summit."

Angel comes back in from the cold.

"Ok, we have a solution," he says. "A Sherpa will bring up the food – "

"Finally, progress," Greg says.

"But he won't do so until the twentieth."

"The twentieth? But we'll have left that morning."

"The Sherpa will bring the food up to Camp 3," Angel says. "We'll set out and it should arrive about the time we get there."

"And what have we got here to eat till then?"

"It won't be great, but it should get us through."

"Ok. By the way, Angel, I didn't mean to shout at you. I was pissed off with Base Camp, not you. You were the conduit to there. Nothing personal. Sorry again," I say.

"No problem."

The dust settles.

Angel tells Roger he cannot continue. He believes Roger has HACE (high altitude cerebral edema). His climb is over. The update shocks Roger. Angel explains that fluid leakage causes a potentially fatal brain tissue swelling. The person is not aware it has occurred, and deterioration can be very quick. Early symptoms include confusion, a change in behaviour, unclear speech, and hallucinations. Prompt prognosis is usually only possible by a trained professional or a buddy who may note unusual or out of the norm actions. Roger refuses to step off the team. An argument develops. I feel gutted for Roger. I'm just as surprised by the sudden turn of events.

Angel has to step up his persuasion. Untreated HACE progresses into blindness, partial paralysis, unconsciousness, coma, and death. The dangers are compounded by the victim denying there's a problem. The treatment, if recognised in time, is simple: immediate descent and then complete rest.

Angel recounts to Roger that on more than one occasion he was not connected to the fixed rope while descending the Lhotse Face. As a result, Angel had spent several hours performing a double clip-in, whereby he ensured Roger was always tied to him on the descent, while he in turn was linked to the rope. The argument heats up. I think back to what Hugo told me about HACE: when a person is irrational, they'll have no memory of it after the event.

Horrid as the situation is, I can't leave Angel swinging by himself. I apologise to Roger in advance. In front of the team, I detail my encounters with him over the last two days. It's as unpleasant a task as I've ever had to do. I lay down the facts, as seen through my tired eyes, and then let the decisions fall where they may.

Greg speaks up and confirms that he believes Roger has HACE.

"Roger, you must descend. You have HACE," Nurhan says. "There is no choice."

I now realise I'd seen a few irrational climbers over the last two days. It might have been best if someone had sent them back early. I saw a man at the Yellow Band hold a metal carabiner in his bare hands. The task he performed was meaningless. There was also the person with no oxygen tank, who twice this morning tried to kill me.

Angel and Roger continue the argument outside the tent. A sombre Angel returns to say that Roger will descend in the morning.

The radio crackles to life. We hear Ted's voice from Base Camp. He asks why we didn't stay at the South Col and attempt another summit after the botched effort. No one says anything. I swap glances with my climbing buddies. Heads shake. Eyes close. Greg's head slumps in both hands.

Ted suggests that Ade should continue the descent to Base Camp and quit. The words scandalise me. We stare at each other. A firm response is given. The radio is set down on the table.

"Up to us from here on in, lads," Greg says.

It's May 18th. The on-going sleep and oxygen deprivation has sapped my energy. The thought of having to start all over again has drained my spirits. This is life high in the mountains. I'm sitting in the mess tent looking at the plate in front of me. A dozen chickpeas stare back at me.

"This is not mountain food." Nurhan, our legendary climber, thrusts a hand towards his plate.

After our Pumori climb, I'd filled in a questionnaire for Ted and added several paragraphs of suggested improvements. Among other items, I can remember writing "a better quality of food is needed; I will not get up Everest on the same diet." It kills me to be now playing with the same food again.

Private grumbles have been bubbling to the surface. Greg had confided in me that he expects no miracles from Base Camp in our bid for the summit. Ted's public lack of faith in Ade has walloped him. His climbing buddy, Martin, has already dropped out, and now he appears to have no team support. Ade's initial anger has been replaced by a deep sense of being abandoned. I assured Ade that I've got his back, but countered that by reminding him that I'm thrashed and won't be able to step into the breach should he need a hand.

Our reduced numbers leave plenty of space around the stone table. Yet still, we eat in our tent, while the Sherpas squeeze around the pots in the kitchen tent. No one questions the arrangement. Perhaps language has created the barrier. Maybe we represent the latest batch of egotists; we've travelled to their country to defy dangers that our Western lifestyle already protects us from. In that process, we'll force them into harm's way for a handful of dollars. Or is it that simple human shyness, on both sides, hinders the breakthrough?

"Khalid, thanks for helping me yesterday. How did it work out with the guy at the Geneva Spur?" I ask.

"Which guy?"

"My buddy: the man who tried to untie the fixed rope."

"Oh yes. He was in a bad way. He'd tried to summit the night before. His Sherpa had got frostbite, I think in his legs, so they'd turned back. The man had given his oxygen tank to the Sherpa."

"Where was the Sherpa's tank?"

"I don't know. We got the man down the Geneva Spur, and I gave him a bottle of water. There's more oxygen there, and he was able to walk down further."

"There were a few injuries on the summit push. Angel pointed out a Mexican guy in that camp just there." I point to a tent, twenty metres away. "He got frostbite, supposed to be pretty bad."

"What happened?" Khalid asks.

"I don't know."

We learn that the body tied to the fixed rope was that of Sergei Duganov. He was on a Russian or Kazakhstani expedition. One person said it was cerebral edema; another said it was a fall. He died a few days ago at about 7,800 metres while descending Lhotse. A team of Sherpas had been carrying down his corpse when we came across it.

It's mid-afternoon. I'm standing outside my tent. Hugo strides into camp, grinning.

"Congratulations Hugo, nice one." I stretch out my hand.

"Thanks Fergus, good to have done it."

"How was it?"

"Not too bad. Now it's your turn. You guys get up there."

"I'll do my best. You'll be down the valley drinking beer in a few days?"

"Oh yeah."

"It hurts me to hear that. Any tips for up there?" I ask.

"Yeah, don't take any crap from the Sherpas. They're here to do a job, and it's well they know it. It's up to them to carry the oxygen tanks. Do not walk out of Camp 4 with more than one tank in your pack. Do you understand what I'm saying?"

"Got it. One tank only, they carry the spares. But I thought this'd all been arranged ages ago."

"So did I. Pete, always the gentleman, gave in and carried tanks up."

We're sitting in the mess tent eating dinner. Questions fire at Hugo. About 6pm, Pete stumbles through the entrance. I've known this man over six weeks, a silent machine. No one tames this mountain. I thought he might be the first. I was wrong.

"Congratulations Pete," Khalid says. "Sit here, just here, there's space. Greg, pass down the flask."

Pete looks like a man who stared into hell and didn't like what he saw. The bookies' odds for me have just gone through the roof.

A paraffin lamp throws shadows around the tent. We've zipped up our down suits. About 7pm we hear voices outside. Charlene enters to a chorus of cheers. She slumps onto the rock bench. She smiles. Mingmar stands tall behind her, beaming. He has given six weeks of outstanding service. In one more day, he can rest and put himself first.

Greg – Week Seven
The elements have taken their toll on Greg. The liquid in the bottle is fluid he has coughed up from his lungs.

The 19th is a day of waiting. I nibble biscuits and hydrate in the mess, or lie low in our tent with Greg.

"I heard no one summited from this side yesterday," I say.

"I think that's what we expected. That was a good call by Nurhan. It wouldn't have been good up there," Greg says.

"We'd have been in trouble if we stayed."

"Too right."

"Pete looked shattered last night. I didn't expect that, Greg."

"It won't be easy." He turns sideways and coughs up more phlegm. "Pete told me he passed Navy Seals near the summit. One of them was literally crying. He didn't want to go on."

"Serious?"

"Yeah."

"Well, Pete would say that; he's Air Force."

Tomorrow we set off for the final attempt. There will be success or failure, nothing in between.

MAY 20

Climb Up from Camp 2 to Camp 3 on the Second Summit Push

P ressing the backlight on my watch, I understand what it means.

"Five o'clock, Greg. Time to rise."

We sit up in our bags, head torches on, postponing the cold's attack for another few minutes.

"I can't go." Greg's head drops.

"What? What's up?"

"My lungs are a mess. I'd a rotten night. I can't climb coughing up this rubbish."

"You could try, I mean, it's not the end."

"I won't make it. Wearing a mask tomorrow, no way. Up above the South Col, with lungs full of fluid, I wouldn't stand a chance."

He's had this problem for two weeks, but this is not a Greg I've seen before.

"Is that it?"

"I think so. I could stay here today, see if I improve. Set out tomorrow morning. If it works, I'd skip the sleep at Camp 4 and join you guys for the summit push." He coughs up phlegm.

"Will a day make a difference?"

"I don't know. I can't go today."

"That means getting hydrated in a few short hours at Camp 4," I say.

"I'd leave Camp 3 early, about 4am. Get there for noon."

"Well, it's worth a try."

"It's a fifty-fifty chance." He coughs. "Tomorrow, I'll go up or down."

My chances of reaching the summit are hardly fifty-fifty; his are much less. He's been a great climbing buddy for seven weeks. He was always the stronger of us two. But now our paths will diverge.

"I'll let Angel know in the mess." I crawl out into the black.

Angel looks like he's been hit by a freight train.

"Morning, Angel. You ok?" I sit on the stone bench.

"Not really. Terrible toilet troubles." He rubs his hand on his brow.

"You've been like that for days. Is it worse?"

"Every couple of hours now."

"Oh no, that bad? Where do we go from here?"

I'm chewing tasteless food with half closed eyes. The Sherpa cook has laid out a few flasks of hot water. Without the mugs of tea, the nourishment would not pass my throat.

"We go as planned. The window is there."

"Angel, I'm not sure you should go up like this."

"There's no choice. There's one window. This's your chance. I'll go up with you guys."

"That's some huevos, but there's a limit." I crunch on a biscuit. "Greg can't go up today; his lungs are rubbish. He'll try tomorrow and then join us at Camp 4 for the push. How about you go up with him?"

"Tomorrow?"

"Yeah, you might be better by then. You can't be any worse. Greg is the sick guy climbing alone. It makes more sense that you go with him."

"And what about you guys?"

"Jingbar's going up with Khalid. He knows this mountain backwards. Ade and I will tag in with them. I think Khalid also has a second Sherpa. He grabbed one from one of the guys that went home."

Ascending without a guide to 8,000 metres was never on the agenda; this is extreme high altitude climbing. But this is what we came to do. If required, we'll be medics, stretcher bearers, water carriers, solo-climbers, maybe even Everest summiteers. It's all improvisation from here.

"Makes sense."

"Why not? You're the guide; you should be with the person in most difficulty. We know the route. If it hits the fan, Jingbar's in charge," I say.

"Ok, let's go with that."

"Right. And Nurhan and Yener, they'll go up tomorrow?"

"Yes, on their own schedule. Perhaps Greg and I will climb with them."

Ade, Khalid, Jingbar, Khalid's second Sherpa, and I stand outside the mess tent. I've a single packet of biscuits in my chest pocket. It'll be at least four days before we return. The planned food delivery to Camp 3 better happen.

"Up to us now, Fergus." Ade seals his black hood across his mouth.

"Left foot, right foot, you know the drill." I clip on my helmet. "Keep going till we get there. Khalid, looking good?"

"All set." He tightens his waist harness.

"Ok guys, take it steady today," Angel says. "I'll join you at the South Col in two days."

We stride onto the snow as a tight team of five. Our numbers have been decimated, but in this small, self-contained unit, we'll look out for each other. Ade is a fabulous man: steady, deliberate, upbeat. Not since the brutal ten hour ascent of the Icefall have I toiled side by side with him. His climbing buddy Martin has descended, and I in turn am without mine. A new alliance may form. Being leaderless is almost refreshing. Today, I'll mature into a mountaineer. We'll look to no one else. Our squad will not wait on the direction of another.

Up above, in the cold morning light, we see Camp 3. We must close off six hundred and fifty metres of altitude. We lessen the gap to the Bergschrund on a quiet route. Most teams will start the big push tomorrow; they'll not spend a night at the South Col.

The last time I set out from Camp 2, my climb almost ended. Today I feel better. My mind is clear, my vision crisp. I must stay upright today; there's no Angel to save me if I collapse.

An hour and a half has us at the Bergschrund.

"Let's take a break here, guys," I say. "That was a good start."

The extreme cold relents as the sun rises over Lhotse. The snow around where we're sitting glistens.

"That's colder than normal," Ade says from behind his hood.

"Yeah, that wind's coming off Everest," I say. "I'm glad of the sun. A biscuit?" I pass the packet over to him.

"Thanks."

"That was the last pack I could find. Here, Khalid, fancy one?"

Three biscuits won't put much fuel in my body. I'll try to reach the summit and return before I disintegrate. I sip water and gaze down the white valley and at the mountain ranges beyond. The four lads hunker down beside me.

I pull out my camera. I capture Ade, protected in his black down jacket and hood. His dark shades hide the man within. He cuts a fine silhouette against the outline of the Western Shoulder. Cold, blue Himalayan skies complete the frame.

Ade Takes a Moment before the Bergschrund

Jingbar, half the size of Ade, is wrapped up in a bright, yellow down suit. Reflective shades obscure a brown, weathered face. He's stood on top of this mountain before and intends to summit again within the next three days.

Khalid's orange down suit sports a large Omani flag on the left breast. He's climbing for national honour and personal pride. The shutter catches a picture of concentration as he adjusts a glove, oblivious to the camera.

"Pass that camera here, Fergus." Ade reaches over to me. "Let's capture those good looks."

Might all five of us stand together at the summit in three days' time? The law of the mountain dictates otherwise. Nature will whittle our numbers down further.

"Are we ready?" Khalid asks.

"Ok, let's go." Ade pushes himself up.

We ascend the Bergschrund and climb up the Lhotse Face. Up front, I inhale and exhale between each step. Calm, relaxed progress carries us to within three hundred and fifty metres of camp. Three more hours will get us there. We almost have the slope to ourselves. I concentrate on lifting one boot up and over the other. My hands move in sequence as I clip in and out of the fixed rope.

"Hey Ade." I face him below me and fight the wind. "Your pace, there's an easier way to do this. You're taking several quick steps and then stopping to catch your breath. That'll kill you. Slow pace all the way. Try a full, slow breath in and out between each step. I know it sounds silly. Never let your breathing rise. Time is on our side."

I'm nervous giving this survival expert my wilderness advice. But this is our team today; we must look out for each other.

The wind hurls in from the left and scours across the surface. Our faces point right, hoods pulled tight. Every ten minutes a biting gust punches us. We hunker down on the slope, backs to the gale. Left arms protect our heads; right hands grasp the jumars. Snow and ice particles shoot across our vision on their own Himalayan adventure. The journey pauses. Is this a passing squall or the start of a tempest that will end our exploits for good? But as quick as they strike, they relent. In between, we edge up the mountain.

A glance at the altimeter every half hour rewards me with the knowledge that our exertions are not in vain. Metre by metre, our summit push moves higher into the blue sky.

Halfway up the slope I reach a metre high ridge. I crouch against it, take a gulp from my bottle, and slide it inside my open down suit.

"Let's take five here, Ade. I don't see any more shelter between here and camp."

"Sounds good." He drops onto the snow, panting.

I lean down to share what's left of my biscuits with him. My water bottle slips out. As it bounces off the hard snow, Ade catches it.

"That was close. Thanks Ade. That would have been in the Bergschrund."

Khalid and Jingbar squeeze beside us. In clipped conversation over the wind, we acknowledge we've had none of the drama that accompanied our last climb up here. We agree we should reach the tents in less than two hours. The only concern is food.

I've slipped ahead of the lads a little. I turn around, dig in my crampons, sit down, and enjoy the view. I've afforded myself few opportunities this past month to smell the roses. Often I've been too tired, but mostly, I felt there was a job to be completed first. It'd be a shame to arrive home successful, having not taken time to appreciate the journey. But I'd feel worse smiling for the camera for two months and then not completing what I'd set out to do. When I'd trained for the last year, it wasn't to kick back on a Club Med holiday in the sky. There's climbing to be done, and it will demand everything I possess. But right now, I'll steal a few moments for myself.

The wind has eased. Sitting at 7,000 metres, the great Himalayas once again stretch out in front of me. Even through my shades, the snow and ice sparkle under the noonday sun. Pumori, as ever, nods to me, confident I shall never climb her. The Cwm Valley, silent and white, runs down to the Icefall. Camp 2 is reduced to specks of colour on the right side, crammed between the glacier and the sheer, brown wall of Everest. A blue and grey sky extends out over Asian peaks I cannot name. And much closer, just ten metres below, Ade, Khalid, and Jingbar ascend. I reach for my camera. Khalid, his orange hood tight around his face, waves to the lens. Tall Ade, beneath a yellow helmet, smiles for the shot. Jingbar, just behind, shoulders a heavier pack than each of us. From my brief viewing post, I see that he too is human; he labours to lift one heavy boot up above the next.

Our Small Group Closes in on Camp 3
From left to right: Khalid, Jingbar, Ade.

We Know that Another Day's Target will soon be Reached
From left to right: Khalid, Jingbar, Ade.

"Keep going, lads, looking pretty," I say as they toil past.

"Get off your butt and join us." Ade throws me a smile.

The gradient increases over the last fifty metres. Winston Churchill said it best: "KBO, keep buggering on." We reach the hard ice. It rips at my muscles. The mountain wants to throw me down into the Bergschrund. The fixed rope strains. My shoulder begs for relief. The crampons scratch the surface, searching for grip.

I disconnect from the rope and step onto a level platform. I am here. We are all here. I slump onto a snow shelf, tired but not exhausted.

"Ade, have you got any food? I'm starving." I release my helmet.

"Try these." He hands me a packet of raisins the size of a matchbox.

I pour them down my throat and look at him. He hands me another.

"Thanks," I say.

It vanishes. I can't remember ever being this hungry. I'm not sure how much longer I'll last.

"Damn, there's been a half a metre of snow since we were last here." I look at my tent. "I better do this while the weather holds."

I pick up a shovel and start digging. We're far above the rescue limits of a helicopter. My breathing increases. This tool is my friend, and it better find a way into the tent.

I drag my equipment inside and set up the tent for the night. I clamber back out and glance over to the Sherpa's shelter. The sight stuns me. They've several MRE bags coming to the boil in a pot.

"Where did this come from?" I ask.

"Come inside," one says.

I crawl down.

"What on earth," I say.

Aladdin's Cave never had it so good; food lies everywhere. Half the tent floor is hidden under grub. I see chocolate, Kellogg's bits and pieces, MRE's, packets of dried noodles. Coloured labels abound. Has the damn chain of command between Ted and these guys been completely severed? Was I supposed to starve to death on the side of this bloody mountain?

"What is-" "When was-" "Were you guys ever going to tell me?"

I grab items and stuff them inside my down suit: Snickers bars, Kellogg's Nutri-grains, silver MRE bags, white packages, something sugary. I spy a small, plastic zip-lock bag, crammed with coloured packets. Written on it, I read the name "Fergus." I think one of the team who pulled out, perhaps TC, put some thought into preparing food for each of us.

"I, it, what-" I point to the bag and then me.

I stare at the Sherpa. I hold up my hands. I shove the zip-lock bag into my suit.

As I walk back to my tent, some of the bounty slides out the leg of my down suit and pops onto the snow. I grab it. Nothing will go to waste.

I look like a hyena over a carcass. Three Kellogg's Nutri-Grains, slim and moist, disappear. I find a protein bar, its amino content lower than the ones Charlene gave me but so much more palatable. I wolf it down; my broken muscles cry out for it. I think these were TC's reserves. She didn't make it to the top, but her decency might put me there.

The party's over. Discipline is required once again. I must boil two litres of water and pour it into my blood stream. I have to fill a bottle for the night ahead. Once that process is started, I'll return to the treasure. I must be deliberate and make no mistakes; this is thin air at 7,100 metres. I craft a little platform for the stove.

I light a feeble flame from a frozen canister. As the water warms, I place the next canister into the liquid. Once it's hand hot, I turn off the stove, switch in the hot canister, and restart. It blazes, roaring, as the fire attacks the pot.

Two hours pass. The temperature has plummeted, but my down suit matches the challenge. A full bottle, too hot to drink, is heating my sleeping bag. Soon it'll warm my insides. I've set up the tent for the night ahead. Water has not been a problem as

I didn't have to split it. But this has been weird, Greg is missing. This is the first time on the mountain we've not shared a tent. Cooking and recovering in the confined space required mutual understanding and economy of movement. Over the last month we learnt each other's ways. We could have done with more space, but tonight's shelter feels empty and lonely with just one occupant. I wouldn't mind being cramped by another person right now. What in God's name am I doing up here?

I try to settle down. The gale increases. The tents suffered a hammering at Camp 2, but nothing like this. Sleep will not come quick. Only a madman could doze in this. The wind attacks from every direction. A battalion of soldiers beat and tug the material from all sides at once. I try to spread my weight, so the gusts cannot raid underneath and toss my lodgings into the air as a dog might a rag. Locked into a mummy sleeping bag, I can do little.

Not here. Not now. Not like this. Not alone. The prospect of going to a solitary demise becomes much less appealing than doing so in company.

Ade lies just two metres away in the next tent. The wind will not pick him up. But he might as well be on the far side of the planet. An un-roped walk on snow, in pitch black, separates us. We're perched on a ridge just wider than the tents. Many climbers have met their fate at night stepping out to answer the call of nature. One misstep and it's into the Bergschrund, to join the collection of bottles, gloves, XTC's, and cameras. In 2002, after a fierce storm hit the Lhotse Face, the body of a British climber was found there. But from up at this height, I'd bounce right over it and end up far down the Cwm Valley. Either way, I'd hope to be long dead before stopping.

The wind delivers its assault in surge after surge. The tent feels massive on my own. I hope Greg improves tonight and reaches Camp 3 tomorrow. But I'm not certain what he might find. Flying debris has loaded the black glacial air. Will the material withstand the night? One airborne sliver of ice will be enough to pierce it. If it tears in this gale, I've no Plan B.

MAY 21

Climb Up from Camp 3 to Camp 4
on the Second Summit Push

I open my eyes. I see tent material. I'm relieved.

I'm almost through my preparations.

"We'll be leaving soon." A Sherpa's head looks down into my tent.

"Give me fifteen minutes."

I calculate how much food to carry. Hugo had told me to expect no appetite above Camp 3. He'd planned to eat little more than a few energy gels over the three day push. My legs already look like something from a famine. I must eat to succeed, but I don't want to over-pack and carry nourishment I'll never eat. I'll be gone for between two and a half and three and a half days. I decide on an MRE, a packet of dry noodles, some snacks, and my three remaining gel pouches. It's precious few calories. It pains me to leave grub behind, but travelling light is crucial if I'm to reach the South Col today.

Breathless, I stare down the Lhotse Face. Early risers dot it on this clear, crisp morning. Three times we've toiled up the beast below; there will not be a fourth.

At the edge of camp, Khalid and his two Sherpas are clipping into the fixed rope.

"Morning Fergus. How're you today." Ade screws his regulator into an oxygen tank.

"Good, set for another one. And you?" I clip my mask to my regulator.

"Good, thanks. I'm glad that wind disappeared."

I strap on my crampons, and yank them tight for the blue ice just outside camp.

"Ade, can you double check my set-up? Put me on one and a half litres."

We tighten the straps on our cheeks; the need for oxygen supersedes ease of conversation. The heavy tank, hose, and mask now feel like a second skin. We communicate via hand signals. Packs are secure. Harnesses are snug. Helmets are fastened. Our outer gloves envelope our intermediate ones. Ade gives me a thumbs-up and a nod. We stride out to a quiet fixed rope. Most mountaineers aiming for our window have just set out from Camp 2. Very few will stay a night at the South Col as we plan.

Ade and I tackle the sheer ice face just outside camp. This had been a brutal start to the morning last time. But a week of climbing by hundreds of boots in both directions has kicked in steps. We take advantage of the grip and slog beyond it.

I'm setting the same pace as when Greg and I were here: left foot forward, two slow breaths in and out, and then lift the right foot. The thin air takes its toll on me. Ade labours just behind; I can hear him breathing through his mask. There'll be no Olympic medals for either of us. But we progress, and with each step, with every two inhalations, we push upwards.

Every ten minutes I glance back over my shoulder, nod to Ade, and receive a thumbs-up by way of response. We're climbing as a pair, but each exists in his own cocoon. In my bubble I concentrate on ascending, saving energy, breathing to a measured pace, staying calm, and holding it together for another forty-eight hours. If I get to the top, it'll have been worth it.

First success of the day, we reach the traverse. We turn around and plant our backsides on the snow. The Himalayas stretch out in front and beneath us.

"OK?" Ade stretches his mask down over his chin.

"Yeah. That was good, steady progress. And you?" I fish out a chocolate bar.

"Yeah, not bad." He reaches for his bottle.

"Half a Mars bar?"

"Thanks."

A few mountaineers labour past us on their way to the Yellow Band. Beneath us, few climbers pepper the route. The sugar and water should keep us ticking over till noon.

"Let's stay another five minutes. We've plenty of time today." I take a slug from my bottle.

The traverse across the face is mild on my legs, after this morning's relentless incline.

Failing to reach the summit was a desperate let-down, but we are at least familiar with the route. No sooner am I at the bottom of the Yellow Band, than I'm clipped into the vertical rope and pushing myself up the snow and rock features. I switch at the next knot, try to calm my breathing, and ascend further. Below me, Ade searches for a handgrip, inhales, and pulls himself higher. I do not question why I am here; I just keep climbing.

We plod up the long, white trek to the Geneva Spur, encased in the valley between Everest and Lhotse. Ade's pace has been dropping for the last hour. Behind us, the trail lies empty. Slogging at 7,700 metres, the highest and fourth highest peaks on the planet encircle us. Apart from the ever shrinking few specks of climbers up near the Spur, we're all alone out here. If someone was to look back from the top of the ridge and see us now, they might think: "What great mountaineers are these?", "Now that's how to climb, two men in a sea of white", "No fear", "Old school, give it socks, gentlemen", "Climb on you heroes!"

If only they knew.

Ade's pace falters a touch more. I've eased off a little. I can hear his heavy breathing behind me. Regardless, we're making progress, which is all that matters at this altitude. We should reach camp in an hour and a half, where we can start the recovery and hydration process. We're aiming to recoup at close to 8,000 metres, in one of the world's most perilous places.

We arch our heads upwards and take in the sheer face of the Geneva Spur. Ade has dragged himself to here over the last hour. I've a little in reserve; the pace is slower than I'd otherwise set. The oxygen in my tank has kept me alert. On our left the drop has grown. As it's increased, the afternoon has slipped away.

"Last challenge, Ade. Over this and then a thirty minute walk to camp." I transfer my jumar to the vertical rope.

"Good." He sits down to regain himself.

"See you at the top. Take it steady."

Hand over his mask, he draws in air.

I try to leave the hard work to my legs. I control my effort and take breaks for a few seconds as needed. Within ten minutes I'm crawling over the crest. I catch my breath on a rock and wait for Ade. A carpet of cotton wool clouds floats below me to the horizon. Some of the biggest mountains on the planet jut through it.

View from the Geneva Spur - Nuptse Stands above the Clouds

I lean over the edge and snap a few photos of Ade ascending. I'll send them on to him when this is all over. Turning around, I capture the massive brown and white colossus that is now the last nine hundred metres of Everest. Only those who've scrambled to the South Col can appreciate the boldness and majesty from so close. It stands, oblivious to me, Ade, and the other climbers who are now up at Camp 4. Pyramidal in shape, it taunts me, its presence now magnetic. This is why I am here. Tomorrow I will give it everything to reach the summit.

Peering Over and Down the Geneva Spur
Camp 2 is pressed up against the right flank of the valley on the grey rocks, one and a half kilometres below.
The broken, slate-like rock of the Spur is in the foreground. A misstep here will lead to a fall off the Spur, a
tumble down the Lhotse Face, big air over the Bergschrund, and a final stop somewhere down the Cwm Valley.

Ade's head appears over the rim. He hauls himself over the top and sinks onto a
rock.

"Go on ahead." He slides his mask back over his nose.

"No, no, we're fine, no rush."

He leans forward, elbows on his knees.

"No, you go on. Get settled in. Unpack your stuff. Easier, more space."

"Ok, that makes sense. You're cool to walk in from here?"

"Yeah."

"Thirty minutes, slight uphill. No rush. Ok?"

"Yeah. See you there."

I round an outcrop of rock and see coloured shelters a couple of hundred metres
ahead. I expected to see more. In a stiffening wind, eight kilometres up in the sky, I
close the gap over loose rock and snow. I can't find our camp. I'm in the right spot.
I'm standing beside two orange tents. What on earth happened here? The sight
shocks me. I stare down at a flattened mess of what had been our Sherpas' main

tent. I see a tangled mass of string, bent poles, and ripped material. What struck our settlement?

"Hi." Jingbar pokes his head out of the tent at my right knee.

"Jingbar, what happened? What's left?" I bend down so I can hear him.

"The storm. Three tents finished. Two others ok. We make from pieces."

If Angel, Greg, and another Sherpa had climbed with us today, we'd now be in serious trouble. Of the two tents standing, the fly sheets are torn and the outer zips look busted. They wouldn't fetch a dollar apiece in a shop. Up here though, tonight, they're all that stands between life and death.

"Angel wants you." He passes me a walkie-talkie.

"What does he want?"

"He wants to know. He does not understand."

"This is the button, Jingbar? Just press?"

"Yes."

"Fergus to Angel. Fergus to Angel. Over."

"Fergus, this is Angel. Tell me the situation. I do not understand the Sherpas. Over."

I strain to hear his voice above the wind.

"A storm has hit Camp 4. Two tents remain. I repeat. Two tents remain. They are damaged, but working. Over."

"Can you find the two down suits of Nurhan and Yener? Have they been damaged? They cannot summit without them. Over."

"Let me check. Over."

I stick my head into the tent.

"Hi Khalid, all good?"

"Hey Fergus. Yes, I'm fine."

"Any sign of the Turks' down suits here? There should be two somewhere."

"Not in here," Khalid says.

I riffle through the debris of the main tent. It's just twisted metal and fabric, no suits.

I bend down to what will be my home for the night. The outer tent zip has jammed three quarters of the way up. Above and below the fastener, the zip teeth have not bound and defy my attempts to fix them. The wind is swirling around the small vestibule. The inner zip functions. I open it and crawl inside, dragging the oxygen tank behind.

A few stuff-sacks of equipment lie in front of me. I identify the one that contains my sleeping bag. Another one looks like Ade's bag. At least our vitals are here. I rummage through the other packages. One of them contains a red, fluffy material. I recognise the sponsorship logo of a Turkish company sewn onto it. The outer sack is sound; I can presume the suit inside has survived. Burrowing within the next piece of baggage, I find yellow material that has the name of a Turkish company embroidered on it.

"Fergus to Angel. Fergus to Angel. Over."

"Go ahead, Fergus. Over."

"I see two down suits. They are good. Over."

"Please confirm. The suits are ok? Over."

"Yes. The suits are ok. Over."

"Thank you. I will meet you tomorrow with Greg at Camp 4. The Sherpas will bring up tents from Camp 3. Over."

"Understood. Over."

"Over and Out."

I start to unpack my stuff. Khalid pops his head into my tent.

"Hi Fergus, you ok?"

"Yeah. I must get hydrated. I'll have to go now and collect ice. Bloody tired." I take a breath through the mask. "It'll be an hour before I get a drink."

"No. The Sherpas should get the ice, not you."

"You sure? I don't think so."

"Of course. They should have bags of ice. You stay here. Do not get ice."

Two minutes pass.

"For you." A Sherpa pushes a heavy sack into the vestibule.

"Thanks." I check its contents.

How does Khalid do this? I start smashing its contents.

"Coming in, Fergus. Grab my pack." Ade pushes his pack into the vestibule.

I update Ade on the situation as he sets up his equipment. The first pot of ice has melted.

"Throw me those boots, Ade. I'll block up these gaps as best I can. There's still wind everywhere. The flame is hopeless."

"Well, we'll not set the stove up in here with us like last time."

"Damn right, that was some screw up." I place a frozen canister into the water. "Once this can heats up we'll get a decent flame. Just a few minutes."

A blast of wind and snow blows in on top of us.

"Damn." I stretch the mask down over my chin. "Those zips are useless."

"Let's close up this inner zip while the water heats. We can check on the stove every few minutes."

"Sounds good." I grab the zip on the right. "Grab your one. Ok, up."

Our efforts begin to produce food and liquid. The large down suits and heavy tanks complicate the preparation process. We're operating from half inside our bags. We explain each move to the other in advance; the water is precious, the flame dangerous, the tent damaged, and our location precarious.

"We did well. I wasn't sure we'd get anything boiled in that wind," I say.

"That was two good hours."

"I was hungry. My appetite's fine up here. That's a surprise." I shove an empty wrapper into a tent pocket.

"Right, that's boiled. Let me fill this bottle." Ade leans over the stove.

"Hold on, let me get out of the way. Ok, all yours."

"That's the last one?" Ade tightens the lid onto the full bottle.

"Yeah, that should do us. We can spend all day tomorrow boiling water."

By the light of our head torches, I turn off the stove and close up the inner zip for the night. To my left, Ade locks himself into his mummy bag. The down-filled material will protect us from the ravages of a night at the South Col.

I might never climb beyond this point. I find my camera, and stretching out an arm, take a snap of myself for posterity. I view the display screen. My black, fleece hat sits under the blue, bulky hood. The mask hides my nose and mouth. An air hose trails out of shot. The only visible skin is a pair of sunburnt, windswept cheeks. Cracked and worn, I ask a few extra days sacrifice of them. Just above them, tired eyes stare back at me. Shell-shocked, red at the edges, they've seen much that is new these last seven weeks. Hopefully they'll view something higher, newer, and more spectacular in thirty-six hours' time. But for now, they must rest.

MAY 22

Dawn at the South Col

My mind keeps running over the plan. To reach the summit, I must do the following:

Walk out of camp at 6pm and climb up to the Balcony. That first challenge will take us to a height of 8,400 metres. The first two thirds look to be a consistent thirty degrees on snow. Then the route turns right and gets steeper. It's to the far right of Everest as I look at it. Once there, we should get a fresh oxygen tank.

Then we'll turn left and ascend a long, steep snowy ridge. I'd seen a massive drop on this side of it. I've no idea what's on the other side. An ant-like line of mountaineers had moved along it last week. It had broken me to watch them; hopefully, there'll be no repeat. The route then turns right to head straight up a slope of about sixty degrees. In low snow years, smooth rock is a challenge in crampons. Deep drifts create their own problems. From what Hugo reported, conditions are good. This'll take us to the highest point that can be seen from here, the South Summit at 8,700 metres. We'll get another tank there. Above it, there's little if anything that can be done to help an injured person. Even strong, experienced climbers will have their work cut out to get themselves back to Camp 4.

The Cornice Ridge follows next, a hundred metre long horizontal section of rock and hard snow. Jagged and uneven, in places it'll be less than two metres wide. The Southwest Face plunges down 2,700 metres on its left. A misstep to the right promises a fall off the Kangsung Face of more than three kilometres. I'd heard someone refer to the view of the Rainbow Valley below. It sounded romantic, until the vista was explained. The rainbow spectrum is composed of a variety of coloured down suits. Inside each lies a mountaineer who'd slipped off the ridge over the years. This mountain has ended the lives of more than two hundred climbers. It has kept and preserved scores of them.

That ridge will deliver me to the Hillary Step, a twelve metre wall of rock and snow. First climbed in 1953 by Edmund Hillary and Tenzing Norgay, I hope it'll be the last obstacle en route to the ever nearing summit at 8,848 metres. If conditions are favourable I can expect about -25C, but down as far as -50C threatens.

MAY 22

At the South Col

"God, it's cold up here." I push the mask back over my nose.

"Yeah, this morning sun makes no difference. What time is it?" Ade asks.

"Eight. I'll get the stove going."

"Good man. We'll spend the day drinking. Let's have two bottles each ready before six."

I'm half in, half out of the sleeping bag as I crawl to the vestibule. Cold air attacks my socked feet. The night's body heat escapes. The oxygen hose tangles in the pack. My gloved fingers fumble with the lighter. The flint will not ignite its frozen contents. I slide the frigid lighter inside the elastic of my underpants.

"I'll give it a few minutes and then retry."

We're boiling the second pot.

"I can't keep my feet warm. Every time I move, the damn cold gets in," I say.

"Try sticking the next bottle in your bag. It'll be too hot to drink straight away anyway."

"Will do. You're in good shape today. Nothing wrong with your appetite."

I slide a silver packaged MRE with the words "Vegetable Jalfrezi" into the pot. I doubt it'll bear a resemblance to the Indian dish of the same name. I've only eaten one MRE on this expedition, after our first climb through the Icefall. It promised barbequed chicken but tasted dreadful. I threw up just afterwards. But I've no choice; I must eat.

The once frozen bag of Indian promise has been bouncing in the boiling water for over ten minutes. If nothing else, its warm contents will heat me up. I drag the mask down under my chin and take a forkful.

"This tastes great." I push my fork in again. "It's fantastic."

The aroma, the taste, the heat, this dish has everything. Why did I not pack a pile of these for the mountain? I should have carried several for today. Perhaps I was dehydrated and wasted when I had that first MRE. I've been a little hasty writing these off. In a foxhole, this small, silver bag is a lifesaver.

All too soon it's gone.

"Man, I'm hungry. Hugo said it would be impossible to eat up here. I'm ravenous."

I snack on the few remaining bits of food I have. We place another lump of ice into the pot and seal up the inner zip. The only grub I've left is a packet of dried noodles and the three small gel pouches I'll need for the climb itself.

"How are those feet?" Ade asks.

"Impossible to keep warm. I've got a bottle down the bottom of the bag. I'm playing with it, keeping the feet and toes moving."

But as soon as I move it away from my feet or attend to the stove, they remind me again just how high up in the sky we are. We're at 8,000 metres; this is the edge of my tolerance.

Noon has passed, and we're hydrated. It occurs to me that the boots will be a problem. They'll be frozen solid and inflexible, probably about -20C. If I put them on just before we leave, I'll be in big trouble. My feet might not recover from that. Usually on the mountain, they heat up by 9am as the sun rises over Lhotse. Today will be different. We'll set off at sunset and climb through the night. The rays will not come to save me for twelve hours. It'll be colder than I've ever experienced. Less oxygen than ever before will float in my blood stream. I have to face reality: if my feet are not warm before the off, they'll not survive the push.

I pull down the zip of the rear vestibule to get my boots. The space is half the size it should be; tattered material flaps in the wind.

"Bollox, there's snow everywhere." I lift in my boots and close the zip.

A thin covering of snow coats the inside of both boots. I scrape it away, cautious not to melt any, which would refreeze as ice.

I take the chill out of the inner boots, one at a time, with a bottle of hot water. Then I place my feet into them while still in the sleeping bag. I'll leave them there till the last minute. For as long as I've a hot container to hand, I'll leave it down the bottom of the bag and massage my feet with it. I must keep my toes moving all afternoon.

Ade sits just to my left elbow, half wrapped up in his bag. The masks limit a good natter, but the tent karma is positive. In this extreme environment, this ex-paratrooper is as good a friend as I could hope for.

"Damn."

"What's happened?" Ade asks.

"This suit is rubbish." I hold the zip handle up in my hand.

"Will it still work?"

I wrestle with the zip.

"I can push it down, but I can't bring it up."

"Let me try."

I hold the jacket closed as Ade tries to force the zip up towards my neck. He cannot.

"What sort of mickey mouse material was used to make this? I've not even tested it in anger yet. I can't go out there tonight like this."

"It won't budge," Ade says. "Let me get my penknife. What else do we have that'll help?"

We try various options for twenty minutes. A key ring attaches an emergency whistle to the shoulder strap of my backpack. I'd spent time getting its placement just right, putting it where I could reach it with my mouth if my hands were unavailable. Change of plan, I attach the key ring to the zip and throw the whistle into a pouch at the top of the pack.

"Does it work?" Ade asks.

"It's flimsy, but yeah. Up and down. It's moving." I hand the penknife back to him. "Thanks."

It's early afternoon, and we hear voices outside.

"Hi guys." Angel shoves in his head. "Make space."

His red suit and equipment fill the tent. He positions himself between Ade and me.

"Greg and the Turks are here," Angel says. "The Sherpas brought up a tent from Camp 3. How's that stove going?"

The three of us are lying on our backs with our heads raised. A movement by one is felt by all.

I keep wiggling my toes in the bag. It's mid-afternoon and my appetite rages. I drop half the packet of frozen noodles into the empty MRE foil pack and pour in boiling water to the brim. Huddled over it in the cramped tent, with mask under my chin, I spoon it into my mouth. I'm careful not to waste any. I repeat the process with the remaining noodles. They're plain, half-cooked, and delicious. Hugo got this one wrong; I'd eat the tent if I could.

It's 5pm and time to get serious. After hours of massaging my feet and toying with bottles in the sleeping bag, they don't feel cold. I place a bottle in the outer boots for several minutes to take the subzero chill out of them. Then, in a swift movement, I tie up my feet in their home for the night. They're warm; I'm relieved.

Now for the final call of nature. I crawl out of the tent into the frigid air and walk twenty metres through shallow snow past the edge of camp. I've tied the tank over my shoulder with a piece of string I rescued from the destroyed Sherpas' tent yesterday. There's been a lot of foraging and jury rigging of late. Money has no value up here. Guts and experience are the currency of the South Col. But too much of the former, and not enough of the latter, is the worst of all combinations.

I pass a few corroded metal items of rubbish from previous expeditions. I can imagine the state some climbers may have been in when they dragged themselves off this mountain. A little litter was probably the last thing on their mind. A few years ago, Sherpas undertook a clear-out and hauled old oxygen bottles and destroyed tents from here. Apart from a little old rope, I've seen no rubbish all the way back to Camp 2. Given the enormity of the Himalayas, nature will handle our laziness along this narrow trail from Base Camp to the summit.

A thirty centimetres high ridge offers little to protect my modesty, but at least it shows I've made the effort. I need to be quick. I zip open the bum flap on the down suit and attend to business in the arctic temperatures. I may as well not have bothered. Days of eating almost nothing produces, not surprisingly, almost nothing. But I can tick the action off the checklist. Having to expose myself on the mountain tonight could cause frostbite in the most tender of places.

As one might do when walking a dog, I scoop the deposit into a biodegradable plastic bag. I'll tie that knotted gift to my pack tomorrow and then spirit it back to Base Camp. Once there, I'll throw it into the Base Camp toilet. An unknown local will then collect the contents, and they'll be dumped in a pit or incinerator lower down the valley.

I walk back to the tent, surprised my rear end is still attached in these bitter conditions. There must remain a little fat back there to protect me. I'd been anxious about that necessity all afternoon. It had to be performed before setting out and I wasn't sure I'd recover from the exposure. I've no idea how I'd perform such a feat clipped into a rope on sloping terrain. I'd overheard that one of the lads has no rear flap on his suit. Lower down, he had a pressing need. He zipped the suit open at the front, pulled it down off his upper body, and squatted down. Unfortunately, the delivery landed in his hood.

Back in the tent I swallow an anti-diarrhea tablet. That's it now: lock down. The next time I sit on the throne, I'll have climbed this beast or failed in the process. Like a scorecard in golf, there'll be no room for comments. One massive, one final, one all-or-nothing, ball-breaking twelve hours and this will be behind me.

I zip up the suit and adjust the pack. I've already switched the regular padded waist strap for a simple, lightweight belt. Every gram shed before tonight's altitude and gradient could make the difference between success and catastrophe. I know it's not vital equipment, but I shove the camera into my left chest pocket. On the right side wait three energy gel pouches. Inside the down suit jiggles a seven hundred mil bottle of water; in the backpack it might freeze. But regardless, I've put the one litre container in the pack. It should be fine. I can't have two bottles bouncing around my body with only a dodgy zipper keeping them in.

I pull on the large double mitts but have no dexterity in them. I change back to my regular gloves. Up to now on my right hand, I've just worn the inner glove, so I can operate the jumar. The inner and outer gloves should be warm enough. I can always switch to the mitts later if needed.

I'm kneeling down outside the tent, tightening the crampons. All around me, everyone is busy in their own world, ensuring their equipment is set-up right.

Camp 4: 5:45pm – The Team Next Door

A Sherpa in a red suit drops an oxygen tank outside the tent. He says something like he'll be climbing with me, and walks away. I don't recognise him, but he must be with our team. I presume this is the man who's been tasked with assisting me on tonight's push. This is not quite the buddy system I'd imagined. I remember Hugo's

285

firm advice to me. For better or for worse, this is the job that red suited guy signed up to. Carrying cylinders on summit night is the occupation description. I should get a fresh one at the Balcony and another at the South Summit. Pete had been shattered when I last saw him. I can't risk my legs buckling on a rock face in a few hours because this Sherpa has a problem with his employment. I recall Greg's advice to expect no miracles of management from Ted. I'm sure Hugo has given Angel a heads-up.

"Angel, a Sherpa left a tank at my feet over there and walked away. I'm not sure what's going on."

"Which Sherpa?"

"Just there, in the red. Sorry about this."

"That's ok." Angel walks to the man in the red suit.

The tank that had been left at the tent disappears. I hope it goes upwards.

Our group is standing close together with packs on backs. The two Turks look professional in their sponsored suits. Jingbar assists Khalid with a final adjustment. No teams have set out yet. It's still daylight, but our lengthening shadows portend a coldness, like never before, that will descend upon us. Once the sun dips beneath the South Col, there'll be no hiding from the havoc of the night.

"Fergus." Nurhan beckons me over. "You need mitts. Gloves are no good. You need to keep your fingers together, much warmer."

I struggle to take off the pack; the oxygen tank is inside and the hose gets wrapped around my neck. I dig out the mitts and make a quick switch to preserve heat. I try to seal them, but cannot. I feel myself getting agitated. I try and try, but cannot grip the forearm sections and close them over the sleeves of the down suit. My hands have not recovered from last week and have little strength. I heave the pack back up and fasten the straps. There's a gap between the mitts and my sleeves. If I set out like this, I'll lose my hands.

Through the mask, I try to explain my problem to others. They also have their mitts on and cannot straighten out my sleeves and seal me tight. I'd a close call last week. If my hands get cold again I doubt they'll survive. I'm losing my calmness. Perhaps Angel can help.

I explain the problem to Angel. No doubt he has his own concerns. Regardless, he slips off his outer mitts. He tugs down my sleeves, yanks the mitts up my forearms and pulls the draw strings tight. Not a puff of wind will get in. This man has saved my bacon several times already. Once again, he's stepped into the breach.

I realise Nurhan's advice has been priceless. Had I tried to switch over tonight, after my hands were cold, in the dark, into mitts that would be -20C, I'd have fallen short. The blood flow to my hands would have ceased.

I regain my composure. I take a slow and steady breath in. And out. Now I am set.

My hands are warm. The inside of the mitts are soft and comfortable. Their luxury feels out of place in this unforgiving environment. My feet are not cold. I wasn't sure in the tent today if they'd come round. The oxygen tank is full. Helmet secured, harness tight, my hood is up.

Everyone else looks ready. I nod to Greg. He nods back. Who'd have thought that when he made that indecent proposal to me seven weeks ago, that we'd both stand here to have a shot at the final hurdle? We're less than half a day from the top.

A Sherpa in a red suit, twenty metres out of camp, is shouting at me. He's standing alone in the snow-covered field on the way to the Balcony. He summons me to join him. No other squads have started. He's roaring at me. I presume this is the man who'll assist me tonight, who earlier pushed his luck and dropped a tank at our tent. I know nothing about this guy. There's no way I'm heading out now with him. He can screw himself. I'm waiting for the team. I climb one step behind Angel.

MAY 22: 6:30PM

The Summit Push

Angel leads. I fill third place. My Sherpa walks close by. Ahead of us lies an empty trail. If I can stay with the pace, I'll avoid the worst of the jams that'll occur at the bottlenecks and vertical sections. I'm in no rush, but waiting at the base of a rock face will risk frostbite and waste oxygen.

Angel sets an even tempo. I don't think he has been this high before. He's never been to the top of Everest, and less than nine hundred metres now separate us from the summit. Every step tonight will carry me into unchartered territories and new elevations.

For half an hour we progress up the slight snow slope. I take measured breaths through the mask. The light dims as the colossal, triangular lump fills our view. I glance behind. The sight blows me away. Over a hundred climbers trudge in a long, slow line. If it weren't for the bright coloured suits, it would be a death march. Heads point down and shoulders hunch as the stream shuffles forward. No one speaks. Each mountaineer is following the boots in front. I feel under pressure; I hope I don't cause a delay.

My mind concentrates on what lies ahead. Two months of climbing will yield a result, or nothing, in the next twelve hours. Anyone who says the summit is just a bonus, that it doesn't define an expedition, has never pried everything out of their body.

We reach the fixed rope, clip in, and push up an increasing gradient.

Angel moves onto the next rope. I cannot unclip my jumar. The mitts and damaged hands have defeated me. A line of climbers stretches hundreds of metres behind me, but I will not take off the outer mitts to fight this spring. I know if I do, my limbs are finished. I struggle as a climber comes past me. The Sherpa takes off an outer mitt, yanks off the jumar, and pushes it into my palm. I muffle thanks through my mask.

The light fades. My eyes adjust as the sun dips west and the moon rises high in the sky. The moon's reflected glow illuminates the way. For now, I'll save the batteries in the head torch.

The gradient slaps me. Every step hurts. Perhaps I'm going faster than on the Lhotse Face with Greg. I'm troubled, conscious that I'm blocking those behind. But I don't want to lose my place in the line. At almost every connection point I fumble on my knees for twenty seconds, breathless, trying to unclip the jumar. In the dark, bungling with a small spring mechanism, my inability to perform the simple task embarrasses me. Then the Sherpa pushes me aside and jerks it free. We speak no words; masks hide faces. His attitude isn't helping.

I scramble up a rock and snow vertical face. My breathing increases. I'm not climbing well. Darkness surrounds me. I'm focused on the fixed rope. That is what I must follow. I'm aware of people close to me. Just ahead, mountaineers push upwards. Someone stands right beside me. So many behind are trying to get past.

I reach a wider section. I plod upwards, every step painful. The light of head torches reflects off snow or is absorbed by rock. The Sherpa unclips my jumar again and again. I must stay in the train. I must follow the person ahead. I must push up along this rope. I feel coldness in my toes. The sun will not rise for hours. How will they warm up?

I should take some food. The sugar may work its way down to my toes. I stand to one side of the rope, clipped into a connection point. I open the small zip on my chest pocket. I manage to grip one of the three-inch long pouches through the mitt. I tear it open with my teeth and squeeze the gooey contents into my mouth. I should not lose my place but better to take on grub early rather than later.

I pull down the main zip and grab a few swigs from the water bottle. That should help. The mitts complicate every task, but they're warm and comfortable. I wiggle my fingers to be certain I'm not imagining how good they feel. I need to rejoin the line and try to stay close to Angel.

I think we left camp two hours ago. My legs cry out for a release from the pain. The mountain has stolen the heat from my feet. Otherwise I'm not cold, given that it's far below -20C, and the mercury is still dropping. But so little oxygen fills my blood stream, it's no surprise they're starting to suffer. I was worried this would happen. I must keep going, keep my place in the line. Stay in touch with Angel; he's just a few climbers ahead.

I wish I could manage this damn jumar on my own. Where's Greg? I'm wrecked.

Climb over this steep rock, gasping. Now left boot up. Push myself. People are close to me. It's black. Turn on my head light. Moving shapes. Keep going. Where am I going? Just follow the rope. I'm slowing up the people behind me. They want to get past. Where's the rest of the team? Just go up. Shit, my feet are cold.

I look back over my left shoulder. Piercing the black, a trail of white lights, hundreds of yards long, snakes down from where I'm standing. It looks like Christmas. Underneath each bulb, a climber pits themself against this monster tonight. There're so many behind me. I cannot linger. Get moving.

Oh man, that's sore. What the hell is that? It feels like someone has just poured acid into the veins in my feet. It's as if my ankles have been cut open, and someone is packing ice down the void. This is a new sensation. I feel pain. But mostly, I just sense ice. I don't know what this is. Fuck, I think this is my feet switching off. I think my system has made its choice. My body is cutting off the extremities to save the core, to save me. Stupid damn system, send blood down there and don't quit now. Now what? Turn back? I must make a decision.

What's the intelligent choice? Go back, do so now. I'll lose my feet if I continue. That is certain. I must return to Camp 4.

But what's there? I'll sit in a tent on my own through this subzero night. The bag of ice we had is finished. Boiling water will take ages. Damn, I may lose my feet there as well. Last week, I sat at the South Col while others made it to the summit. Those climbers have stood on the peak of this brute and are now far down the valley near Namche. To turn around and still damage my limbs is the worst of all worlds. Either way, I'm going to suffer harm. Shit. This was a call I didn't want to make. I have to choose. I have to stop now and decide.

Go back now. Write off seven weeks of suffering. I could try again in two years. I've learnt a lot. I might be stronger then.

Will I ever get this close again? It's just a few more hours to the top. Where do I draw the line?

What does going on mean? Is it madness and stupidity? Is it balls and determination?

What does descending entail? Is it failure? Is it common sense?

It's only a mountain. But damn, I came here to climb this thing. I'm still alive. I'm still breathing.

Oh shit, I must decide.

My left foot will be beyond repair. I'm right footed. I knew coming here was a risk. I don't need to be the healthiest corpse in the grave.

Ten seconds, and I must make a choice.

Sit in Camp 4 on my own, in glacial conditions, surrounded by the stench of defeat?

Make the most foolish decision ever and press on. Complete what I started and write off my feet for the rest of my life?

Decide.

I may as well be done for sheep as for lamb. Let's get to the top as quick as I can, then turn around, and get the hell off this mountain. Tomorrow I'll deal with the consequences. No second thoughts from here on up. Right or wrong, judgement has been made. Left boot forward.

I concentrate on each step. I switch to the next rope. I follow the Sherpa. I must keep going.

I'm staring up a short, dark wall, waiting for the rope to clear. I peal back the forearm of the mitt to glance at my watch by the light of the head torch. It's 10:30pm, later than I expected. We've been on the move for four hours. It doesn't seem like I've been slogging for that long. I must have put a chunk of the mountain beneath me. But in the dark, on this unfamiliar route, I don't know what progress I've made. The altimeter suggests I'm on track. I'm standing a few hundred metres above Camp 4. The Balcony cannot be much further. The line clears, and I push myself up the rock.

Panting, I force myself up a slope that's steeper than the Lhotse Face. My feet are so cold. I need to warm up my body. I must go faster. I'll get a fresh tank at the Balcony.

"Turn up my tank to two." I tap the Sherpa on the shoulder.

I set the pace of a lunatic. I'm in oxygen debt, but I must generate heat in my body. I slurp in air and then blast it out. I've almost doubled my speed. Over and over, I lift my boots in quick succession to defeat this steep section. The noise of my breathing blocks out all other sounds. But nothing hides the pain. The Sherpa is bound to notice that something has changed. The pace murders me, but I must keep it up. My feet are in a place I've not felt before. The sun will not appear for hours; there's little if any chance they'll warm up.

This must be the Balcony. A dozen climbers stand in the dark on a flat section. It's the size of a living room. It's almost pretty in the glow of the head torches. There's a wall beside me. At the end is a service counter. There are lights on top of it. I think those two guys are attending to people. I've nothing left, exhausted. Chunks of ice form my feet. Let's do this oxygen change as quick as possible and move on. My Sherpa makes the switch. I mumble thanks and help him swap his tank.

I'll take two minutes for a snack. I squeeze the second gel pouch into my mouth. I lower the main zip of the suit and draw out the bottle. I gulp back a few mouthfuls, no point in just carrying this liquid to the top. That's the basics taken care of: oxygen, sugar, and water. I push the container down into the suit and pull the zipper back up. Oh bollox. My repair job from this afternoon has come undone. The zip jams mid chest. I cannot budge it. The Sherpa assists but to no avail. Now I'm screwed. I stick the Velcro pads together to give me some insulation, but a lot of body heat will escape up past my neck.

"Let's catch Angel." I stretch my mask down over my chin.

"Angel is behind us," the Sherpa says.

"What? Behind? He is not up there?" I point to a ridge on my left.

"No, he has been behind since the bottom."

Who was the tall guy in the red suit I was following? When did we pass Angel?

"Hey Fergus," a voice says.

I turn and look over my right shoulder. Ade stands a pace below me. I thought I'd raced up the last section. He must be strong tonight, or maybe I'm slow.

"Hi Ade," I say. "How're you?"

"Not good. My throat. It's hard to breathe. Can't breathe."

"That bad?" I slide the mask back up.

"I don't think I can go on."

"Take it slow."

"I'll rest here. See if it gets better. You go on."

"Ok."

The Sherpa and I pull out of the Balcony onto a steep, narrow ridge. My crampons bite into the hard snow. He leads. I see white to the right. I've no idea what's to the left. Two climbers ahead slow us. We adjust to their speed. I'll freeze solid at this pace.

"We must pass them." I hold the mask at my chin. "I'll get cold at this pace."

"You are cold?" he asks. "We must turn back."

"No, no, I'm fine. But this pace is too slow. It will make me cold. In the future."

"This is ok."

"No. We must pass."

"Ok."

We press up right behind them. They hear us, step aside for half a minute, and let us pass. We pick up the pace again.

I feel nothing but frozen winter beneath my ankles. The damage will get worse and worse as I ascend into this night. My hands and fingers, however, are snug and comfortable inside these extraordinary mitts. Whoever designed them is a genius.

I'm right behind the Sherpa. No one is near us.

"Go past." He steps to one side. "I cannot go faster. I am tired. Sorry."

I push past. He's carrying a heavier load than me. Every kilogram up here feels like twenty. If I do not keep my body moving my feet have no chance.

I labour up the ridge on my own. Fifty yards ahead of me I see the glimmer of two or three head torches. Beneath me, the light of the Sherpa fades into the night. Where did all those mountaineers go? Where's that trail of lights I saw a few hours back? I'm clipped to the rope and climbing upwards; so, I must be on track.

Panting, I fumble with the jumar for half a minute at a connection point. I clip it to the next rope and plod upwards. I have to keep moving. I must lift up my left boot, breathe in, and then the right. The pace is too fast for this altitude, but I must do it to pump blood around my body.

I reach another knot. I kneel on the snow and fight the spring. I can do nothing in these mitts. No matter what: do not yield to the temptation and take off the outer mitt. I work with computers: no fingers, no job. Gasping, head slung, I pop it out. I clip to the next rope and toil higher.

This is surreal. This is the weirdest place I've ever been. I'm walking in a dream sequence. I'm on my own, climbing through the night, amidst a cold hell. The Darth Vader noise of the mask fills my ears. Outside of that is silence. Darkness surrounds me. My life, my everything, is contained within the narrow beam of this head torch. There is nothing else.

I battle the jumar. I'm agitated, spent. I have nothing left.

Three or four people ascend a distance above me. Below, I see the odd glimmer of a head torch. I must keep climbing.

A near vertical rock slab stands in front of me. Two ropes stretch up it, one red, the other lighter in colour. Pete's advice springs to mind: avoid the red rope, the other is easier. I look up and see two mountaineers on the red option. I force myself a few yards past it and clip in to the green one. It moves around to the right of the face. The ascent exhausts me. The crampons scrape the rock. But I find just enough foot holds in the boulder to allow me use my legs and save busting my arms.

I have to keep climbing. Most of the mountain must be beneath me now. Up and up through the snow I labour. The pain will end. Just do this. I cannot move what's within my boots. I feel ice below my ankles. Forget it; keep going.

Another rock face blocks the route to the summit. It looks to be seven metres high. Four climbers are standing at the top, leaning against the old stone house, just by the window. I stretch up an arm to find grip. My legs push from below. I clamber up. I try to let my legs do the work. My fingers search for a hold. I scramble over the crest as the four move on. I tussle with the jumar. Hands on my thighs, I try to slow my breathing. I squeeze past the old wall and follow the trail.

I press upwards, exhausted. How much damage am I doing to my feet?

Where am I? What is this darkness? What's beyond this black? How much energy do I burn fighting this jumar every ten minutes?

What is over there? Where is this? Where am I? What the fuck am I doing here on my own? This is freaky. Jesus, what am I doing out here on my own? There's no one ahead, no one behind. I must wait. I must. I'll kneel here and wait for the Sherpa. I hope he comes.

I wait. Blackness and the resonance of Darth Vader surround me.

I stay on my knees for several minutes. I must hold it together.

MAY 23

Sometime after Midnight

"I am tired. I cannot go faster," the Sherpa says.

"No problem."

I'm just glad to see another human being.

I must be near the top. It can't be that much further.

Up ahead I see a small flat section. I can't see any snow above it. Is that the finish? This might be it. I check my altimeter. No, it displays 8,750 metres. There's another hundred metres of altitude. Damn. It's not accurate to the last metre. It could be out by fifty or more. The reading is based off Camp 4 being at 8,000 metres; that's what Hugo told me to set it to. I think the South Col is less than 8,000 metres. That means there's more than a hundred.

Panting, I lift a boot up and continue.

What's that, up in the sky? It's a shape. It's dark. It's massive. No bloody way. It can't be. It's the damn silhouette of a mountain soaring up forever. Jesus Christ, it goes halfway to the stars. That's a lot more than a hundred metres. I won't make it. My feet will be lost for nothing. Either way they are gone; just plod on. Just keep going.

The two of us reach a level area. Snow does not stand in front of my face. We're turning right. I think there's a view. This must be the South Summit. On the left, as before, looms a dark, black void. Up above and in front stretches the night sky. Below my right arm, miles and miles of dark clouds extend out farther than I can see. I'm on the other side of the mountain. That's Tibet or China. If this is the South Summit, then I've another hundred metres to go. Ok, the altimeter was out but not by much. Let's count this as a mini-achievement. I've nothing left, but a last hundred metres may be possible. Wheezing, I bend down as the jumar hits a knot. The Sherpa clips me out. I grunt thanks. We continue.

I labour along a snowy ridge. My thighs can give little more. I sense a massive drop to the right. I'm not sure what loiters to the left. The dark clouds, beneath me on the right, shimmer. I might be looking fifty miles across them. The black rug bubbles with a white glow. I don't see streaks of lightening, but the sky below me is on fire. Hugo told me he saw it too. I cannot enjoy it; I must press on. I must get up, get down, and get out of here.

The end can't be too far now. Hold it together. Stay cool. I force myself forward.

In the east I see a thin shimmer, just a faint line against the black. It's so far away. The sun is heating mainland China. I drag in air. Get up here you bitch and blast me with your rays.

I must turn away and follow the rope. I must not stand still.

It's maybe 4am. I trudge along the ridge. The Sherpa and I, more or less, have it to ourselves.

We climb down through a narrow, jagged passage. Rock and snow presses against my shoulder. I focus on the rope. The cold attacks me. My feet are beyond repair. I'm unsure how I remain upright. The thin air has drained my body. Frigid vapours find a passage through the damaged zip. The route angles up. I raise the left boot. My arm strains on the jumar. My right boot searches for grip on the stone. My head slumps. I wheeze. I look up again. I drag myself upwards. The incline flogs every muscle. The crampon slides across the hard face. I have nothing left. What comes after exhaustion? My left thigh squeals as it pushes me higher. I scramble over the top. I must follow the rope.

Three Sherpas are huddled in the dark on the ground. Orange oxygen tanks have been tied to a large rock just to the left of the trail. The Sherpa is changing his tank. I kneel down and assist him. What sort of place is this? The narrow trail is hemmed in by a ridge along the right. On the left, just at my backside, threatens an endless drop. Where on earth is this? Jesus, this must be what hell looks like. I help the Sherpa lift a tank. He lowers a fresh one into my pack. Good stuff, but I didn't expect a fresh cylinder. He's snappy at switching tanks. He points forward; he doesn't want to hang about either.

Panting, I force step after step along the slender, serrated, rock and snow ridge. How are my legs still moving? I have nothing, nothing at all. Those feet are finished, definitely the left, everything below the ankle. The summit must be around one of these outcrops. It has to be. It can be no more than a few minutes away. I must get there and exit.

The glimmer to the east increases. The west remains in darkness. The sun has not yet revealed itself, but I can see where I'm placing my boots. I switch off the head torch. I've climbed right through the night, yet still no sign of the summit. It must be around the next bend. It must be. I may make it. Just follow the rope. Keep lifting my feet uphill. I'm finished. Focus on the rope. Keep pushing up. There can only be seconds to go.

That is spectacular. It's criminal not to be able to enjoy this. To the left lies probably the most extraordinary thing I've ever seen. The shadow pyramid is laid bare. It's just like the photo I saw in Pheriche. I never thought I'd see it. A perfect triangle stretches for fifty miles, maybe a hundred, maybe more. Half a nation rests in shadow to the west. Linda has a snap of this. She did well to take it. I cannot ass about with my camera. That picture stays in my mind only, what's left of it. I've never known such pain. I cannot stand still.

I round an outcrop. I look up. A grey ridge extends out into eternity ahead of me. It snakes to the right and soars up into the distance. The huge, dramatic, ragged mountain astounds me here. Snow clings to its edges. This must be the range on the other side of Everest. I didn't expect to see such a spectacle so far up in the sky.

Wait. No. Fuck no. No. No. No. I'm climbing Everest. There's nothing higher. It's impossible. No way, it can't be. Oh shit, I'm doomed. That up there is the damn mountain I'm climbing. It's so far away. How can it be? I can't make that. It's beyond me. I've already given everything. I've lost my feet for nothing. At this pace it'll take over an hour. My feet, my damn feet, they're destroyed.

Nothing.

Nothing.

Nothing.

Just keep ascending. But I won't make it; I cannot climb what I've just seen.

I push upwards. My pace falters. I've moved far past exhaustion. I trudge up the narrow ridge. I round jagged walls that twist left and right. I aim for the next bend. In between, my eyes look down. I must keep lifting my feet. I will never see the top.

A sheer face, several metres high, stands in front of me. My legs give what they have. I heave on the jumar. My arm aches. I search for footholds. I need my arm to pull me up a few more inches. Breathless, I make a huge effort, and another. I push again. I drag myself over the crest. I pick myself up. My eyes drop. I pant. I continue forward.

I follow the rope. I must keep it together. I must walk upwards.

I stand at the base of another rock face and stare up. The Sherpa climbs to the top and beckons me. His rear crampon spike presses into the rope. He knows what he's doing. He's been trying to kill me for ages. Why did he drag me up so far to kill me here? It would have been easier, for both, if he'd done it hours ago. It would have been quicker down lower. I don't understand this guy, but I'm onto him. The line to the left looks old but reliable. I clip into it and test the jumar. It takes my weight. Mask pressed against the stone, I lever and scrape my way up. I heave myself over the edge. I stare him in the eye. I'm on to your game, buddy. But he could take me at any time. I'll keep a careful watch on him.

I toil on. There is no top. I'll never see it.

The sun blasts onto us. I cover my eyes. I lean against the ridge on the right and take out my shades. The Sherpa slips on his. I slide mine towards my ears. They get caught in the hat, helmet strap, and mask elastic. I push them back, agitated. Bollox, I don't believe it. The arm has snapped. What a time to break. This is all going wrong. Ok, stay cool. They're just glasses. The Sherpa pushes them into my pack. I keep walking. I'll get my goggles later, if I ever see the top. My feet. Oh God, what have I done?

I lift each boot in sequence. I struggle to stay upright. I follow the ridge. There is no top. There is nothing but snow beyond each turn. I expect nothing but white after each twist. I heave in empty air on this endless trail. I trudge around corners. I push up. The pain stabs me. How am I still standing? I must stay calm. Hold it together. Concentrate on each step. Each step is important. Each step counts. Just one at a time, and breathe.

Half a dozen colourful climbers stand ten yards away. A snow slope leads up to them. They are not in a line but clumped together. They converse. The Sherpa taps my right shoulder. I look at him.

"That's the top," he says.

Silence.

Disbelief.

Stationary.

Nothing.

His words have stunned me. I'd given up all hope. I didn't expect this suffering to deliver anything but abject failure. I've damaged my feet beyond repair, but I'll make it to the top. A year of training, two months of torment, the reward is just a few paces away.

I take two steps forward and then think better of it. This guy has been trying to kill me, but he's been with me all night. He's not so bad. I go back. I put an arm around him. We walk up the last few paces together.

I'm here. This is it. It's 6:30am. Twelve hours of slog.

Prayer flags and string encompass a mound of snow, three yards long and a yard high. I put celebrations on hold; I must take off the pack and find the goggles, or I'll suffer snow blindness. The hose tangles around my neck. I get agitated. I cannot free myself. I gain a man's attention and point to the pack. He spots my predicament and steps towards me. He untangles me. I give him a thumbs-up.

I protect my eyes with the goggles. I must get that litre bottle of water. I'm parched. I'll take half straightaway. That'll make a big difference. Shit, it's frozen solid. Not even a drip. Nothing I can do. Damn, I needed that. What a waste carrying that kilogram. Ok, so be it, what's done is done.

Fiddling with the pack, goggles, and bottle took ages. I still haven't taken in the view. The clock is ticking.

I unclip myself, move out of the shade of the snowy mound, and sit down.

I take in the vista over Nepal and Tibet. Ridges of mountains and snow stretch out in all directions. For the first time in a long while, there's nothing but sky above. This is the top of the world. This is what I set out to do. I am here. The cost will be high; my feet will not recover from the last twelve hours. There will be trouble ahead. I should exit as planned. But screw it, I'll sit and enjoy the moment. This pain and damage won't be in vain. The sunrays find me.

A few climbers push up the last yards. Behind me, mountaineers from the Tibetan north side ascend towards the apex. I take out my camera. The lens or electronics have frozen; an error displays on the screen. Then it works. I take a snap of ranges in every direction. So many mountains squeeze between me and the horizon.

"Take a photo?" I pass my camera to another climber.

He aims it at me and obliges.

"More, more, be sure," I say.

He clicks off a few shots and passes it back to me.

I can't confirm if the camera has worked. Either I've forgotten how to review a picture, or I'm pressing the wrong button through these mitts. I ask a few other climbers and my Sherpa to take a few photos as well. Hopefully one of the shots will come out.

I wish Greg was here. We could share this. We've gone through much the last two months. I played this moment out in my mind many times. He was always standing next to me. I hope he makes it.

Wouldn't it be super if Nurhan was with us also? Such a great climber, he could point out and name all these peaks below. I don't have an idea what I'm looking at. I can't figure out which way is Base Camp. Nor can I trace out the route we followed through the night.

I've been sitting for ten minutes. The Sherpa indicates we should descend. I know he's right. But so what, I'll take five more and soak in the occasion. I may regret all this; so, I may as well enjoy the panorama and the moment. I take a few more photos. I relax a little and let the location drift over me.

That was some night, but what's done is done. I've made it to the top of Everest. How did someone like me scramble all the way up here?

With calm breaths, I absorb all that extends out below me.

If I get down in one piece, I'll remember this tale till the end of my days. Fifty years from now, I'll be the old man in a leather chair beside the fireplace. Slow of movement, time will have taken its toll. "He doesn't do much but sip whisky," the bartender might say, "but rumour has it, that he once climbed Everest." My youthful years are almost behind me. I'm not too far off forty. Plenty of decades lie ahead, but from here on, I'll take them slower and enjoy them more.

Some people journey here thinking that the summit will alter them, add something to them. I hope it will change me, but perhaps by taking something away. Leave me a bit more chilled, less to prove, no more hills to climb. That's for younger men. That's for the next generations. If they pursue thrill seeking exploits and world records as much as I'll enjoy reading about their daring acts, then I reckon we'll both have a great half century.

Sitting here has magic. I allow myself a cheeky grin. Was it worth it? Ask me when I'm in hospital next week. Ask me in that leather chair fifty years from now. Ask me on my death bed. For now, I've done something beyond myself. The closer I got to the top, the more I knew of its hardships, the more I wished I'd never started. But I had begun, and I had to see it through. It is done.

I take a last gaze in all directions. The landscape melts me. I'm sitting on the same spot where Hillary rested five decades ago.

It's time to descend, to my life below. To the life I left two months ago. That is where I belong.

The Sherpa pulls on the end of my safety. I must get down alive and then do what I can to save my feet. Goodbye summit.

We walk off the slope, the downhill allowing for bigger steps than when we ascended.

A line of mountaineers ascend against us. If I stop for even one, the following climbers will presume to come past also. I cannot remain stationary. The clock is ticking. Every minute up here tempts death. A fearsome drop terrorises the edge, but escape is my only concern. We waste little time getting past them. Rather than spend time clipping and unclipping ourselves as we move around them, I just grip their upper arm as we step by. My legs hurt so much. As others see us coming, they'll know we're now descending summiteers. If they stay cool and still for a few seconds, we'll be through and on our way.

Angel stands inches from me, masked-up, but recognisable in his red down suit. He should make it to the top in less than fifteen minutes. I stop for just a second and give him a thumbs-up. He nods back. He has not been near me all night, but he's done more than his share to get me to the top. An avid mountaineer for years, his reward is close.

We follow the ridge left around a spur and come upon the two Turks. The thin air has smashed Nurhan's hope to be one of the few to climb this mountain without a tank. He gave it a good shot. I wonder where he had to admit defeat and put on the mask. Beside him stands tall Yener. We exchange a thumbs-up and squeeze past.

We race past climbers. I look down a near vertical rock face. The Sherpa descends first, and I follow him. I arm rappel down with the rope running through my safety. I place all my trust in the rope. Gravity tears at my shoulder joint. I don't have time to mess about looking for perfect foot grips. I must descend and get my feet out of their icy prison. Breathless, the crampons scar the rock. Those ascending step aside, for their own safety.

We put most of the twisting ridge behind us. The Sherpa is behind somewhere. I don't need his assistance at the connection points, as the jumar has no value descending. I can manage the simpler clipping and unclipping of a safety carabiner by myself. Panting, I concentrate on keeping my legs moving. I'll keep this momentum going for as long as they last.

A vista opens up beneath me. Under the intense rays of the sun, I see red rock and sand in the panorama below. It looks like Arizona. It stretches for miles. Wait a sec. Slow down. Take a breath. What's going on?

I stare back up and see snow. I know the summit is up there. I know I just sat atop Everest. That, I did not dream. That was not my imagination. I was there. It's one of the coldest places on earth. I see snow above but a desert landscape below. Only one can be real. I must make a decision. Which is the illusion?

It's the desert; the desert is fake. It has to be. Oh shit, my mind is gone. I'm loopy. I'm hallucinating. How long have I been out for? Five minutes? Ten minutes? Longer? On the way up? The Sherpa trying to kill me? Of course he wasn't. Oh God, I've been a basket case for ages. Reaching the top is tainted. I was at the summit; that, I know. But there's no pride in getting there like this. It doesn't really count. I'll have to be honest when I meet people at home. What I did is hardly half a summit.

I keep descending, but aware that I must focus from here on in. I'm not sure how much I can trust my own judgement. Most people who don't return meet their end on this journey back down. I must move fast, but steady, insofar as such a thing is possible.

The scorching rays of the sun take up the assault where the intense cold of the night left off. My body heats up inside the suit. I hope the warmth can reach my feet. Very few climbers dot the route near me. Most climb above, or they turned early, and are long back at the South Col.

I can see the end of the ridge. Up ahead the route turns left. I scan the mountain to trace out the trail. I follow the rope's outline for a hundred yards before it blends into the snow. This is a new experience. For the last two months we've walked up and down on acclimatisation hikes. I know the route up to Camp 4, but everything above it is alien. I climbed it in the dark of night. Standing here, I recognise none of it. I've no idea how far I have to go or in which direction are the tents. I'm beyond dehydrated. But every step down is a step into thicker air. I'll descend as fast as my legs can carry me.

I reach the junction where I'll turn left. Three climbers are sitting on the snow. I recognise Khalid and Jingbar. I collapse down beside them, panting.

"How're you?" Khalid slides down his mask.

"Water. Have you water?" My elbows on my knees, my head slung. "Mine frozen. I'm wrecked."

He hands me a heavy bottle. I'm too tired and thirsty to be bewildered. I gulp back a few mouthfuls. This could be the difference between reaching the tents and not.

"You ok?" I exhale.

"Jingbar's ill. He has a headache. I've been with him all night. He cannot continue."

Jingbar, this great climber, looks ashamed.

"I was on the radio. I thought I should go down with him. They told me to go on. Jingbar agrees."

I take another gulp of water.

"Is the summit much further?" Khalid asks.

I must answer him, but this is no time for foolish encouragement. I must be honest. I cannot send him into danger. The peak is far from where we're sitting. I've been descending for about an hour and a half, as fast as my legs can move. That means it may take over four hours to get to the top from here. A hundred climbers will descend against him on this single-rope narrow route. I'm not sure he can reach the summit and return to safety.

"It's a long way, a long, long way. Several hours at least."

"Sure?"

"Yeah, I've been descending about an hour and a half. It's maybe five hours further. There's a lot between here and the top."

He is silent.

"I will go on." He turns to his right. "Jingbar, you're ok to get down alone?"

"Yes." Jingbar does not look up.

"I must get down." I reach out my hand to Khalid. "He'll be safer without me. Good luck."

Old ropes entangle me as I try to stand up. I fight them for a minute and then turn left down off the ridge.

My body has warmed up. Apart from my feet, I'm too hot. If I root my gloves out of the pack, I'll save time at each connection point. My agitated, confused mind complicates the simple switch. I manage to not expose skin during the exchange. The nimble gloves lose their chill as I open and close them several times. I examine the water bottle. I see a little movement inside it. I try to force out a few drops but cannot break the frozen first inch.

I must get lower. I remind myself that I'm walking on snow, not sand, whatever my eyes might tell me.

I'm looking down a near vertical rock slab. I should abseil. Screw it; I need to get down as quick as I can. My muscle cries with the pain of the arm rappel. Panting, the crampons slide across the surface. I remind myself that it is rock, not sand. I must keep it together. I grip harder. I cannot give up.

I'm walking down a snowy ridge. I've dropped a huge distance since the top. My brain will get a bit more oxygen. My legs just about keep me upright. I cannot see the Sherpa behind.

Fifty yards ahead, a climber sits in the snow.

I have to do the right thing and check on his condition, but there's nothing I can do if he needs assistance. I have no food, no water, no brain to speak of, and it's all I can do to put one foot in front of the next. I lean down and tap him on the shoulder. We exchange muffled words through our masks. He's conscious and no worse than me. I must continue.

I don't recognise any of this trail. Without the rope I wouldn't have a hope. I remind myself that every step down is a step into oxygen and a step out of danger. The gloves make short work of the anchor points. This is good progress. Hold it together. I must get back to Camp 4, take off these boots, and warm up my feet. The quicker I arrive, the sooner the damage will stop. God knows what I'll see when I peel off the socks.

I descend further, drained.

I have the route to myself. This is all good metres to get behind me: more oxygen, more heat for my feet. God, I need liquid. I boil under the rays. My blood must be solid. I was at the top of Everest today, but it's a tainted achievement. Climbing with no mental capacity, with no ability to help others, counts for nothing.

The route spins right. Beneath me I see coloured dots. Camp 4 lies hundreds of metres below. I remember this white slope. Perhaps one hour more. This can be done.

I must go as fast as I can. But don't fall over and break something.

To the left I see a platform of snow and rock. It must be the Balcony. I think I saw a pub there last night. I cannot trust my spaghetti brain. But it's better than it has been for the last twelve hours. At least I can now tell the hallucinations from reality. Hugo had said that when people get HACE, they've no idea of it the next day, if there is a next day. They believe their actions were rational. Not me, I'm a basket case, and I know it. I have been for ages. How did I think my Sherpa was trying to kill me? And where is he?

I concentrate on my foot placement and staying upright. At any stage my system might switch off. It's so far to the tents, but I'm making progress. Every hundred yards in distance I'll stop for a minute break to catch my breath and minimise the chance of a mistake.

The tents grow in size. I think I'll make it. I'll live to fight another day. A climber descends above me, perhaps the guy who was sitting in the snow.

I scramble down a ridge and then lean back against it to calm my breathing.

I must keep descending into oxygen and heat.

My right foot, I can feel it. I can wiggle the toes. It is alive. The nerves must have survived. The foot lives.

I feel nothing in the left boot. I keep stepping downhill.

The slope below drops another hundred metres before the walk into camp. A guy ascends against me. He's the second person I've seen in an hour. I've got to get down. I've got to hold it together a little longer. I must drink water. I have to remove these boots. Take it easy, one step at a time. The slope punishes my legs. I should make it.

I reach the long walk into camp. The rope ends. I will make it. I'm a mess. I must drink. The left foot is frozen solid. Steady now, just a few more minutes and it's done. I suck in air. I must concentrate all the way. I must cover another few yards.

I reach the tents. What will I see when I take off my socks?

MAY 23

Camp 4

It's 10am. Camp 4 looks deserted, just a collection of tents and colours on a rocky field high in the sky. I presume the only people here are the few that descended before me and those who turned around. I collapse beside my tent. I pull out the water bottle from my pack. I shake it. Nothing moves inside. One of our Sherpas appears at my side. I don't know who he is, but I'm glad to see another person.

"Water." I hold out the bottle.

My head limp, the pain eases from my body. He returns after two minutes and stuns me, the bottle now full of liquid. I gulp down mouthfuls. The midmorning sun finds me sitting in a down suit. I slip off my gloves as my breathing slows.

My hands pulsate with pain. I'm an idiot. I remember Greg's warning. The air bites my flesh. I cannot stop the throbbing. I dive into the tent, my boots trailing in the vestibule. Ade is sitting inside. I shove my hands into the sleeping bag and rub them together. The air's a little warmer in here.

"Sorry, Ade, hands."

Against the heat of my face, my hands re-start. I glove them. My brain is hazy, but I remind myself that they stay covered until I escape this mountain. My breathing calms again.

"Ade, sorry again. I'm good. That was close." I look up to him.

"Did you make it?" he asks.

"Yeah."

"Well done."

"How about you?"

He does not respond. He stares down.

"No." He swallows. "I had to turn, at the Balcony, just after we met. My throat closed over." He stops for air. "I could hardly breathe. It's still bad. I'm getting ready to leave and descend."

I know that decision killed him. We slogged through the Icefall together. I heard him drink in air, refusing to quit, as we acclimatised. I saw him on the Lhotse Face, doubled over, put that slope beneath him one step at a time. Snow blindness stabbed his eyes, but we heard no more about it. His throat must have been shut for him to turn around. I'd been gutted the last time I was here. Just above me people were summiting while I lay in a frozen, dark tent. I presume he was visited by the demons of what might have been last night. He may never get this close again.

"Sorry man." I roll over to face him.

"Thanks. I'll be gone in half an hour. Get down to Camp 2. What's your plan?"

"I'm in no condition to move. I'll stay here for the day, I think. Are you descending alone?"

"Yes." He shoves equipment into his pack.

"I've a problem. Frostbite. My feet."

"Really? Is it bad?"

"Don't know. The right foot has some movement. Not sure of the left. You might take a look with me. See what you think."

"Of course."

"Screw triage. I'll do the right first. Good news before bad."

I'd rather spend a little time on it before seeing the horror of what lurks in the left boot. I expose the right foot.

The big toe and the next one are dull in colour, but the main body of the foot appears perfect. There's been a little damage, but overall the limb looks good.

"Wow, much better than I thought." I examine the foot with my gloved hands.

"Should be fine," Ade says.

"I can move it. I've got sensation."

"I can't see a long term problem there," Ade says.

"That's a weight off my mind. I expected worse." I exhale. "That should recover, I hope."

The prognosis for the left foot must be better than I'd feared. It'll not be pretty, but it must be comparable to the right.

"Ok, let's get this left sock off."

I slide it down. We stare at the sight.

The toes have taken a pasting. We see purple, grey, and touches of black. All five have been overwhelmed. But the rest of the foot looks healthy. A future that involves walking is on the cards again.

"It could be worse. I have a foot."

"There'll be some trouble ahead. But a lot worse happens up here," Ade says.

The Sherpa appears at the entrance.

"Can you get a basin of warm water?" I point to the damage.

For ten minutes I immerse the foot. I'm agitated. I know I can't trust my senses or instincts. For the first time in twelve hours, the blood in five toes de-ices.

Ade has departed. The sleeping bag surrounds my lower body. The mask covers my mouth. I only remove it to sip through what remains of the litre of water. Hydration will make a big difference to my predicament. I wiggle my toes and massage the feet at intervals.

I need more water but decide I shouldn't play with gas and matches, not in this distressed and confused state. Angel will arrive an hour or two behind me. He'll fire up the stove as soon as he returns. I'll wait and keep my feet warm.

I hear noise outside about 11am.

"Greg, that you?"

"Yes."

"Did you make it?"

"Yes."

"Well done. How you doing?"

"Tired. Very tired. How about you?"

"So-so. Frostbite in my feet. It could be worse." I press the mask back against my face and breathe. "My brain is a mess."

"Ok. We'll stay here for the day. Descend tomorrow. Drink plenty and stay rested for the feet."

I hear the zip close on his tent.

The heat builds in my shelter.

I try to open the down suit. The damaged fastener breaks in my hand and pulls out some of the zipper's teeth. Sweat is running off my brow. I try to squeeze my shoulders and arms out of the half open suit. I cannot. I feel myself getting agitated again. I must force this blue bulk towards my waist, but it won't budge. I draw up the lower zip from the crotch to the missing teeth. Heat escapes. It's the best I can do. Had there been wind last night, this outfit would have killed me.

The afternoon passes. I've not moved. Angel has not made it back to camp. I think I hear the Turks but am only half-aware of what's going on outside. I should have collected ice and tried to start the stove. Dehydration will exacerbate the frostbite. This morning's litre is long gone. I need to douse my insides and send thin, oxygenated blood down to my toes. But placing my feet in freezing boots for ten minutes to collect ice carries its own risks.

"Fergus!" Greg calls from his tent.

"Yeah. What's up?"

"I got word that Angel's waiting for Khalid."

"Thanks."

If I'd known that, I'd have amassed snow while the sun was high. I'm damaging my feet by not drinking. It's after 5pm; he should be back any moment.

When I left Khalid this morning, he was facing four hours plus to the summit. He'll have had to deal with traffic also. He'll descend a little slower than me, at least he will if he has any sense. Adding those numbers together, he could be eight hours behind me, which means it'll be 6pm by the time I see them. It'll be dusk, a full twenty-four hours above the South Col for him. Even with a dodgy mind, I should have put a match to that gas at noon.

Darkness closes in. About 6:30pm I hear their voices. They've made it off the mountain just before the intense cold descends again. Angel crawls into the tent.

"How're you doing?" I ask.

"Not good. My fingers. I think I've frostbite." He kneels up, panting.

"Bad?"

"I waited at the Balcony for hours. Cold. Waited for Khalid. He summited."

He grimaces as he takes off his gloves.

"Seems ok." He flexes his hands.

"The colour looks good from here," I say.

"Have we got water?"

"No."

"What?" He looks in the vestibule. "Is there ice?"

"No."

"What? Nothing? Nothing? What have you been doing?"

If I'd been in any decent condition, I would have exited long ago to the safety of Camp 2. That was the original plan. As it is, it's about all I can do to stay calm and not do anything stupid with fire.

He clambers outside to get snow.

As he boils a pot by the light of his head torch, he understands I have frostbite problems. He offers me half the water, which I take.

The gas runs out. We prepare to settle in for the night. I stay sitting, thinking. I know that for the sake of my foot I must get more water.

"Greg!" I call out.

"Yes."

I only just hear him over the wind.

"Have you a spare gas canister over there? We have none."

"Yeah, come get it."

Boots on, I drag my tank outside into the dark. The wind bites at my face. I've only to cover a few paces, but it feels like I've stumbled into Scott's nightmare.

I spend half an hour boiling up three quarters of a litre of water.

"Angel, half for you?"

"It's ok, take it," he says from his bag.

The water will slow the continuing damage to my toes; although, I need about three times as much as I just drank. Oxygen will provide the other vital ingredient for recovery. I've set the flow to a trickle. The tank will run out about 2am. The last few hours of sleep will edge me close to my limit. Not only will my toes degrade, a lot will be asked of my brain. I'm not sure how it will cope in the cold of the night when the mask stops hissing. I switch off the head torch and pull the mummy bag tight around my face. I've no thoughts of mountaineering success or achievement. We face another two days of toil, out of the death zone and into the Icefall, before we elude danger. This will be another harsh night at Camp 4.

MAY 24

Climb Down from Camp 4 to Camp 2

ngel and I shove our gear into our packs in the tent about 7am. For the last few hours I've had no supplementary oxygen. I struggle to force my sleeping bag into its stuff-sack.

"We'll leave in a few minutes." A Sherpa's head appears in the vestibule.

"I'm not leaving till I boil a litre of water for now and another one for the journey."

"There is no time. We're leaving."

"If it takes an hour and a half, then that's what it takes. I am not leaving this time without water."

"We must leave."

"I am not leaving. I did that last time. It nearly killed me. Do what you like. I am drinking water before I leave. That is the end of the matter."

With two months of suffering under my belt, injured feet, damaged hands, a sore throat, an empty belly, and an oxygen depleted brain, I'm in no mood to take orders to set out on a dehydration march for six hours.

"Ok," he says. "Go to our tent and get water there."

His words stun me.

I crawl out into a frigid, dull morning. People are packing. I slump onto a stone and tighten my boots.

"How're you, Fergus?" Teshi asks.

"Ok. No oxygen. Tank's empty. I'll need one for descent."

"I'll get one." He walks away.

We click in the hose to a fresh cylinder, and I pull the mask down over my mouth and nose. The oxygen courses through my veins. In just a few breaths, the day takes on a different complexion. It's still overcast. I'm still in as dangerous and bleak a place as I never hope to be. But the transformation astonishes me. The elixir washes away the fatigue and confusion.

How did I not think to grab a tank from the pile last night? They've always been rationed. I just felt I shouldn't dip my hand in there.

"Thanks Teshi, much better."

I consider Nurhan's attempt to get to the top without a tank. He had to surrender before the summit, but the shot took some guts.

"Hey Fergus, how're you doing?"

"Ok Greg. There's water in the Sherpa tent. I'm getting some."

"I'll join you." He follows me.

We step into a much bigger tent than ours. What I see blows me away. A huge pot of boiling water sits on a stove. A Sherpa tends to litres and litres of liquid. Food litters the floor.

"We came for water." I stare at the bounty. "We were sent."

He hands us each a full mug. I sip it. It's hot, sweet tea. Light brown in colour, I taste cardamom or another exotic flavour.

I cannot comprehend that this much hot liquid has been available all the time. I suspect this Sherpa has been on unofficial kitchen duty. I should have cracked Ted's balls the first time he passed those busted-up, old stoves off on us. But given our current location, I figure it's not the time to dwell on the fact that I've stumbled on these riches so late in the journey, but rather time to revel in my discovery. Our mugs are refilled.

"Can you boil me up noodles?" I point to a packet on the floor.

He does so straight away.

"Greg, a packet for you as well?" I ask.

"No, I'm ok."

"We've got a six hour hike. Good to get something in."

"Ok. One for me too."

Five minutes later, calories find their way into our systems. The oxygen and hot beverage slap my senses awake. Sitting in this tent with head room, I feel like I'm at a campfire. This is the way it's supposed to be. This is the first chat I've had with Greg since we separated four days ago. He says he feels strong and has no injuries. He tells me the two Turks set off yesterday for Camp 2 about 5pm. As we chat, a third mug of tea each arrives.

I complete the last of my packing and strap on the crampons. The Sherpas roll up the sleeping tents; they want to get out of here. I drop back over to their shelter where my bottle, now full, awaits me. I've been upgraded to the platinum package. Sometimes you have to earn privileges in life; other times you just demand them. With a bellyful of hot liquid, and a small meal inside me, I'm in better shape to set off than I've been for several days. Back on track, I push out of Camp 4, with Greg at my side.

I know we're not out of the woods till Base Camp. But it is done. We have climbed Everest. Nothing can ever change that. It feels odd to have the task behind me. At the edge of the South Col, we stop and gaze back at the cloud-covered summit.

"Greg, I know there's plenty to do. But congratulations." I stretch out my hand.

I cannot tempt fate more than that.

"Thanks. And yourself."

Looking up, the failure I felt yesterday dissipates. It sinks in that I've been successful. Maybe the report card won't be too severe after all. If someone asks if I've summited Everest, then I suppose there is only one answer.

Perhaps it's the knowledge that there's no more uphill. Maybe it's because I'll never have to push myself higher for as long as I live. Possibly it's just the hot tea. But this is the best I've felt since we arrived at Base Camp. We have done it.

I take a final glance at the mountain that challenged me for the last year. I turn and stride out of the South Col, once again through the snow, with my climbing buddy Greg. I leave sixty-five straight hours in the death zone behind me.

We walk along the brown slate of the Geneva Spur. To our right, a large boulder hides the body of Scott Fischer. I'll not detour and disturb what I presume is his final resting place.

The clouds drop, and visibility reduces below a hundred metres. Back on snow, through the yellow tint of my goggles, I see a featureless landscape. Walking down the narrow trail off the Spur, aware of a cliff to our right, I push them up onto my forehead.

Leaving the Geneva Spur Behind

Descending the valley above the Yellow Band, we join up with Khalid and Jingbar. His other Sherpa takes a few photos of us, shrouded in cloud and light snow. In large coloured suits, masks on faces and with full packs, we give off the look of hardened explorers. Khalid's national flag hangs from his pack. He'll be the toast of Oman.

Descending through a Whiteout towards the Yellow Band
From left to right: Khalid, Greg, Me, Unknown climber, Jingbar.

Greg abseils down the Yellow Band. Half a dozen climbers wait at this bottleneck. I'm up next.

I balance on a ridge with my nose close to the snow. The rope has iced up. My damaged hands struggle to bend it into the XTC. I cannot make a strong fist and loop the line into the carabiner. A climber, with a British accent, shouts down a comment that is intended for all to hear. I'm embarrassed. I'm furious.

My obscenity doesn't go beyond the mask. I don't have the energy to climb back up and dare him to repeat it. There's no point in continuing a war of words with an ass up here. Most, if not all, of this small group have just climbed Everest. This guy reckons the mountain is his and his alone. Khalid, who's beside the stranger, instructs him to watch what he says. It's a shame Khalid is such a gentleman.

We start descending the Lhotse Face. We'll now put serious altitude above us. My leg muscles strain under the full pack. Oxygen thickens the air with every step. Visibility improves. Protected from the rays of the sun, and hydrated, I cannot compare my progress to the last time I stumbled down here.

My biceps ache as I arm rappel. My breathing quickens. My face heats up under the mask. But the summit has dispelled the fear of failure that haunted me for the last two months. I'm not elated; there'll be trouble ahead with my foot. But confidence creeps over me as we move out of danger.

Khalid and his two Sherpas descend just behind me. The pain moves up a notch as the gradient increases. But the recent snow, and bashed in footsteps, lend a hand on the sheer ice.

I won't need to stop at Camp 3; I've half a bottle. I glance to my left and see only a ridge of snow. Our Sherpas have already pulled down the tents.

"Khalid, let's take five."

He gives me a thumbs-up.

Just below the old camp site, we park our bums on the snow. I feel the efforts of the last three and a half hours drain from my legs.

"How're you for water?" Khalid asks.

"No problem, thanks. That was good progress. Not too far now. How you doing?" My head rests on my hands.

"Good, thanks." He pushes the mask back over his face.

I'm exhausted, but not in the same way I've been for the last two months. This feels like the tired fulfilment after a hard day's work. Beneath us in the grey light, two dozen climbers are descending the Lhotse Face towards home.

We push ourselves back to our feet for the last challenge of the day, reaching the Bergschrund. Under a heavy load, I'll need steady footwork and alertness. Each step takes its painful toll. I disappear back into my bubble.

I hear a constant hiss from a Sherpa just ahead. An unused tank is strapped to his pack. He has opened the valve to lighten the load. Yesterday, that would have been a crime. But today we travel to a place where oxygen is the norm; we're heading back to our lives.

I pull the hot mask down to my chin. The fresh, cool air lifts me. I can better see my boot placement. I'll still get a benefit as pure oxygen drifts towards my nose.

Greg has disappeared into the grey soup below. Above, Khalid clips his safety to the rope and descends towards me. I wait a minute for my legs to stop burning. Then I hook up my abseil gear and walk backwards down a steep section into ever more oxygen.

The Bergschrund and today's dangers behind me, I set out for Camp 2. I staggered along this section last time, but the murky sky and breakfast gave me a great start today. It's 3pm and the clouds have lifted. I slide the goggles back down from my forehead. I pace myself in the last kilometre.

I fall in behind two climbers in matching orange suits. They sound Australian or New Zealand. I follow them over the glacier's melt water streams. On this near flat surface under a warming sun, I enjoy being here. I've made it to the top and returned to Camp 2. One more day and I'm out of harm's way.

I round the last of the three-metre high glacial formations that surround Camp 2. The mess tent has already disappeared, as have most of the sleeping shelters. These Sherpas may be all about climbing Everest, but they don't hang around when it's time to get off the mountain. I dump my pack on the snow and walk into the kitchen tent.

"Nice one, buddy." Greg passes down a flask.

"Fergus, congratulations," someone says.

I look around. I see Teshi and a few Sherpas crowded around the cooking table.

"Thanks guys. It's good to be back."

Two mugs of warm water are dispatched. Chatter jams the air around me.

"Fergus," Teshi says, "this is the man you climbed with." He gestures to a Sherpa.

This is the first time I've seen his face.

"Thanks mate. Thanks for the help with the jumar. My hands were hopeless. Sorry about that."

"No problem." He stretches out his hand to mine.

"And I think my mind might have abandoned me up there."

Laughter fills the tent.

"Sorry if I was a hassle."

"Not necessary. Everything fine."

I feel strong. My body bathes in what it thinks is a sea of oxygen.

"Some food?" one of the Sherpas asks.

"Sure, load me up."

We exchange tales of adventure around the table. In two months, this is the first time I've sat in the kitchen tent, the Sherpas' tent, and chatted with them. We should have done this from day one.

"Are the Turks down at Base Camp?" I ask.

"Yeah, but not without incident," Greg says.

"Why, what happened?" I dig a fork back into the rice.

"They set out from Camp 4 yesterday about five pm. It struck me as late, but they're the experts."

"That is late."

"Nurhan was behind Yener. It was dark. Coming down the Lhotse Face, Nurhan went down an old rope."

"No way, you're joking."

"Serious. Well, he reaches the end of it, and there's no more rope. He called out for Yener, but the wind just sucked his words away. He tried to climb back up and rejoin the route, but he couldn't find it."

"So what did he do?"

"Well, he knew that one misstep was a one way ticket into the Bergschrund. Eventually he found a tiny ledge. He took out his sleeping bag and bivouacked."

"What? He spent the night on the face? And where was Yener?"

"Well, after a few hours at Camp 2, he figured something was wrong."

"Yeah?"

"He went back out into the dark and spent hours on the lower slopes, searching and yelling out for Nurhan. He feared the worst."

"Did he find him?"

"Gone all night," one of the Sherpas says.

"About six this morning, some passing Sherpas find this guy sleeping on the Lhotse Face. He was only a few metres off the route."

"Brilliant. Better him than me. Lads, pass over that flask again. I wish I'd been on the summit with him. He could have pointed out what I was looking at. It's a shame I wasn't on the top with you as well, Greg."

"You were, you idiot," Greg says.

"What?"

A Sherpa spoons more rice onto my plate.

"I was a few metres away. I tried to get your attention after I arrived. You ignored me," Greg says.

"What? No way."

"You were handing out your camera, getting people to take a shot."

"Maybe I just saw another mask in a red suit. Not intentional. How stupid. We spend two months climbing together, and then I miss you on the summit. Well, at least you can vouch for me. You saw me at the summit?"

"Yeah."

"I'm afraid I can't return the favour."

Greg recounts how his Sherpa's oxygen seized as they climbed up a rock slab above the Balcony. It had probably frozen. They were half balanced, half suspended off the rope for twenty minutes as they tried to get it flowing again.

"Where're we sleeping tonight?" I ask. "I see the tent we were in is gone."

"We're sharing. Here, I'll show you. I'm going there now." Greg stands up.

A beautiful afternoon has unfolded, the sky a deep blue. If it wasn't for the trouble lurking in my boots I'd be exhilarated. I unpack my sleeping gear into the tent and have a short rest.

Back in the kitchen tent about 6pm, food is dolloped onto plates. Angel, Khalid, and Jingbar have arrived. The cramped conditions are irrelevant as we savour the success of the last few days. Appetites return. Conversation flows as we drink mugs of tea. I'm within a day of cementing our achievement but will take nothing for granted yet. My eyes feel irritated, probably the smoke from the stove.

As the sun dips, the chatter continues.

"Is it smoky in here?" I ask. "Are anyone else's eyes stinging?"

I'm met with blank stares.

"No problem here," Khalid says.

"Let me see." Greg turns to me.

He examines my eyes.

"It's snow blindness."

"What? It can't be."

My shades broke yesterday. I wore goggles this morning. They were hot and limited my vision. When we walked through the clouds I saw a featureless yellow / grey tint.

"I pushed up my goggles." My head falls into my hands. "But there's no way. It was cloudy, completely grey."

"There's no smoke in here. It's snow blindness," Greg says.

Darkness has fallen, and we've returned to our tents about 7pm. Greg studies my feet.

"The right foot is fine. Those toes should recover. I can't see a complication. The left has taken a beating, but the toes aren't dead. They should heal, as long as you don't do anything stupid."

"Hi guys." Angel crawls into the tent. "I'll take a look."

He's seen a lot of frostbite from his days as a mountain guide in Argentina. His opinion will be appreciated.

"The left toes are in a serious condition, but I've seen worse recover. Keep them warm, drink lots, and don't do anything foolish. Ok, put that sock back on and get it into the bag."

"What's the plan tomorrow?" I rub my eyes.

"We'll get up at six. Base Camp says the Icefall is moving. I want to get through it before the sun gets too hot. It's becoming unstable."

"Ok. We'll see you then. Good night." Greg zips up the tent.

Feet wrapped up warm in the sleeping bag, Greg and I settle in for the night. But the nagging irritation in my eyes has spiralled to something far more painful. It feels like someone is grinding sand into my eyeballs. My vision has become patchy behind a curtain of tears. The pain intensifies over thirty minutes. Groans and curses fill the air.

"This is killing me."

"There's no relief?"

"It's getting worse. My eyes are burning."

I can't think of the last time I felt such pain. The damage to my feet is much more serious, but I'm consumed by this agony. Sleep is out of the question for both of us.

"Some snow might cool them." Greg fills a small plastic bag from the vestibule. "Try that."

Lying on my back, I hold the cold bag on my closed eyelids. It cuts the pain in half. The heat of my face and eyes melts the snow at the bottom of the bag. For thirty minutes I shift the contents, so the coldest part is against my eyelids. When it's all melted, Greg refills it from the vestibule. I can no longer see.

I will not drift off in this condition. Moans and curses will not let Greg sleep either.

"Should I take anything for this?"

"How about a pain killer?"

"Yeah, anything."

Greg picks through his medicine kit.

"Here, take this. It's codeine." He places something in my hand.

"How long will it take to kick in?" I swallow it.

"Thirty minutes."

"Thirty minutes! Jesus, I can't wait that long. Is there nothing quicker?"

"Not orally."

I rearrange the snow in the bag. A few minutes later, Greg refills it.

Twenty minutes pass.

My next noise is not a roar, not a growl, not a curse. Air flows from my lips, a quiet groan. The torture subsides. Bearable pain returns. Calm revisits the tent and Camp 2.

Nature has thrown another spanner at me. How will a blind man descend the Icefall?

MAY 25

Climb Down from Camp 2 to Base Camp

I can only open my eyes for a second or two before the pain overwhelms me. I see blurs and water.

"Let's have a look," Angel's voice is in the tent.

I try to hold my eyes open.

"Ok, we need to change the plan," he says. "You can't travel during daylight. You won't be able to leave the tent until late this afternoon. Greg?"

"Yeah."

"You leave as planned with Khalid. Keep packing."

"Fergus, let me see those feet."

I pull off my socks.

"This thin air won't help your foot. You've got to keep drinking all day. I'll have a word with the teams around here and see if someone has a spare oxygen tank. Get you on it for a few hours." Angel crawls out.

I take an aspirin for the pain. I give it a few minutes, and then I swallow a Brufen for my feet.

About 8am, Greg and Khalid set out for the Icefall. The last piece in their Himalayan jigsaw commences.

Angel arrives back with a tank. I place the mask over my nose and mouth and settle in for a day of waiting.

He keeps an eye on me during the day and makes sure my bottle is full. As the sun rises the tent heats up, and we strip down to our base layers. We snack on the remaining food and stay hydrated with the water the Sherpas boiled.

By early afternoon I can keep my eyes open and see. I hear the Sherpas dismantle tents and pack them away. As the hours pass, the noises outside diminish and the mountain is returned back to nature.

"I was on the radio to Base Camp," Angel says. "I wanted the ER doctor to examine your foot as soon as you arrive. Unfortunately they'll be closed by the time we get back. But you have an appointment with them first thing tomorrow at seven."

"Thanks. We'll see what the damage is."

"We'll set out at five. Your eyes should be able to take the sun behind shades."

I examine my toes. They don't look too bad. But it's clear from Angel's concern that the damage, while confined to a small area, is severe. I keep my feet warm and wiggle them to encourage blood flow. I think back to the few hours I spent in Camp 4 without oxygen. That will have done a lot of harm. I can't figure out why I didn't get a tank when I left the tent to get a gas canister from Greg. That was a bad mistake.

We start packing at 4pm. It's warm, but the temperature will plunge by the time we move through the Icefall. I'll have what I need close to hand.

"You said your shades are broken?"

"Yeah, they snapped near the summit. I've got goggles."

"Let me see them."

I hand them over.

"These are too bright. The yellow tint won't block out the light." He rummages in his pack. "Here, try these. These are my spare shades." He places them over my eyes.

"Perfect. Thanks. That's dark."

"Now put these over them." He hands me his black goggles.

"Who turned the lights out? I can't see a thing."

"Excellent. That's what you'll wear outside till night time."

I drag my pack outside. Our camp has been reduced to this single tent and a few pieces of equipment. The Sherpas are long gone.

"The arrangement is that we've to carry whatever's left down to Camp 1," Angel says. "There's a pile of gear down there. Some Sherpas will bring it all to Base Camp tomorrow. Give me a hand with this tent."

"Ok, I'll go this side."

We fold it into its stuff-sack. Angel straps it to his already enormous pack. We divide the remaining equipment between us. I tie his sleeping mat to the side of my pack; there's no more space in, or on the edges, of his. I heave the bulky weight onto my back. Angel, who always carries a large load, is dwarfed by his cargo.

At 5pm we set out on the final chapter. Everest stands to my right. I have climbed it. I cannot think of any reason why I will return. I cannot ascend any higher. Even if it were possible, I'm not sure I'd be able. With every trip here a climber pushes his luck. I must tackle half a dozen more hours in the belly of the beast before I can be counted as one of the fortunate ones. Laden down by our packs, we trek out, leaving just rocks and snow behind us.

The weight of our loads demands concentration and effort through the scree, but I know every step down is a pace into thicker air. Angel drops off the oxygen tank that he borrowed earlier. I've no idea who gave it to us, but I suspect I'll benefit from its few hours of use in the recovery months ahead. My mind keeps returning to the frostbite, but I must postpone such thoughts until we make it to Base Camp. A handful of toes will be neither here nor there if something goes wrong in an upcoming crevasse or in the Icefall.

We descend a hundred metres to the edge of the rocks and attach our crampons. We press out onto the Western Cwm glacier. The weight and bulk of Angel's load exaggerate every move he makes.

Angel Hikes down the Glacier

We have the windless glacier to ourselves. I only hear our footsteps crunching the snow. The sun has not yet dipped behind Nuptse. The valley, through a double set of shades and goggles, looks stunning under the deep, blue sky. Snow blindness has shattered my eyes, but I can see enough to appreciate the beauty of this gorge as it basks in the late afternoon sun.

This is the first time I notice how spectacular it is. Every other hike through challenged me. I strove to reach the day's target; I was on a mission. So often I hear it's all about the journey, rather than the destination. Perhaps that's true, or maybe that's too easy an excuse when we fall short of our ambitions. But I know why I came here. It was not for the journey. The destination was the draw.

On April 1st, the menu listed two rough months, and that's what's been served. Now, out the far side of it and with the accomplishment sinking in, I can stop to smell the roses. I come to a halt, turn three-sixty degrees, and breathe in the vista. White surrounds me. On two sides, the Nuptse Ridge and Western Shoulder soar up towards the sky. Under my boots sleeps one of the most famous glaciers in the world. At its head looms the daunting Lhotse Face. It taunted and scared me just a month ago. I never really expected to climb it, let alone to then tackle the romantic sounding Geneva Spur. For much of the adventure I didn't know what form that outcrop would take, just that it was an obstacle between the bottom and the top, one of nature's many hurdles. But I no longer see impediments. I see beauty. I see stunning, enormous creations. I marvel at millennia of tectonic movements that keep pushing this point higher. This is the Himalayas. This is the great outdoors. It has stood here for weeks in front of me, and now, finally, I see it. I pause. I will never view this again. I bid it adieu.

We descend the moderate slope towards Camp 1. Angel stumbles and falls forward. The pack gives him no chance of recovery. He's lying on the snow cursing. A fall like that in crampons could be nasty. He hauls himself up with my help, still swearing. By jovial Angel's standards, he's in foul humour. I don't think it's just the fall; I think he's annoyed about something else. He's gone above and beyond the call of duty looking after me this afternoon, even if it is the job he signed up for. But I'm not sure he should help an injured climber off the mountain and carry such a load at the same time. He committed to be a guide; he didn't register as a concurrent porter. I'm not sure if that's what's eating him. Maybe he's just fed up saving my ass. But this is neither the time nor the place for the discussion. He dusts himself off, and we continue.

A little over an hour after leaving Camp 2, we see the first target of our last day on this mountain.

"There's hardly anything left," I say.

"Yeah, everyone's clearing off the mountain. That's our gear there." Angel points to a pile of equipment. "Let's drop the stuff beside it, and take a few minutes."

I chew on a bar and take a few slugs from my bottle.

"That sun's disappearing. It's got cold all of a sudden. I'll put on my warm stuff here. There's no point in waiting," I say.

"That makes sense. How are those eyes?"

"They sting like a bitch, but I can see. Let me try without the goggles." I take them off. "Yeah, that works. I'll leave on the shades till it's dark."

I tighten up the fleece zip to my neck and then attach the head torch to my helmet.

We stride towards the Icefall. The lighter load frees Angel. We reach the fixed rope and negotiate the crevasses that act as a warm up to the monster ravines and ice boulders that loom ahead. When I first saw these obstacles over a month ago, they struck me as foreign features, not from the world in which I lived. But I now recognise each one of them. I notice where they've changed. I spot where the ice has moved. I can identify where a succession of climbers over five weeks has altered the landscape. I can distinguish where the ice doctors have reassessed the placement of a rope or ladder, and repositioned it to a safer location. The moving glacier has warped several aluminium legs; they're no match for nature's power. Every day it moves. Each day these ladders bend. I don't care that it shifts today, just as long as it doesn't do so tonight.

"Do you recognise that smell?" Angel stops walking.

I breathe in. I catch something but can't place it. I sniff in again and try to categorise the odour that surrounds us. It's not something I've smelt before.

"I get something. What is it?"

He points to a small pile of equipment fifteen metres away. On its fringe lies a parcel, two metres long, thirty centimetres high, and half a metre wide.

"A body," Angel says. "I think it's a climber who died some time ago, maybe two years back. Sherpas are carrying him down."

"How can a corpse smell after two years?"

"Most likely the body was down a crevasse, out of the sun."

"But even still?"

"Now, under the sun, the gases are released. It's no different than if you'd a piece of fish in the freezer for two years. You take it out and put it on the window sill. Same thing."

On top of the many new experiences this adventure has gifted me, I can now add another item to the list: the smell of death.

Daylight has slipped away. We're standing at the edge of the colossal crevasse that marks the start of the Icefall. I take off the shades, no longer troubled by the sun's rays. The pain has waned. The darkness of the night will help my eyes further. In the distance, and six hundred metres below, the lights of Base Camp glimmer.

Head torches on, we stare down into the final challenge of the expedition. This last stretch lies between us and success.

"Fergus, on the steep sections, walk with your left foot sideways. You don't want to bang those toes against the front of the boots."

"Thanks, I'll do that."

With that in mind, there's nothing more to be gained by considering what lies ahead. It's time for action. We clip ourselves in, turn around, and abseil over the edge, into the blackness of the Icefall's biggest crevasse.

Silence surrounds us. We concentrate on what we must do to descend in safety. The narrow beam of our head torches confines our focus. Outside the shaft of light lie the Himalayas, odd shaped forms of ice and snow, and a starry sky above. We progress from rope to rope. Every step down carries us closer to home.

We've put the difficult upper section behind us and continue our steady progress. A crevasse, which had two ladders tied together across it a fortnight ago, has widened. The ice doctors have been busy, and we're now challenged by four ladders, bound as one, to bridge it. It'll make for a fabulous photograph with a flash bulb. Four ladders straining and bulging downwards under the weight of a climber, the unknown darkness gaping below him, alien ice forms as the backdrop. But this is not the time for frolics. Angel has waited all day at Camp 2 to protect my eyes. He put me on oxygen to save my toes. I lug a heavy load, he a heavier one. Whatever energies I've left I'll direct into exiting here as quickly and safely as possible, so we're both out of danger.

We overcome twists, turns, and crevasses. Angel, ever the professional, insists on clipping into two ropes while crossing the ladders. I only do so when he's looking. Otherwise I just clip into a single rope to keep our speed up and save energy. On the regular sections he always clips in. Moving behind him, I often just run a gloved hand along the line, in a less safe habit I picked up from Hugo. Bending down to a connection point under a heavy load breaks momentum. Unless a section looks very dangerous, I take my chances that I won't slip, nor the glacier shift.

Half the challenge remains. The extra oxygen boosts me. I've hit my left toes off the inside of the boot a few times, but Angel's tip has kept it to a minimum.

I think he's tiring. He's suffered his own health problems in the tummy department, but he put his personal requirements second to those of the team. Crossing a ladder, a rope tangles in my pack and dislodges his sleeping mat that I'm carrying. Once safe, I take off the pack and mat to retie it. I've confused Angel. I think he presumes I'm just dumping his mat and refusing to take it. He tries to add it to his pack. It takes a few moments to explain that everything is cool.

We attack the last three hundred metres of altitude. Over the night sky floats music and the sound of high spirits. Celebrations will have surged for the last twenty-four hours as climbers arrived back, flushed with success. Some of those echoes must emanate from our tents. Angel talks into the radio to inform them of our progress.

"Fergus, two Sherpas are on the way up. They've got food and a flask of tea for us."

"Great stuff."

"We should meet them below somewhere. We'll stop for a break when we do."

The thought of imminent grub and copious fluid lifts me. But with no danger of hunger or dehydration and so close to home, I'm bewildered why Ted is sending up this Sherpa party now. Plenty of times over this last fortnight we were slammed by a lack of such basics. If Sherpas are available, he could at least have arranged for one to clear out Camp 2, rather than force a tent onto Angel's crammed back.

I should come face to face with Ted in about an hour and a half. I've better things to do than get into a petty argument and listen to excuses. As resolved in Camp 4 on the night of our bungled attempt: we made it to the top, we got back down, end of story. I gave Ted my constructive criticism six months ago; the less said about such matters from now on the better. I hope I can keep my mouth shut.

We climb down, peering into the darkness for the glow of a head torch that promises food and hot tea. We round ice formation after ice boulder and still nothing. Rope after rope is left behind us, each one for the last time, and still no sign of the Sherpas. And then as we round a chunk, we see a glimmer of light just twenty metres below. We link up.

We're sitting on a snow ledge, with Penba and young Deshi from the kitchen.

"Thanks guys," Angel says.

"It took a lot of effort to get up here, lads. Thanks." I loosen my pack.

"Here you go." Deshi hands us a mug each. "Keep steady." He tilts the flask.

As we gulp back lemon tea, he places food on two plates.

"No way, is that chicken?" I ask.

"And potatoes? And vegetables?" Angel takes a plate.

We lean back against the glacier and relish the taste of real food, real meat. Deshi refills our mugs. Few people relax for a picnic in places as dangerous as this. As we're sated, conversation increases. More grub is added to our plates. Penba has suffered no ill effects from his extended stay on the mountain ten days ago. That was the last time I saw him.

"More potatoes?" Deshi asks.

"No, I'm done. Thanks man. That was good."

"Ok, let's pack up, guys, and get ready to move," Angel says.

"That liquid and food will make a difference. Less than an hour from here, Angel?"

"I reckon so."

The four of us stand up and push down into the night. The passage becomes less challenging, at least compared to the previous two hours. A moment I'd envisaged so often while trying to fall asleep in my tent arrives. I always presumed I'd be in Greg's company when it occurred. He's not here, but against all odds, the two of us made it to the top and back. Barring the absolute unexpected, success can now be registered. Below this point the ice doctors saw no danger; I stand at the end of the fixed rope.

We walk the last twenty minutes into Base Camp, up and over the ridges that hide it from view until it's almost upon us. The ice turns to snow, and then to rocks and water. Sometime after 10:30pm I crouch down for the final time and unstrap my crampons. Penba insists on carrying them in the last fifty metres.

I've sailed pretty close to the wind these past few weeks, sometimes on the wrong side of it. But now my secret millstone can drop away: that my shortcomings might drag a conscientious climber or Sherpa into jeopardy. However, this is not the way I'd dreamed our return. I know I've injured my left foot. I can't celebrate when there's a good chance I've inflicted permanent damage. While I knew the chances of making it to the top of Everest were less then fifty-fifty, I'd imagined what arriving back successful might look like. I'd pictured a beer at the edge of camp. I'd seen a big smile on my face. I'd envisioned a hearty handshake with Greg, perhaps even a big bear hug. I'd considered dipping my bare feet into the icy stream that I'm now crossing. I'd even thought of stripping right down and jumping in, a moment of unbridled festivity and madness. But it's not to be. I cannot allow myself any sort of festivity; there may be trouble ahead.

We walk into the bright mess tent.

"Fergus, Fergus, congratulations, well done." The boisterous and lovable Finns jump to their feet.

I've not seen them since our sojourn at Pheriche. Half-empty vodka bottles litter the table.

"Well done, buddy," Greg says.

"Congratulations." Ted shakes my hand. "You'll have a drink."

"Best to skip that for now." I drop into a chair at the rear of the tent, next to the heater.

"I'll try a slice of that cake though, and a mug of tea."

Questions fire at me from all angles. Angel relaxes in a chair on my right. I pour another cup of tea amid the high spirits.

"Bring in a basin of warm water." Ted turns to a Sherpa. "Not too hot."

"Ok, Fergus, let's have a look at those feet." Ted pulls up a chair beside me.

The conversation around the table stops.

"I'll do the right first. It should be ok." I untie the boot.

Ted holds the foot in his hand. The big toe and next one are blackened.

"They'll recover. There'll be some pain. Ok, let's see the other one."

A Sherpa places a basin of water on the ground beside me. Ted dips his hand in it. He adds a touch of cold liquid. No one speaks. I slide off the left sock. Ted kneels down. He's holding the foot with both hands. All five toes are a mixture of light black and grey. I feel little pain.

"I hope summiting was worth losing your toes for," he says.

I look down, presuming he's kidding. No one knows what to say. The Finns lower their drinks.

"The top of the middle toe will be lost, probably the top of the big toe. The tips of some of the others may be lost also."

I struggle to take this in.

"The grey at the top of the middle toe indicates dead flesh."

Angel leans forward to look.

"The black isn't too bad. It shows the flesh is alive. It's trying to recover," he says.

Blood is not flowing to the grey areas. Without oxygen or heat reaching them, they're as good as gone. The prognosis slays me. It's a lot to take on board. The trade-off, of aims achieved versus disfigurement received, is not a debate I wish to consider right now. Making it to the summit is a hollow victory.

Success is meaningless without a risk of failure. I knew the hazard of injury was a constant companion on a venture such as this. But I'd banked on something mendable like a broken leg. Losing a body part for good, however tiny, feels very personal. The thought of asking a surgeon to cut off a piece for ever sickens me to my core. The night's elation in the tent has been killed.

"Don't give up, Fergus," one of the Finns says. "Nothing lost yet."

"Heat, oxygen, rest. You never know. Stay positive," another Finnish voice says.

Greg seems unsure what to say. My toes have deteriorated since he saw them yesterday. Angel examines the foot.

"I've seen worse recover," Angel says. "Many of these toes can be saved. But there'll be a lot of pain as the blood flows back in. Once you fly to Dublin, you need to go to Spain. The best frostbite clinic is there."

I nod my head.

"In Kathmandu, go to Ciwec Clinic. They're very experienced with frostbite. They'll help."

For twenty minutes I sit with my left foot in the basin. Every now and then, Ted adds a little hot water to bring the temperature back up. I don't wish to take everyone down from their exuberance.

One of the Finns made it to the top of Everest. The two who'd tried to summit Lhotse turned back several hundred metres below the endpoint. Ropes, which they'd expected to be fixed in advance, were not there. Discretion was judged the better part of valour. I'm astonished they got as far as they did; I could never have survived this altitude with a hangover. Not reaching the peak has not diminished their enthusiasm, and they're busy devising the next adventure. If someone doesn't write it down, the finer details may be lost in the ensuing bottle of vodka.

As of now, nothing else can be done for my foot, other than keep it as warm as possible. The appointment at 7am tomorrow in Everest ER will reveal more. Ted fetches my booties from my tent, so I don't have to put my feet back into freezing boots. A few heat packs are rustled up. They don't work higher up as they can't activate in the thin air. But here at 5,350 metres I'll get a benefit from them. I bid the lads goodnight and hobble to the tent with Ted. Good wishes follow me out of the mess, with encouragements to stay snug and reminders that all is not lost.

I crawl into my tent. Two weeks of glacier movement has dropped its height and width. It feels more like a coffin than a tent.

"I'll be back at six forty, and we'll walk over to ER," Ted says. "Keep the foot warm till then."

"Ok. Night."

He pulls down the outer zip. I'm on my own.

I'm wearing the same clothes I've had on for days. I've packed two heat packs into the left bootie and can feel their warmth. A hot bottle lies in my bag near my ankles. Despite the subzero temperatures, this'll be the warmest night for me in over two weeks.

The full weight of what has happened lands on me. In this thicker air, my mind becomes sharper. It does not like what it finds. Lying in the dark, I go over and over the events of the last few days. I keep returning to the prospect of presenting myself at a surgeon's office in Dublin next month, to have the tops of two toes cut off. I consider if this was an adventure too far. I try to balance the achievement of climbing Everest against a permanent injury.

I never intended to live forever, or to be the healthiest corpse in the graveyard, but I know I've made a mistake. Parts of toes will be lost. I've never been overly bothered about my toes, nobody is, but I now feel like a damn fool having caused the loss of them. Neither the nights at Camp 4, nor the illness down the valley, or the sleepless, headache-filled darkness on this mountain compete with the depths of my despondency now.

Hours of blackness pass. My mind will not let me sleep; it torments me. The accomplishment of summiting is buried somewhere within me. It cannot be taken away. But it has come at a price, a very personal price.

My watch reads 3:30am. What will the doctor say tomorrow? I'll have to grin and bear it, and take the future as it comes.

MAY 26

Last Day at Base Camp

awn has broken, and I'm preparing myself. On cue at 6:40am, I hear footsteps outside.

"You up, Fergus?" Ted draws open the outer zip.

"Yeah."

"Let's have a look at that foot before we go." He crawls in just past the entrance. "Just for a few seconds, keep it warm."

I slip off the bootie and sock. Half sitting, half lying in the slumped tent, I can't see my foot. Ted touches the end of it.

"Yes." He touches another toe. "Yes, they're warm. They look the same as last night, but they're generating heat. It's not just the heat packs. The toes themselves are warm, even the middle one. It's not cold. There must be some blood flowing."

My spirits soar on this prognosis.

"This is better than I expected. Wrap them up. Let's see what the doctor says."

I hobble the few hundred metres to ER, supported by a trekking pole. I'm wearing a thick sock, bootie, and a soft over-boot on my left foot. It offers no grip or protection on the rocky trail. If I stub my toes on a stone, there may be no pain, but that doesn't mean there won't be damage.

The doctor is waiting for us.

"Come in, gents. Take a seat there. It's frostbite, isn't it? You made it to the summit?"

"Yes."

"Well done." He shakes my hand.

"I had a quick look this morning. There's some life there," Ted says.

I sit on the patient's bed. The doctor drags over a gas heater and positions it by my left knee. He sits on a chair in front of me.

"Ok, let's have a look."

I strip down the layers and leave the foot exposed to his expert eye. He holds it for a few moments.

"Is that it?" he asks.

"What? I-" I fall silent.

I look at him. I fear I've misunderstood. I read his face. He looks genuine.

"It's ok?" I ask.

"Frostbite damage for sure. But this will recover."

Worry, fear, the shame of losing a small body part flows out of my body. Now I can enjoy the achievement. A smile creeps over my face.

"I'll clean the foot and then rub aloe vera cream on it." He walks to the medicine counter. "That'll help the skin. Then I'll put a dressing on it."

As he gathers what he needs and tends to my foot, we discuss the season ER has had. Many patients have had less serious injuries than me, but for a few, there's been a high price to pay.

One climber spent a night just below Camp 4, too exhausted to cover the last hundred metres. He slept without a tent or bag. Confused and probably suffering HACE, he lost his right mitt. He was assisted down the next day. He suffered severe frostbite to his hands and ears. He was helicoptered out from ER. Amputation of fingers on the right hand is expected.

An exhausted mountaineer stopped at the Balcony while ascending. He waited five or six hours as his teammates summited. He could have descended; the route back to Camp 4 is roped. Angel performed a similar feat at the Balcony, but he bit the bullet to ensure no man was left behind. The halt has extracted a heavy penalty. Most of the climber's toes and one finger will be lost.

Danish climber Tom Jørgensen got HACE on the north side in Tibet. He was descending to safety when his condition worsened. Despite rescue efforts, he could not be saved. He died on the 19th.

Japanese climber Hiroshi Ogasawara died at camp 3 on the north side after summiting. The details have not yet arrived.

While I lay awake in my tent in the early hours this morning contemplating my injury, I was one of the lucky ones. Others suffered a long night of desperation and frostbite to save an injured climber. Scotsman Peter Kinloch summited Everest yesterday about 1pm. Blindness struck him on the descent, and his condition then deteriorated. Sherpas ascended to assist his teammates with the rescue. Eventually, the harsh night-time weather threatened the lives of all who remained on the mountain. There are reports of extreme frostbite. Those involved were unsuccessful. Last night was the Scotsman's final night. He rests in an icy grave.

A ladder across a crevasse, at the top of the Icefall, collapsed yesterday while a Sherpa carried a load over it. He fell thirty metres and broke several ribs. A female climber also fell; it's presumed the two accidents were linked. ER received a message that her head was bleeding, she was vomiting blood, and could not use one of her legs. Several hours later, and with assistance, the Sherpa descended to Base Camp. The woman is thought to have suffered a broken hand, broken knee, broken back bones, and facial injuries.

Also yesterday, a climber with severe frostbite presented himself at ER. His oxygen flow had ceased on the mountain. A Sherpa found him and got it restarted, but the mask may have been silent for thirty minutes. The man only remembers the incident from that time forward, at which point he noticed he was missing a mitt. It's expected he'll lose several fingers. He refused the helicopter option and is trekking back to Lukla.

At the same time, another drama unfolded near the Balcony. A mountaineer became irrational and combative. He refused help and had to be dragged down. Several climbers and Sherpas assisted. They gave him dexamethasone and encouraged him to take oxygen. Even at the base of the Lhotse Face, he insisted they were trying to poison him with argon gas. A helicopter evacuation was planned for Camp 2, but I'm not sure if this took place.

I'm the second from our team to sit here in as many days. Ade, whom I last saw as he set out alone to descend from Camp 4, has withstood a harrowing episode. On the night of the summit push, he had to retreat as his throat's swelling restricted his breathing. That condition did not improve, probably worsened, on the two day slog back to Base Camp. By the time he arrived, he had to walk with his head pointing upwards to keep a clear passage open in his throat. He spent just ten minutes at his tent, to drop off equipment, before presenting to ER. His speech was limited. They were appalled by the gravity of his ailment and set about treating him straight away.

He'd suffered an airway obstruction due to swelling and accumulation of dried secretions. It's common up here, as the fast breathing of cold, dry air damages the airway tissues. Dehydration further dries the tracheal emissions. A few nights ago at Camp 2, the same affliction almost killed a woman. ER pumped Ade with medicine, pain killers, and hot water to open his throat. They kept him under observation here for about three hours, in case an intervention was required. He moved out of danger, and they released him. But they're still concerned for his recovery.

ER received almost four hundred and fifty patients. Nineteen were evacuated by helicopter, or otherwise carried or assisted out of Base Camp. While people presented with all manner of problems, the following groupings were recorded:

> High altitude pulmonary edema (HAPE): 8
> High altitude cerebral edema (HACE): 3
> Frostbite: 17
> Urinary tract infection: 29
> Bladder and / or kidney infection: 7
> Acute mountain sickness: 5

Perirectal abscess: 2
Asthmatic bronchitis: 5
Bronchitis: 19
High altitude cough: 66
Cough: 17
Dehydration: 3
Diarrhoea: 19
Gastritis: 25
Headache: 8
Haemorrhoids: 5
Laryngitis / Pharyngitis / Tonsillitis: 29
Insomnia and periodic breathing: 7
Palpitations: 2
Sinusitis: 9

I made my contribution to those numbers.

"Take Ibuprofen for the foot." The doctor sits back up in his chair.

"I have loads." I look at the dressing on my foot.

"And if the pain gets too much, take these." He places a plastic bag containing a few tablets into my hand. "There'll be a lot of pain as the recovery starts."

"I don't mind that."

"Keep the rest of this aloe vera and apply it." He hands me a small plastic bottle. "And here's a clean bandage. Replace the dressing tomorrow."

"Ok. Can I walk out of the valley?"

"No problem."

I feel like Lazarus. For all this good news and treatment, he charges me twenty US dollars. He could have hit me for twenty thousand.

"Will you need a receipt?" he asks.

I'm hobbling out of ER with ten toes.

"I think we can skip the paperwork this time." I smile to him. "One last thing, can I have a beer tonight?"

"As many as you want."

I limp back to camp with Ted. I feel great. It is done. I have climbed Everest and returned in one piece.

"Ted, I know he said I can walk, but the boulders from here to Lobuche, I'll bash my toes for sure. There're a few places where you have to jump. And there's loose rock underfoot. Should I risk that?"

"A horse might be better. I'll see if I can arrange one down to Pheriche. It'll be five hundred dollars."

"It is what it is. I can't see any way I could walk out of here without doing more damage."

"It might be tomorrow before I can get a horse. It certainly won't be early today."

"Whatever can be arranged, I'll take it."

We reach the edge of camp.

"Can you believe that?" Ted asks.

"That's the first one I've seen up here," I say.

A battered old mule, with a light load, stands metres from us.

"Keep going, Fergus. I'll see if I can find the owner and strike a deal."

Back at camp I share the good news with Greg. Sitting in the mess tent, enjoying a breakfast of muesli, yogurt, and tea, we discuss the events of the last two months. The yogurt adds unexpected flavour, and the grub slides down. Everything is going my way.

"Hey Fergus." Ted steps into the tent. "That horse will take you down to Pheriche."

"Brilliant. Thanks."

"Ok," Greg says. "Let's get our tents down, and be out of here in an hour. Another mug?"

"Please. Pour away. I can't wait for Pheriche. A decent bed and a beer."

I'm sitting on a rock, just in front of my tent, packing my gear. The injury limits my movement, and I'm aware that my bandaged foot is susceptible to damage. My celebratory shower at Base Camp, to wash away the summit push, must be foregone. I'll carry two weeks of toil and sweat to Pheriche and rinse it off there. But a set of clean underclothes for the trip down makes me feel more human, and prepares me for integration back into civilisation. Whatever I need for the three day trek back to Lukla goes into the backpack. I keep it as light as possible. I shove the remainder into my two duffle bags, which will be transported by yak later this morning.

Ted shouts over to a Sherpa to give me a hand to take down my tent. In less than ten minutes, two of them have stuffed it into its sack.

Greg has packed away his tent. He's squeezing the last few items into his duffle bag. Ten metres away, Angel's backside pokes out of his shelter, gear everywhere. It'll be another hour or two before he's ready to move.

I see clouds over the valley. I'll be stationary on the horse today and will take no chances. I zip up my down jacket. Insulated pants cover my legs. On my left foot, I'm wearing a bootie plus two soft over-boots (the left and the right). I've packed fresh heat packs around the ankle. Goggles are at the ready, and my gloves are already on.

With the duffle bags ready for transportation, and the pack over my shoulder, I limp to the mess tent where my chariot is being prepared. This old mule has seen better days. A Sherpa adjusts a saddle. Old rope has been knotted to the reins. Twenty minutes pass as modifications are made.

As I wait for the mule to be readied, I'm told the story of the last person who left here by horse. Two weeks ago, trekkers stayed at our camp. One of them was struck with altitude sickness. It was determined that she should descend several hundred metres by horse to safety. On the way down, her stead reared up. She was thrown off, landing on her face. Her injuries necessitated helicopter evacuation to a hospital in Kathmandu.

"Let's get moving," Greg says, about 10am.

I mount the mule. I think he's unimpressed by my presence. I place my feet into the stirrups.

"No, no." Deshi, from the kitchen, rushes over. "Do not put your feet there. Best to get thrown clear."

Greg throws his pack on his back. We say our goodbyes to the Sherpas.

"I'll see you guys in Kathmandu in a few days," Ted says.

"I'll follow you down to Pheriche in a while." Angel waves from his tent.

A young boy takes the reins. He leads the mule out onto the rocky trail. I take a last look back to the colourful tents, to Nuptse, and to the Icefall. The summit is already hidden from view.

Every hundred metres, the mule stops and kicks up a storm. The boy shouts at him, tugs on the reins, and threatens violence, before we restart. Trekkers pass against us. I'm ashamed to sit on this stationary animal that's fit for the knacker's yard. We've not even passed all the tents of the other teams.

"I'll have to go on, or I'll get cold," Greg says.

"No worries. We won't be far behind."

Within minutes, he has disappeared.

For two to three hours, the sequence of stopping, tugging, pushing, and shouting repeats itself. We've made pitiful progress. This is more dangerous that what we did on the mountain. I'm astounded Ted put an older lady on such an animal. On the steep, uneven downhill sections, the horse's head is far below me. It's all I can do to hold onto the saddle and not get thrown forward as the animal lunges for a rock lower down. I might not be using my legs, but my upper body is working overtime to keep me in the saddle. One hand grasps the front of it, while the other clenches its rear. I return to my bubble. I presume I will eventually make it to Pheriche.

My mind drifts to the thirteen year old American who'd set out from Base Camp on the north side. What was I doing when I was his age? Word on the mountain is that the Chinese authorities, who control Tibet, will now copy Nepal, and ban under-sixteens from attempting to summit. It can never be tried again. Records are made to be broken, but perhaps this one will stand the test of time. Jordan Romero, at thirteen years and ten months, has walked off the mountain. Four days ago he achieved the impossible, and stood atop it.

Halfway between Gorak Shep and Lobuche, a local man with a horse meets us coming in the opposite direction. A short negotiation ensues, and I'm informed that I'm to switch rides. I think the boy has realised we'll never make it to Pheriche at this rate. The new, bigger horse has a lot more interest in the task. The local knows how to handle his steed, and there's no more stopping and starting.

The sky has clouded over. The temperature has dropped and a light snow falls. Sitting stationary in snow is about the worst thing I could be doing right now. It's mid-afternoon, and my patience has worn thin, but I know it's not the fault of the two locals.

We reach the graveyard. I'm apprehensive as to how the horse will descend a two hundred and fifty metre drop through boulders, with me on his back. Just before the crest of the hill, he stops and will not budge. He cannot see the incline but seems to know what waits ahead. He's given the rough end of a stick. I hang on to the roller coaster.

With the second most risky descent of my life behind me, we reach the green fields that separate us from tonight's lodgings.

Another hour brings us to the edge of Pheriche. I relish the extra oxygen, the green colours, and the sight of basic civilisation. But my focus is on dismounting this animal and warming up by the hostel's stove. At 5pm, seven hours after leaving Base Camp, I shuffle into the hostel.

"You made it. I heard you reached the summit. Congratulations." The owner stares down at my footwear. "Oh dear. A problem?"

"Small problem. A little frostbite, but I'll recover."

"Painful?"

"A little. There's much more to come I'm told."

"A speedy recovery to you, sir. Let me take your bag."

"Thanks."

Over in the far corner sits Greg, all smiles, enjoying food and a beer. Khalid and the crazy Finns fill the table. Glasses are raised as I limp over.

"How'd it go?" Greg asks. "I've been here for hours."

"Don't talk to me about that damn horse."

"Fergus, we hear great news on your foot. Fabulous." One of the Finns rises and holds up his arms.

"Great news. Success." Another Finn lifts up his glass. "A drink."

"I'll hold that off for a few minutes, lads. I best get this foot warmed up."

I know the stove in the centre of the room is not the place to dry off gear, but I'm in no mood to compromise. I pull up a stool, whip off my footwear, and hold my feet to within centimetres of it. Within ten minutes I can feel the heat and life return to them. Sitting still in the cold and snow for seven hours was not what the doctor ordered. His words this morning were nothing short of miraculous. But as with all miracles, I have to keep my side of the deal.

Young Kieron approaches me.

"Sorry about this, I've got to keep it warm." I point to the bandaged foot.

"No problem. Frostbite?"

"Yeah."

"Get well quick. Can I get you anything?"

"I'll need a room in five minutes. And once I'm settled, I'll have a few more orders." I indicate to the bar.

Kieron shows me to a bedroom. He gives me the first one in the corridor, to lessen the distance from the main room. It has a double bed and an en suite toilet.

"Thanks Kieron. This is perfect. Appreciated."

"My pleasure." He places my pack at the end of the bed. "You need hot water for shower?"

"There's no point in wrecking the bandage. I'll wait till tomorrow. I can put on a fresh one after the shower."

Back in the main room, I'm standing in front of the beverage selection.

"That bottle of red there, please Kieron, and a few glasses."

Hands full, I return to the lads and place the reward on an already full table. The Finns let out a cheer as the cork is liberated.

Laughs and tales follow each other in quick succession. Some of us are men who've summited Everest; some are not, it matters not a whit. Excluding Sherpas, just over a hundred and sixty climbers reached the top from the south side this season. The Finns inform us that the Nordic woman, Anne-Mari, touched the summit the same morning that we stood there. Whether setting out from Nepal or Tibet, and including all nationalities, over three thousand one hundred people have now stood at the peak. Glasses are charged. Glasses are emptied. Angel joins us after dark. Kieron brings forth more beer. Future plans of epic proportions are traced out on the table. Food, good food, fills our bellies.

As the drink flows, the banter increases. The other patrons have retired by 10pm. The Finns bribe Kieron, with a few cans of Red Bull, to keep the bar open. I stay till the end with them. I have nothing more to prove, just good times to be enjoyed. I will sleep tonight.

MAY 27

Out of the Himalayas

"That was a great sleep." I lift a mug of coffee to my lips.

"How's the foot?" Greg asks.

"No problem. A big cosy bed and the extra oxygen probably did a world of good. I had the booties on and a heat pack in the left one. I didn't look at them; there's no point in letting cold air at them. I presume the toes were warm inside the bandage."

"That's good news." Angel arrives at the table.

"This breakfast will help too. It's nice to have some decent food," I say. "We'll head to Namche today?"

"Yeah," Greg says, "within the hour. Khalid has already left."

"Early to bed, early to rise." I dig my fork back into the plate. "I'll grab a shower in a few minutes, be the first one for two weeks."

"Are you going to change the dressing?" Greg asks.

"Yeah, I'll do the iodine rinse on the foot after the shower. Then I'll put on the new bandage. You might give me a hand with that?"

"Sure. Just shout when you're ready."

"Thanks." I glance at my watch. "We should be out of here by ten thirty."

"Fergus, the shower is ready." Kieron arrives at the table.

"Thanks buddy. Greg, I'll give you a shout in ten minutes."

Sitting on a plastic chair beside the shower, I take off the right sock. The big toe and toe next to it have swelled up and are black. I feel no pain, but the appearance surprises me. They look worse than I expected.

I begin unwrapping the bandage from the left foot. It doesn't look as fresh as when the doctor applied it; this concerns me. A drop of liquid lands on the tiled floor. My anxiety increases. I unwind the last of the dressing. The sight shocks me. The end of my left foot bears no resemblance to when it was examined. It's the creation of a Hollywood special effects department. The digits have swollen so much as to be not recognisable as toes. Black covers all five. Huge blisters have formed. Fluid oozes from several. The big toe has grown to twice its normal size. The nail, by comparison, is dwarfed by the surrounded, bulging black flesh. After yesterday's prognosis, this vision thumps me.

"Greg! I need you."

He steps in onto the tiles.

"Good God." He stares at the spectacle. "I'll get Angel."

The two of them examine the foot.

"Just take a shower and wrap it up as planned?" I ask.

Greg looks at the shower.

"No. A shower is out. With so many open blisters, the risk of infection is too high."

"Ok."

"Can you walk on that?" Greg asks.

"Well, I got down the mountain, but this is entirely different. This is a mess."

All three of us look at the foot.

"This is some frostbite. I should document it. Do you mind if a get my video camera." Angel walks away.

"The trail's covered in yak dung dust," I say. "Two days walking on that could cause a problem. I mean, if you're saying I can't even step into the shower tray over there."

"If that gets infected, you'll lose toes," Greg says.

"I want to get out of here with ten toes. I don't care what it takes." I look down at the foot. "How on earth did that happen?"

"If it gets infected, it could be more than just toes." Greg puts a hand on my shoulder.

"That foot won't even fit in my boot. Walking out of this valley isn't an option. Damn." My head drops into my hands. "Sitting on a horse for another two days might also trash the foot. Look what happened yesterday. And then I might have to sit in Lukla for a day or two waiting for a plane."

"That needs medical care," Greg says. "You need heat and oxygen, lots of it. Let me drop into HRA next door. I'll bring back the doctor."

I fold my arms and stare at it.

Greg walks back in.

"No joy. They're already closed for the season. There's a sign on the door."

"Closed? Sure it's only now that the real injuries are stumbling out of Base Camp. Ok. What now?"

"It's up to you. Maybe you should get a helicopter. If you walk out, you risk losing the foot."

"Decision made. Chopper it is. That'd be a foolish way to lose a foot."

338

"It'll be about five thousand dollars. Will your insurance cover it?"

"That's another day's problem."

Three months ago, I was amazed to be quoted a premium of just a hundred and fifteen US dollars. It covers me for two and a half months in the wild, including a shot at one of the most dangerous places on the planet. The nature of the challenge placed me in harm's way from the moment I stepped off the plane. But the paperwork buried somewhere in my duffle bag suggests that coverage will now kick in. In theory, I can suffer all manner of illness, amputation, emergency medical evacuation, and death, and not worry about the financial side up to a quarter of a million US dollars. Somewhere on the far side of this globe, in a tall building very soon, an actuary will puzzle over how that policy was drawn up.

I'm sitting in the chair. Angel videos the foot. Greg provides the medical commentary. He points out the features of the enigma that resides at the end of my leg.

The hostel owner enters the shower room.

"Oh goodness, I did not realise." He takes a step back.

"Nor did I." I look up to him.

"We need to arrange a helicopter," Greg says.

"Of course, he cannot walk on that. Let me make a phone call." He walks out.

I discuss the situation with Greg and Angel. The owner reappears.

"I've been on to my brother-in-law. A chopper can come. It'll be four thousand dollars. They'll need a credit card number."

"Damn, my credit card is in Kathmandu; I didn't think I'd need it. I've got to get out of here."

"Sorry. But you know how many people take needless helicopter lifts. They say the insurance will pay, but they were never injured. The helicopter company cannot operate without payment."

"I've got a card. We can put it on that," Greg says.

"Man, thanks. As soon as I get back to Dublin, I'll transfer those funds to your account in Australia, straight away."

"No rush."

Greg and the owner stroll to the main room to arrange the helicopter and authorise payment. I see Kieron standing just outside the shower room.

"Do you want to have a look?" I beckon him.

"No, no." He shakes his head. "I do not wish to see such a thing."

"Chopper's arranged," Greg says. "There's cloud in the valley; it can't arrive till this evening. If that's not possible, it'll be here tomorrow. However, they also said it may come at any time; so, be ready."

"Cool, sooner the better. You guys will hop in as well?" I look up to Greg and Angel.

"There's room for one other," Greg says.

"If one of you wants to jump in, please do. There's no point in the seat being empty."

"Do you want to fly out with Fergus?" Angel asks.

"Great, saves a walk down the valley," Greg says.

"Ok, I'll leave soon. I'll see you guys in Kathmandu." Angel walks out.

"Ok, that's all sorted. Give me a hand with this bandage. Then I'll pack my stuff, just in case."

Yet again a shower has been stolen from me. I take a few minutes to freshen up at the hand basin. A mirror hangs above it. I stare at my face, the first time I've seen it in two weeks. I'm bewildered by Angel's assertion that my snow-blinded eyes look much better this morning. They look like strawberries. I'm worried to think this is an improvement, but at least the mind-numbing pain has diminished to just an unpleasant irritation. The bridge of my nose has been cut by the oxygen mask and has scabbed over. My cheeks are weather beaten; the atmosphere has cracked them raw. Two months of altitude, poor appetite, and bad food have hollowed them. My hair flops lifeless and unruly. Fissures crisscross the skin on the back of my sore hands. I hope that thick air, rest, heat, and nourishment will reverse the damage.

Greg and I relax at a table.

A man and a woman, late twenties or early thirties, walk into the room. He's good looking. She's very pretty, perhaps a touch slimmer than normal after a week of trekking. The whiteness of her teeth strikes me. Greg shares my weather beaten face and cut nose. His ribs stab him with pain every time he coughs. We make a harsh comparison to the beauty of the two newcomers. We strike up a conversation with them. I'm flabbergasted to learn that they too summited Everest. Greg and I piece together our experiences over the last two months. We compare our present condition to this couple. Greg needs to recuperate near sea level; I'm on my last legs. This pair looks fresh as daisies. What team were they on, and how did they do it?

Kieron rushes to our table.

"The helicopter's on the way."

"What? I've still got to pack a few items." I stand up.

"Get moving," Greg says.

We thank the owner and head outside. Greg walks the hundred metres to the landing spot. I follow behind while Kieron carries my pack.

"Wait in here for a few minutes. It's warmer." Kieron points to a small hostel.

Within five minutes we hear the thumping sound of rotary blades racing up the valley. They echo off the mountains that surround us. We step outside and look to our left. In the distance, just above the ground, a speck grows larger. The dot becomes red. As the noise intensifies, it takes on the shape of a chopper. The blast deafens us as the machine passes just over our heads. The pilot swings it around to face down the valley and then drops it.

With the blades still turning, the pilot throws a few heavy bags of foodstuff onto the ground. He beckons us to come forward. We shake hands with Kieron. Crouched over, protecting our heads, we cover the last ten metres to the powerful, noisy machine. I climb into the front seat. Greg pushes our packs into the rear and sits beside them. Doors shut, the pilot passes us both a headset. He presses controls and the tone of the engine changes. He gives us a thumbs-up. The noise increases; the blades spin faster. The rear of the chopper picks up and we shoot down the valley, just above stone walls.

Two months ago, I arrived into this valley by air in the company of Greg. That is how I now leave. It was a crazy idea I had: to summit Everest because it is there. I was approaching forty. I knew I'd have to slow down sooner rather than later. It was not a realisation I wanted to accept. But I felt that one last effort, a monumental challenge, would allow me to move on with no regrets, to a quieter, less physical life.

As I slumped on the snow below Camp 4 ten days ago, shattered after our futile summit bid, I knew I'd had adventure. I'd pushed myself to my limit. That escapade has now been trumped with a success that was far from guaranteed or expected. There's been a cost; I'll limp for some time to come. But mentally I'm where I need to be. No regrets. No easy options taken. Nothing left on the table. I can glide into middle age and close off the youthful chapter of life.

Everest stands behind and above me. But I know I've been above it. It will always be the tallest. It will always be better than the mountaineers who climb it. Many will try and many will fail on its slopes, not all will live to tell the tale. I'd not have got there without Greg. Somewhere below us, Angel treks alone out of this valley. Without him, I'm not sure how much of me would have returned. But I have returned. A chair in front of the fire awaits. The adventures are over. Nobody beats this mountain, but for two months I was a worthy contender. And for a few brief moments, I shared that same spot as Hillary and Tenzing.

The End
(Epilogue Overleaf)

EPILOGUE
2 YEARS LATER

After flying out of the Himalayas with Greg and landing in Kathmandu, we went straight to the Ciwec Clinic, as Angel had advised. The doctors started the mending process. They warned of a sixty per cent chance that a surgeon's knife would be required on the left toes. Around me, unknown climbers, with exposure damage to their faces and huge bandages at the end of their arms, were confronting amputation prospects.

The medical staff directed me to stay off my feet completely for several weeks. After each afternoon sitting on my hotel bed, watching TV and downing fruit juice and decent food, I limped out for a little entertainment after dark. The remnants of our team had arrived back to the city in dribs and drabs. Angel, Hugo, Greg, and Khalid revelled in the city, having met the challenges that the mountain had thrown at them.

Greg and I swapped our fatigued conversations in cramped tents for lively banter around tables overflowing with exotic dishes and foreign beers. The two of us relived our adventure as we packed back on the weight. Forgotten incidents emerged from our two memories. One tale led to another. A few caused us to realise how lucky we'd been. Several had me thanking Greg for yet another moment of aid. All the episodes reminded us that we'd pulled off a stroke. It was hard to believe we'd been strangers only eight weeks earlier. And yet, as much as we knew each other, we didn't know each other at all. We had existed only as mountaineers. I'd never seen him in doctor's scrubs; he'd never seen me slice a golf ball out-of-bounds. We'd reached the top of the world together; we would cross continents in the future to meet up, to fill in the gaps, and to remember the time we kept climbing, kept climbing till there was no more.

For Ade and Martin, having come so close, words did little to console them. I was keen to avoid any mention of summits as we'd sit around a table with them and tuck into pizza. They were considering another attempt at a distant, future date.

Charlene had already flown back home before we reached Kathmandu. Before heading, she, Mingmar, and Hugo had hosted a press conference on her achievement.

The mountain had taken little out of the two experienced Turks, Nurhan and Yener. They arrived back in Kathmandu and joined us in the hotel.

I returned to the clinic every day for treatment and fresh dressings. The right foot was declared out of danger; although, it would need several months to recover. The size and colour of my left toes transformed every twenty-four hours. Watching the bandage being unravelled each day was like waiting for a jury's verdict.

Airplanes took climbers back to the four corners of the earth, to rejoin the lives they had put on hold, and our team dwindled. After ten days, I left the foreign city behind me and boarded a flight with Greg and Khalid. Abu Dhabi connections terminal witnessed big bear hugs as Greg, Khalid, and I gave each other a final farewell. A little later, connecting flights took off to Australia, Oman, and Ireland.

On returning to Ireland, I attended St. Michael's Hospital in Dublin every second day for two months. Experienced hands nursed my left toes back from the brink. Every fortnight or so, another digit was deemed to have been spared. The limp became less noticeable with each month. After a year, the last small wound closed. Eighteen months after summiting, I tested running; there was no problem. Barefoot beach soccer will have to wait a little longer, but I'm sure the sand's not going anywhere.

Everest hasn't changed. In this year's climbing window (two months ago), climbers again pitted themselves against nature. Ted led another group of mountaineers to the Himalayas. Many of the Sherpas on his team were the guys who'd assisted us two years ago. One of them was a man who'd ascended through the biting darkness to the summit, on the same night that we'd pushed for the top. This year, however, his blessings ran out. Stepping across the rungs of a ladder, above a crevasse near Camp 1, he stumbled and fell to his death. All counted, Everest took ten lives this season.

Hugo was right when he said there're no old, bold climbers. I pushed my luck to the limit once and got away with it; once is plenty. It brings a smile to my face when

I think back on the feat. Having shown to myself that I'd the determination to see something so difficult through to the end has left me with little else to prove. Every now and then, a memory will surface from the expedition: sometimes funny, sometimes bizarre, usually tough, but always a reminder that I lived through some exploit. But aside from that, I'm little changed. Despite all I saw and experienced, those I meet usually ask for two key nuggets of information: did I see dead people, and how did we go for a number two? That's after their initial reaction: "You ... to the top? No way." When I chat with the lads who were on the squad, at least they believe me.

A year after our adventure, I visited Greg in Australia. We picked up our conversation where we'd left it in Abu Dhabi. He's settled back into his surgeon's role but is keen for another mountain caper. I just heard that he's engaged to be married. I've no doubt we'll meet again, but I don't expect it to be in the highlands.

Khalid insisted that I visit him in Oman for a stopover. He showed me around his country and treated me like royalty. Settled with his wife and children, he's now passing on his rock-climbing passion to his young sons. As the first Omani to summit, he uses his climbing repute to encourage the next generation from his nation to strive hard to achieve something of lasting value.

Charlene wrote her book as planned, and it was published. She resisted the pull of the office job and now leads tours to colourful locations in Africa, Southeast Asia, and beyond. Engagement also came her way since Everest. She's told me to get on a plane and call into her up north. Perhaps next year I'll get there, in the summer.

I've kept in email contact with Doug and Hugo, the two firefighters from the US. Hugo's become a local celebrity. He's the go-to man for TV correspondents and magazine writers whenever a real-life mountain drama or outdoor survival story breaks.

Having not reached the summit, Matthew tried again the following year. He turned around near Camp 1. I heard that Nigel and Amit made another attempt on Everest this season. They called it a day near Camp 1 and Camp 2 respectively.

Angel has since guided more climbers back to the summit. I know they were in safe hands. Back at his home in Argentina, he's recently become a father. We've not kept in touch. I should rectify that. If this were a work of fiction, I suspect the story would close with us meeting up each year for drinks, on the anniversary of our summit.

But that's the thing about real life; intentions don't necessarily align with deeds. Nor do they always blossom into rational consequences. A biography written backwards can be hammered into shape, till themes reveal themselves and float across the pages. Reality, however, rarely surrenders such meaning. Perhaps W. B. Yeats described us best, as that "bundle of accident and incoherence that sits down to breakfast." But this was not about what happens at breakfast. This was all about what ensues afterwards: standing up from the table, postponing hesitation and regret for some other day, and just going for it.

And that's what I did.

The End

ACKNOWLEDGMENTS

Many thanks to the following people for their keen eye, attention to detail, and gracious assistance, which turned a story into a better book:

Ronan W, Sheena L, Sally Mc'G, Neil O'H, Peter O, Anne D, Greg J, Hugo S, Graham G, Suzanne W, Gearoid P, Gav D, Col D, Eoghan B, Barry D, Tony M, Jim O'R, Lorna O'R, Susan W, and Ger D.

Printed in Poland
by Amazon Fulfillment
Poland Sp. z o.o., Wrocław

56293103R00207